MVFOL

More Than Luck

More Than Luck

The Memoirs of
Raymond J. Poppelman

Raymond J. Poppelman

aug 2002

MARION STREET PUBLISHING CO.
3930 South Swenson, Suite 810
Las Vegas, Nevada 89119

Printed in the United States of America

This book is dedicated to

the memory of

my grandfather,

Johann Arnold Poppelman

CONTENTS

ACKNOWLEDGMENTS

The following people encouraged and assisted me in writing this autobiography:

Neville R. Lewis, my sister Florence's husband, a well-known San Fernando, California, lawyer, encouraged me many years ago to write my autobiography. "Write about your fantastic life," he said. "It should be a book!"

Sue G. Poppelman, my late wife, saved notes, photographs, and letters from Iwo Jima that I used in writing this book.

John A. Lewis, my nephew, an attorney at law in San Fernando, California, provided advice on family history and dates and offered suggestions. He knew more about my life than I realized.

Robert McCracken was the "ramrod" of this project. He taxed my recollections, got them transcribed, and interfaced with the editors, typesetters, and printers as the project progressed, pushing it to its conclusion.

Jean O. Charney transcribed the many hours of taped interviews, did a light edit of the interviews, and corrected the files.

Michelle S. Asakawa edited the manuscript from its taped interview format.

Alice Levine provided additional editorial work.

Sandra Rush designed and typeset the book and prepared the index.

Eugenie Rolfs / Soehnge was helpful in uncovering Poppelman history in Germany dating back to 1223. She provided encouragement during the taping phase of the research.

Charles H. Waterhouse, former resident artist of the U.S. Marine Corps, designed the dust jacket.

My very good friend Cristy Estrada prodded me to "keep going on the book!"

Without the help of these people, this book could not have been written.

—Raymond J. Poppelman

PART 1

Growing Up (1907–1926)

CHAPTER 1

How the Poppelmans Came to South Dakota, and About My Family

I was born on March 6, 1907, on a farm near Marvin, a little town of about 300 people, in the western part of Grant County, South Dakota. It was prairie country, so I probably could be referred to as farmer stock. I was born on a farm, and I lived on a farm. So I'm a farmer from South Dakota.

My mother was in labor with me during a bad March snow-storm. Dad hitched up a team of horses to a sleigh with runners. The sideboards were about 30 inches high all around. He filled the whole sleigh with straw and took the team 18 miles to Milbank to get a doctor; it was 40 degrees below zero. He got the doctor and bedded him down in the straw to keep him warm. I remember my father telling me that the blizzard blew about half the straw away and that the snowfall was so heavy they couldn't tell where the road was (it was just a dirt and gravel road with fences). He said the fences on each side saved them for a long time, but when they got within five miles of Marvin the blizzard was so strong that he couldn't stand to keep his face toward the horses, so he turned the reins loose. The horses could find their way in the blizzard; they even stopped at the house instead of the barn.

The doctor stayed all night, and I think it was on the afternoon of the second day, which would be March 6, the day I was born, that my dad took him back to Milbank. So I could start my story by saying that I was born in a blizzard. In cold weather like that, your nose freezes and turns white. (If you were walking down the sidewalk in Marvin during the winter and you saw a man with a white nose, you would run over to him and grab a handful of snow and put it on his nose. Frostbite was a fact of life eighty, ninety years ago.)

On the return trip to Milbank, my dad had to keep his head turned back toward the bulkhead, behind the seat. For a while he was in the seat, and the doctor was down in the straw. Later my dad had to get down there too because he felt that his nose was freezing, so he just turned the reins loose again.

The farm was 160 acres that had been obtained by my father in about 1905 through the Homestead Act of 1862. His father, my grandfather—like many who came west—had secured a farm in the same way some years earlier. As the railroads worked west, they needed customers, so they sent agents throughout Europe and practically all the world, advising people, "Come to America where the streets are made of gold," and where they could get free land. My grandfather and his younger brother Clemens, who were young men in Germany at that time, decided that America was the place to be. So they came in 1873, which was about three years before the Indians practically slaughtered George Armstrong Custer and the Seventh Cavalry in the eastern part of Montana.

My grandfather's full name was Johann Herman Bernard Arnold Poppelman, but he was known as Arnold. He was born in northern Germany in a little crossroads called Dinklage, near a big estate

An early photo of my
grandfather, Arnold
Poppelman

known as Gut Lethe, which means "good river." Originally, Gut
Lethe had a castle, which deteriorated and vanished. Another branch
of the Poeppelmanns was a family that lived at a place called
Grandorf. They were peasant farmers in the same area. (When I speak
of the same area, I mean a radius of 50 miles.) In the thirteenth century, a bishop living in that sector of Germany was passing through
the countryside and was attacked by robbers. The Poeppelmanns
rescued the bishop with the use of pitchforks, and as a reward the
bishop gave the Poeppelmann family an estate of almost 5,000 acres
with a mansion. I visited Grandorf Estate, as it is known, in 1964,
and I was very impressed. The house was built of timbers. The most
recent addition was made in about 1750, when the thatched roof
was replaced by a tile roof. All the beams in the house had inscrip-
tions, giving the history of events that had happened at Grandorf.

In 1981 the old building was hit by lightning and burned. On the foundation is a new home owned by a Poeppelmann. One of the heirs of the original Poeppelmann family that owned Grandorf is now running Grandorf. (The Poeppelmanns of Germany have been traced back to 1224. One of the Poeppelmanns, who would be my great-grandfather, bought Gut Lethe and raised 16 children there; my grandfather was one of them.)

A painting of house and barn at Grandorf, Germany, by John Moll, Oxford, Maryland, 1970. The main structure in the center was originally built in 1224; part of the thatched roof was repaired with tile in the sixteenth century. The entrance leads through the barn section of the combined barn and residence. Animal heat from the lower barn section warmed the upper living quarters during harsh winters. To the right is a chicken house built in 1953; on the left is a modern barn. The main structure burned down in 1981.

According to the law in Germany when my grandfather was a young man, the oldest son always inherited the property, which was never divided up. Since my grandfather had older brothers, there was not much of a future for him in sharing the estate in Gut Lethe. Also, all young men were required to serve three years in the Kaiser's army, and both he and his brother Clemens were eligible. So when he was 25 years old, he and Clemens emigrated to America on a

Gut Lethe, the Poeppelmann family estate;
photo taken during my European travels in 1964.

sailing ship. For the trip across the Atlantic Ocean in the 1870s, you had to carry a small casket with your own food. The ships were crowded and sleeping was difficult. Getting through Ellis Island in New York was somewhat of a problem—all immigrants were examined very carefully. When they got to America, fearful that there might be a technicality about them coming in, they changed the spelling of their last name and tried to disguise their identity as much as possible in case there was something that would send them back and force them to join the German army.

I think Clemens and my grandfather had less than $100 between them. They took a train from Ellis Island west to Milwaukee. It was probably a German friend in Milwaukee who urged them to come there. I remember my grandfather stating that the first year in Milwaukee was spent getting jobs where they could—as manual laborers. Milwaukee was a booming town in the 1870s. Some of America's famous breweries were being built there, and it was an outlet for wheat. A lot of the wheat that came from South Dakota went to Milwaukee for the big breweries that were starting up.

Because my grandfather was a linguist and Clemens could also speak several languages, they were very much in demand in department stores, which hired them to assist customers from many different countries. My grandfather could speak Swedish, German, French, and Italian, and he was well versed in Danish. He eventually got a good job in a department store in Minneapolis, where he lived for most of his prefarming life. As the customers came into the store, my grandfather would be there to greet them in their language and tell them where to go to buy what they needed.

Later Clemens and Arnold traveled to South Dakota and took out adjoining homestead tracts of land of 160 acres. Clemens worked both claims while my grandfather worked in the department store.

My grandfather's younger brother built the buildings and put the farm on a paying basis. Later my grandfather left the department store in Minneapolis and moved in as a tenant, and he and Clemens farmed together for 10 years. Clemens sold out to my grandfather in about 1910 and moved to Milwaukee and started a soap factory, which was later sold to the Palmolive Company.

The history of Clemens and his Poppelman tribe in Milwaukee and Racine, Wisconsin, is quite interesting. They made their soap by buying fat from butchers at slaughterhouses. They rendered the fat in Racine in a small factory they had, and the renderings were taken to Milwaukee and processed into facial and hand soap, which was mostly sold in Minneapolis.

Clemens had built a home on one of the homesteading tracts, which my grandfather moved into. My grandfather was a specialist at raising hogs—he was known as the hog farmer of Grant County—and did very well. He married a woman named Johanna who did not like farm life. I never knew my grandmother. She was Dutch but came from the part of Holland that was not too far from the German border. My grandfather must have known her in Germany. She and Arnold must have married around 1876. They had only one child, my father, Hubert Joseph Poppelman. In August of 1909, my grandmother was badly burned by a gasoline stove that blew up, and she lived only a few days after the accident.

After my grandmother died, my grandfather moved in with my father on his farm, an arrangement that was supposed to be temporary. In time, my grandfather became the patriarch of the family. We had a two-story farmhouse and two Swedish maids who could barely speak English, so my grandfather was the interpreter. My mother would give my grandfather instructions that he would tell the maids. One maid was the cook and the other was the housekeeper. My

My father, Hubert Joseph Poppelman, in 1886, at the age of three.

grandfather had a bedroom upstairs, my mother and father had a bedroom downstairs, and two of my sisters were downstairs in the second bedroom. Upstairs there were also bedrooms for the four boys—me and my brothers, Kenneth, Lyle, and Clyde. So the boys and my grandfather were upstairs, and the girls were downstairs with my mother and father. There was one bedroom upstairs for the two Swedish maids. It was quite a household.

My grandfather was a great outdoorsman. With his double-barreled shotgun, he would go hunting during the pheasant season, which is after the harvest. Kenneth and I were old enough to go hunting with my grandfather. We wouldn't be in the field more than an hour before he'd have all the pheasants we could possibly carry; he was a good hunter. He also liked to fish and would take us with him. He would take a horse and buggy and drive about 15 miles up the mountain, which is a promontory of the mountain range there. It was sort of a nose of a mountain and Marvin was on the nose of it. Beyond that was a town called Summit where there were two lakes he liked to fish in. The third type of expedition we used to make with my grandfather was to the fields looking for horseradish, which grew wild and looked something like a white carrot. All the farmers liked horseradish for their meats and sausages.

I remember one incident that puzzled my grandfather. We had too many cats around, and my father wanted to get rid of one female, so my grandfather decided to take it into the woods to a creek and throw the cat in the water in a sack with rocks to drown it. We got the horse and buggy and the cat and the sack and went down to the creek. My grandfather put a big rock in the sack and threw it in the creek. When we came home, the cat was on the porch waiting for us! My grandfather accused me of cutting a hole in the sack. I never did figure that one out.

Arnold Poppelman stood about 5 feet 10 inches tall and weighed about 165 pounds. At the time we lived on the farm, he had a typical German handlebar mustache. He was quite domineering with my father. My grandfather sat at the head of the table. He insisted we all be there for dinner when we were supposed to be, including my father. He still considered my father his child. My father consulted with him quite a bit and they were good friends, but my grandfather dominated. He still had a lot of German in him. Discipline was his middle name. But he was a soft touch if you wanted something from him.

Once, when my mother and father went to Texas together, my grandfather took over the home in Marvin. He did a lot of things around the house, little things that my father never got to, and he changed the food menu quite a bit. We were getting more good food

Arnold Poppelman, my
grandfather, circa 1900.

with my grandfather in charge. I remember one time as cold weather
approached, my grandfather said he was going to make the house
warmer for the wintertime. My father was away, and when he came
home there was tar paper around the lower part of the house and a
mound of manure all around the house to keep it warm. And it
worked.

Our social life was with the other German families. On Sundays
after church, for recreation we would usually go to the home of one
of the German families that lived near our farm. There we'd have a
big Sunday feast and make ice cream.

There were two churches in Marvin, a Catholic church and a
Swedish church. My grandfather was Catholic. I was required to go
to church and I was an altar boy. Because of my grandfather's influence with the church, I was given the job of kneeling behind the
priest. I was to ring a bell at a certain point in the ceremony. The
priest would wiggle his hand as a signal to me to ring the bell. But
we got our signals mixed up, and the church service was a disaster.

As a consequence, I was "fired." I was so humiliated that, on future Sunday mornings, when my family would get ready to go to church in my dad's REO car, I would go out to one of our small barns that had a hayloft. In the hayloft, I would tunnel way back in the hay where nobody could get me. One day my grandfather went up to get me out of the hay with a pitchfork, and he stabbed me. My mother, who was a Protestant, declared war on my grandfather and supported my hiding in the haystack. So the ritual on Sunday mornings was for me to get up early and tunnel back into the hay. I never did go back to church. Disaster struck, and I hope it wasn't my condemnation: Lightning hit the Catholic church, and it burned to the ground shortly after that.

My mother's name was Thressa Pament. The Pament family were Canadian homesteaders with a farm not too far from my grandfather's. Mother was born on the farm in 1884. The grade school for all the kids in that area was a little schoolhouse on one corner of the Pament farm. So my mother went through grade school on the Pament farm, living in what they called a claim shanty. The family later built a nice two-story home, which is still there. The Pament family moved to Milbank, and my mother went to the Milbank high school. She liked Milbank. It was more sophisticated than her family's farm, where she used to churn the milk to make butter, dress the chickens, and help prepare three meals a day, including meals for the farmhands during the threshing season. It was constant work.

My mother didn't talk much, but when she did you'd better listen. She never interfered with whatever my father wanted to do—his wishes came first. If he wanted to move, they would move—except once.

Mother was always taking care of her seven children—even with the Swedish maids. My brother Kenneth was the firstborn. I,

My mother, Thressa
Pament Poppelman,
circa 1915

Raymond, came second, followed by Lyle and Clyde. Then came three sisters—Evelyn, Dorothy, and Florence. All of us were born on the farm except Florence, who was born in Marvin.

We went to school in Marvin for the lower grades, and my mother would get us ready for school, going through the Sears, Roebuck catalog to order clothes for us. She nursed us if we were sick. When Dad was ready to go to Marvin on Saturdays she had a shopping list waiting for him. She and the maids had to prepare the eggs for the trip to Marvin on Saturdays; there were usually three or four buckets of eggs cradled in millet seeds so they wouldn't break. We went by wagon with a team of horses or sometimes rode in a buggy.

It wasn't until about 1910 that my father bought his first auto-mobile. Riding in it was a great luxury for my mother. She would dress up and go to church or to visit friends on Sunday. The REO car, which you had to crank, had brass rods running from the top down to the hood. It was one of the first cars in Grant County and in South Dakota, and wherever we went curiosity-seekers would gather around. My dad always had it followed by a team of horses. Some-times the car would break down and he'd have to tow it. Sometimes we would get stuck because the roads weren't made of gravel but of mud or dry mud. Each farmer usually took care of the road in front of his farm, but also always had a mud hole in the area, which served as a "tollgate." The farmers would charge 50 cents to get a team of horses to pull stuck vehicles through. But Dad always took his own team of horses. Later, when my dad moved to Marvin, he was ap-pointed by the governor as a commissioner of highways for 25 miles of road along Marvin; then the county started bringing in gravel.

Dad had a drive and a passion to make money. He later became a millionaire as one of the largest real estate brokers in California. That interest showed up early in his life when he left the farm and moved to Marvin to become a land broker.

My father was the type of man who could enter a room and everybody would gather around him—he was a great talker and a very friendly guy. He always had the ability to make anybody he talked to feel important, and he had many friends. That was why he became successful; he knew how to handle people, he was a good salesman, and he had a lot of drive. How many farmers in South Dakota had the guts to take up and go to Texas when they heard of an oil boom? And how many would leave Minneapolis, and take seven kids, two maids, my grandfather, and mother, the whole bunch of us, to California? He had that tremendous drive. Although he

My father's high school
graduation portrait.
He graduated from
Central High School in
Minneapolis in 1898.

had only been a farmer in South Dakota, he became a leader in the
real estate business in Los Angeles. Jannes Investment Company in
Beverly Hills is one of the big real estate houses today. (Some years
ago I went to Jannes Investment Company to look for a house. I was
then about 50 years old, and when I gave old man Jannes my card,
he said, "Poppelman? Where the hell did you come from?" He had
been be a salesman for my father.)

Because of his gregarious nature and love of music, my father
once bought all the instruments needed to make a band and went
through the countryside surrounding Marvin to find out who could
play what instrument. I have a picture of the band he assembled in
one of my books. Later, when word got around that Dad was moving back to Minneapolis, all the band members turned in their in-

struments to him. Dad had all the instruments shipped to Minneapolis, and he distributed them among us. I got a set of drums and a
trombone. My mother finally revolted because all the boys and all
those instruments got out of hand—nobody could stand the racket.
My father was the bandleader. He could play the piano and most
instruments even though he didn't have any training.

Practically all of my dad's grade school days were spent in Minneapolis. He was about 19 when my grandfather decided to move
to the farm. My grandfather urged him to take out a homestead on
his own, and he did that in about 1905. It was about five miles from
my grandfather's farm, north of Milbank. What I remember most
about my life on the farm was being with my grandfather, who lived
with us. He had time to entertain us, whereas my father was busy

My father's farm, five miles east of
Marvin, South Dakota, about 1910.

all the time, going to Texas, to Minneapolis, or to Marvin, and he was showing farms and selling farms. My grandfather was more of a father than my father.

Dad stayed on his own farm until 1914, almost ten years. He realized when the United States entered World War I against Germany that farm prices would zoom up. So he sold the farm when he could get a high price for it. I was about seven years old when he moved us to Marvin. From Marvin, he would make trips to Texas. He invested in oil leases there and made money. Then he moved us to Minneapolis, bought a new car and a big house. Eventually, through his Texas connections, he was encouraged to move to California.

Years later, after my dad had lost $8 million in the 1929 crash (at the start of the Great Depression), I asked him, "Dad, what was the worst thing about the crash that affected you?" He said, "The worse thing about the crash is I wasted all that time making money when I could have been fishing." Although my father loved to fish and liked to be outdoors, he sacrificed all that because of his drive to make money.

Chapter 2

On School in Marvin and Holidays

There was a country school quite a few miles from our farm, but I wasn't old enough to go to it. Kids today go to school earlier than they did in the old days. I didn't start school until we moved to Marvin. Because my grandfather lived with us, he had time to tutor us, so we were probably smarter than the average kid when we started school.

The first school I attended was a two-story frame schoolhouse in Marvin. The upstairs floor had a big tube that you'd jump into and slide down in case of a fire. The lower grades were downstairs and the higher grades were upstairs. We had a recess midmorning and a recess in the afternoon. During recess you could use one of the two outhouses. The schoolteacher had a bell, and when you heard the bell ring you had to get back into the classroom. Girls were always separated from the boys at recess. We played baseball and softball and keepaway—a game like basketball: you chose up sides, maybe 10 guys on each side, and you'd throw a ball to your teammates and the other team would try to get it. Games were quite simple compared to what they are now. And we had running races to see who could run the fastest. There were very few fistfights. If you got caught fighting, you'd be reprimanded by the schoolteacher.

The grade school I attended
in Marvin, South Dakota,
1914

If you were to be punished, the teacher would take a ruler and whip you a couple times on the wrist with it. If you did something serious or stupid, you had to sit in the corner on a stool, facing the wall, with a 30-inch-long dunce cap on your head. Or you might be dismissed, in which case you had to take a note home to your father and mother about what you did, and of course that was tough. But sitting with the dunce cap on was the most embarrassing.

You respected your schoolteacher. She was a goddess. What she said was the law and the truth, and if you got complimented by your schoolteacher it was great. In those days there weren't a lot of students in the classroom. There were a few kids for each teacher, so we got special attention and the schoolteacher was almost like a mother to each kid. You listened to what she said and you tried to please her.

We studied spelling, mathematics, and recitations. We'd be assigned a story to read and then had to recite it for the class. I remember I told a story that was a big hit, and the teachers combined all the students in the downstairs classroom so that I could repeat the

My classmates and me in Marvin in 1913.
I am in the center of the front row,
looking at my brother Kenneth at the right,
who is holding a cap in his hand.

story to them. But in the interim between the first and second tellings, I forgot half of the story, so when I told it the second time, it was pretty lousy.

We also studied the history of the United States and geography— we had to learn where we lived. I was happy to go to school; I liked it. When I look at a picture that was taken of one of our classes in 1913, I can't believe the way we dressed and how we looked then compared to kids today. Boys wore knickers, not long pants, and stockings. The girls wore pleated skirts and blouses. During the winter, we wore moccasins and heavy socks. Of course when it was slushy, we wore overshoes, but in extreme cold weather, we wore

A certificate I received in 1916 for making
45 perfect spelling recitations
at school in Marvin, South Dakota

moccasins that were just like a chamois (they didn't have hard soles), and those kept us very warm. In Minneapolis, if the temperature was 18 degrees below zero we did not have to go to school. We thought that was great because we could go out and ice skate and play.

We liked to read Indian stories. I remember the happiest Christmas I ever had was when my mother and father bought me an Indian suit, including a headdress with feathers, so I could dress up like an Indian. The suit also had a bow and arrow, and I prized them because we were somewhat familiar with the Indians in our territory. The Indians were docile and friendly, but we seldom saw them.

Cowboys came to Marvin, wearing pistols just like in the old days. When we played, I was the Indian and my older brother, Kenneth, was the cowboy. Guns were also very exciting presents. I remember when I first got my first BB gun, and, later, when .22 rifles were the thing. As kids we didn't dare touch a shotgun. It was taboo. My grandfather, father, and the hired men were the only ones who could use the shotguns.

Christmas was probably our most important holiday; it was a religious day, and it was reward time for the children. One present that I cherished, but didn't use too much, was something my father ordered through the mail. (Most of our items came through the mail from Sears, Roebuck and other companies.) It was a small wagon that was designed for a small Shetland pony. It came in a big carton, and my dad had to put it together. It had a green body with red wheels, and I think it must have been quite expensive. The problem was that we didn't have a pony, although my dad intended to get one. He did find a colt that we tried to use to pull the wagon, but it was generally a fiasco—the colt was not easily trained and the wagon was knocked over a few times. I was growing up fast enough to outgrow the wagon, but I liked it.

Our Christmas trees were generally decorated with candles—we didn't have electricity then. My mother went to extremes to make Christmas nice for everybody, and of course we had big dinners and neighbors were called in to enjoy drinks, mostly cider. Christmas dinner would be turkey. But on the farm we had not only turkey but also chicken, pork, and beef. Those dinners were feasts. Sundays were almost like Christmas because we would go the neighbors' homes for Sunday dinner year-round and they'd have a big spread with ice cream, and we served them the same when they'd come to our house.

Thanksgiving was another big event because we had the facilities for it. Easter would be confined to the church and whatever activities the church committee would have. Easter was a good time to get the church crowd together for a day or so, but we didn't roll eggs.

After the Catholic church was hit by lightning and burned down, the second and only church in town—the Swedish church—became quite popular. Because my mother was a Presbyterian—I think she was from a Methodist family—we went to the Methodist Church in Milbank, 18 miles away, on special holidays. The Catholics sometimes had services in the opera house in Marvin, which was quite small but could hold 50 to 100 people.

The Catholic church was never rebuilt, but a new building was recently put up (I don't know if you'd call it a church; it's more of a convention center) one mile south of Marvin. It's very large, and from the yard you can see for a distance of 100 miles because it's right on the nose of a mountain. It's very popular with tourists. One thing that I like about the new building is that it has a large weaving—it must be 10 feet high—with the names of the pioneers of Marvin on it, including my father's name.

The opera house had a stage and seats like a theater. When the early silent movies came out, sometimes we'd see a William S. Hart picture. The piano player would furnish the sound.

In Marvin, there was some property about the length of a football field away from us that was wooded, and a pack of timber wolves used to live there. We would listen to the timber wolves howl at night. It was also fun to listen to the trains coming through town at night. Two trains usually came through each night, and they would toot their horns before they got to the crossroads in town. So we would listen for the train and the toots. After the train would pass, it would be silent. Then we would hear the wolves howling. The rail-road track went past a swimming hole, so in the summertime we would walk along the track and see who could walk the farthest without falling off the rail. That was a favorite sport of ours.

CHAPTER 3

On Building a Farmhouse, Disease and Loneliness, Auctioning the Farm, and Moving to Minneapolis

In the homestead days, an owner would generally go to a lead carpenter and say, "I want you to build me a house. I need four bedrooms and a living room." The owner would never know exactly what the house was going to look like because changes were made as the builder went along. There were also variations in style. For instance, the Swedes had their idea of a house, the Germans had another, and the Irish yet another.

The Swedish houses would have a little more weight to the roof—a steeper roof to shed the snow better. The Irish-built houses were quite simple and sort of boxy. The Germans liked everything strong and rugged. They used as much stone as they could. And they used beams that others didn't use. The stone came from the fields. If the farmer found nice pieces of stone that he could use for corners, a chimney, and a fireplace, he would save them.

Our two-story frame house was built by a couple of Swedish carpenters who specialized in houses. They were master carpenters, as most Swedes are. It was not a typical Colonial-type house, but

Our house on the hill in Marvin, South Dakota; photo taken in August 1949.

like most farmhouses, it had a porch around two sides. All the farm-houses in the early days of the Dakotas had front porches on which people could sit and wave to people in passing vehicles—horse and buggies—on the road.

It was quite a large house. In those days you could build a pretty nice house for $700 or $800. We had a kitchen, a rather large dining room, and a living room, probably about 16 by 20 feet. The utility porch in the back of the house was screened. There was also one bedroom on the first floor, with a small adjoining room for the babies. Upstairs were four more bedrooms.

After the carpenters drew up a sketch to build a house, they would summon all the neighboring farmers and say, "We need you on [a certain date]. We're going to put up partitions and frame up the house [or barn]." Usually when people built barns or houses, the neighbors would all participate in what was called a barn rais-ing. All the women within 10 miles would congregate and furnish the picnic food, and all the men and the hired hands would come in, and the lead carpenter would direct the activity. In one day they would frame up a house or a whole big barn. Then the farmer and his hired hands could finish up the job, but the basic hard work of heavy framing was done by contributing neighbors. That was the way they did it in the early days; it was the only way they could get it done. A farmer who didn't have a house and barn knew that some-day he would need help, so he would always contribute.

Generally, lumber was very cheap. For instance, you could prob-ably buy good framing lumber—2-by-4s, partitions, and so forth—for $50 for 1,000 board feet. And you could buy sheeting lumber with knots in it cheaper. If you wanted oak flooring, you might have to go to $100 per 1,000 board feet. There was so much forest land in the country then that the small mills around Milbank could pro-duce enough lumber for a whole house in a few days. The framing and material for the barns would be full of knots, but the wood used in the houses would be practically all clear.

There was no indoor plumbing. We had an outhouse that could be used except in the winter; in the winter we used an indoor toilet that was store-bought, I think through the Sears Company. It had a large pail that would be carried out by one of the maids or a hired hand every other day or so to a hole that was dug in the ground especially for that use. The contents of the pail would be poured in and would freeze. The toilet that we used normally was the out-house, a sophisticated one that had maybe three or four holes in it. We always had a sack of lime in the outhouse, and once a day some-body would dump in a couple of shovels full of lime for sanitation purposes.

Drinking water came from a well, and the water was carried to the house. Initially, the wells were hand-dug. They would go down around 30 feet, which was very deep. Later, when wells were drilled they would go down perhaps 90 feet and supply all the water you'd ever need. The wells always held up, even through drought seasons. Water was plentiful in that country.

Most of the houses had cisterns for catching rainwater. That water was used for washing clothes, dishes, and so forth. One winter we had to use water from the cistern for drinking because the well was frozen. The cistern pump was outside the screen door by the kitchen, and it would freeze. My father used to pour kerosene on the part that was frozen and then light the kerosene to melt the ice. Some of the kerosene would go down into the cistern and during extreme winter months there would be a kerosene taste to our water.

We had a creek behind the house and the barn. The upper part of it had a couple deep holes that were our swimming holes in the summertime. The creek banks were lined with wild chokecherries. The cattle and horses would, of course, use the part of the stream behind the barn, so we didn't use the creek water below the barn, because it would be polluted from the animals.

Originally we used wood to heat the house. I remember one of my chores on the farm was to carry wood into the house. But we eventually got a coal stove and switched to coal, which was plentiful in the Black Hills area of South Dakota. After the trains came to the area, everybody started using coal because it could be hauled from the coal areas, like Minnesota, to other places. Coal was sold at the general stores. My mother cooked on a big coal range.

The houses were always designed so that the kitchen and some of the bedrooms, or storage places, were to the north, and as many rooms as were possible would face to the south and east to use the sunshine to warm them. My grandfather's German trick of putting manure around the house kept the basement warm and also kept the walls pretty warm. Fireplaces were not used much—they usually had too much draft from the chimney—but we used the coal stoves that were located in different parts of the house, firing them up before we went to bed. They kept us warm if they were banked right and the draft was set properly. Storm windows were an innovation that helped a lot, too. We'd use plenty of covers—quilts were very popular—and we used cotton blankets instead of sheets because they were warmer.

The men usually wore stocking caps to bed and heavy nightgowns instead of pajamas. Two or three kids would sleep together in a bed to keep warm. And generally, you'd rely on your body heat. Of course, we did suffer, there's no question about it. The houses were cold. But in the morning before the sun came up, while it was still dark, the stoves would be going in the kitchen and the living room.

My mother used heated bricks wrapped in cloth and hot water bottles at the foot of the bed for the children and for people who were sick. It was amazing how comfortable a bed could be if you heated a few bricks and had them in your bed wrapped so that they wouldn't burn you. The brick would hold the heat through the night.

Electricity came in just about the time we were leaving the farm. Until then, we used kerosene lamps at night. We had telephone lines, but sometimes they were difficult to use because they were party lines—five other farm houses might be hooked to your line. One reason my father wanted to move out of his office in Marvin was because every time he talked on the phone, people would deliberately listen in to hear what he had to say. If you had an emergency, you'd lift the receiver and say, "This is an emergency. Please get off the line."

Our house stood up on the hill where normally the snow banks wouldn't be very high. But I remember one year, our porch, which was eight feet high in front of the house, had snow banked up all

Main Street in Marvin, South Dakota, August 1949.

around the house. The only way we could get in and out of the house was by the upstairs windows. I wonder sometimes, How did I ever stand it as a boy?

We also had a storm cellar—sort of a small basement with doors on it—on our farm. It was about 50 yards from the house. There were several times when my father and mother would round us up and get us into the storm cellar because a tornado was coming. One hit a barn on an adjoining farm just about at twilight. My father and mother had gotten us all into the storm cellar. My dad was peering through the crack in the double doors and called us to look. I remember that sight; the sky was full of boards flying through the air above the barn. And we could see the funnel—it was very black. But I only saw that one tornado. A few tornadoes hit during the night, but we didn't see them. In those days there was no warning; the tornado just went through and you only knew about it after it hit. But the farmers were good weather prophets—they could look at the sky and know what was about to happen, according to the season.

The thing the farmers feared most was hail. When grain is ripe, ready for thrashing, a hailstorm can flatten it right to the ground and there's nothing you can do about it. There's no way to cut it or shuck it; it's just lost. That happened to my father once, and it's one reason I think he got out of farming. You had tornadoes, hail, droughts, grasshoppers . . . so many things to worry about. If you have a drought in the spring you have no water for your crops. The hail flattens out your wheat, and not only is the drought tough on your crops, it's tough on your animals, especially if the creek dries up. So then you've got to use your well and pump it practically dry to get water for the animals. The farming business had too many dangers and hazards.

Our farmland was very rich, with good drainage. We grew only wheat and enough corn for the animals. In the fall when the wheat was ripe and golden, as far as you could see looked like a big sea of gold. My father started with 160 acres but bought a quarter section from another homesteader who had bought the land for speculation. So he wound up with over 300 acres of cultivation; grains were bringing about $40 to $50 an acre, so that was pretty good profit. He got about 40 to 50 bushels per acre. The lowest price for wheat that I remember, or even read about, was $1 a bushel. When World War I came, of course, prices skyrocketed. We needed wheat not only for ourselves but for our allies. When the price went up, farmland went up, and people made money. My father got out when the prices were high because he didn't want to be a farmer all of his life.

I really marvel at the people who settled in wheat country, ranching country, or any place in the West—any pioneer. Even though you had free land, you had to get trees out (in some places, all the trees) with a team of horses; you had to clear the land and get all the rocks out. The land had been naturally fertilized for centuries, but you've only got a team of horses and limited equipment—a plow, disks, and so on. You had to walk behind your team for miles and miles all day long; 160 acres is a lot of land when you've got to plow it. And then you have the problem of cultivating it and keeping the weeds out.

Hunger was not much of a problem in the Dakotas because the typical farmer was well prepared. He had canned goods in the basement, he had hogs butchered and hanging, he had beef, and he had wild game—geese and ducks—and certainly he had turkeys and chickens. He was self-sufficient for food, but medically he was in trouble. People died young because they didn't have doctors to help them. After the phone lines came in, a farmer could call a doctor on the telephone, and the doctor would get in his horse and buggy and try to get to the farmhouse and do the best he could. But he could not operate—he couldn't take his patient to the hospital; the best he could do was to give the patient some medicine, which might help the patient at least emotionally. Often the doctor knew that the patient was going to die and there wasn't a damn thing he could do about it unless there was some way he could ship the patient to Minneapolis.

Of course, lots of people died from diphtheria, which doesn't happen often today. One ailment people didn't suffer from was heart trouble because we got enough exercise. From the time you could walk you were active, and even the farmers in their seventies were still working.

My brother Kenneth—my older brother, who fell off the barn, which caused him to be retarded—is a good example of what could happen in the days when medical science was in its infancy. My father was very concerned about Kenneth, and after he made money in California in real estate, he took Kenneth to the best doctors, but there was nothing they could do for him. Incidentally, Kenneth died from appendicitis in about 1926, when he was a young man. He had been eating grapes from our grape arbor, and the local doctor thought his stomachache was from the grapes, but it was really appendicitis.

The doctors had to deal with mental problems, too. The women suffered from loneliness. The state of South Dakota set up an asylum in Mitchell in about 1850 for women who were suffering from loneliness. A young couple would get married. In her first years, before she had children, the wife was in her house all day long by herself. The nearest farm might be ten miles away. Her husband worked from daylight to dark in the field. When he came home at night, he was the only person she saw all day—and her husband would likely be too tired to engage her in conversation. Maybe she could get to town on a Saturday or to church on Sunday, but she had no companionship. Some of those women suffered—they couldn't take the loneliness—so they were sent to the asylum in Mitchell. I think the physical effort of washing clothes on a washboard in a tub didn't bother them as much as the loneliness did.

We used a lot of home remedies—castor oil, for example. We had all sorts of cough syrups—including some red-colored stuff out of a bottle; I don't know what the hell was in it. I know that sulfur was used—sulfur and honey was a remedy for many ailments. But I think we relied mostly on natural healing. If that didn't work, you would die. God knows how many died of pneumonia.

As I remember, when I had a cold, I'd usually be put to bed. The schoolteachers were pretty good physicians. They would notice when something was troubling a child and would send the child home. And I think the local doctor had some of the advantages of a witch doctor. People believed, "If you go to the doctor, he'll cure you." So no matter what placebo the doctor would give you, it would work.

Once automatic machinery came into use for farming, there were quite a lot of injuries. The thrashing machine would come to farms on certain dates. All the other farmers would work with you to get your crop taken care of; then they would move on to another farm; it was a cooperative arrangement. I never heard of any fatalities, but there were some injuries—people losing an arm and so forth.

In 1914, my dad sold the house in Marvin, the farm, and everything on it through an auction. Farmers came from all around the county. There seemed to be a purpose for everything we had—right down to the washing tubs, so everything went. I was surprised how fast things went. First, the house was auctioned off, with the barn in the back, and the property. Then the furnishings in the house went; the animals were auctioned off separately, including a team of horses that we had used mostly with a buggy before my dad bought his car. When the family left Marvin, there was nothing we had to take with us or have shipped.

My father opened a land office in Minneapolis, and he advertised farms in the Minneapolis papers. The local farmers would come to the land office in Marvin, and my father would visit every so often to look at the listings and tell the farmers what he thought they could get for them. Most of his buyers were immigrants who came west from Ellis Island in New York. The train was a godsend to my father because the prospects would get on the train and go out to Marvin, and Dad would meet them or have somebody else meet them. They'd see the farm, and boom! there'd be a sale.

(Once, my father made a deal with a shoe manufacturer in Minneapolis, and in exchange for some land, my dad took shoes. The shoes were delivered on the freight train, and there were so damn many shoes my dad couldn't get them in his office. So the family had a field day; we all went down and rummaged through all those shoes.

Dad probably had about $5,000 worth of shoes in his office. I think my dad finally had to give most of them away to get rid of them.)

Buying land then was like it is today—you could make a down payment, or you could pay cash. It was amazing how many Europeans who came over had cash. I think that the banks also made out because they would finance farms. The people who got in there early and got the farm on a homestead basis got the land free; they had a free title. So there was sort of an interesting exchange of land. If you had a farm of free land—homesteaded land—any penny you sold it for was yours. You could then move to a town or a city, or go to Florida, or California; you had cash in your pocket from land that had no mortgage on it. When my dad sold the farm in 1914, I think it was in the $200 to $300 an acre range, which was considered very high. You had to have a lot of money to buy 160 acres. Of course, at that time $100 was a fortune.

After we auctioned off the house and furniture in Marvin, we had no beds to sleep in. We stayed in the local boardinghouse, which today we'd call the hotel. Boardinghouses were where people lived and had their meals cheaply. Dad had arranged for all of us—my grandfather, the two maids, my mother and seven kids, plus the dog, Fido—to stay in the boardinghouse that night. There wasn't a darn thing left in Marvin. Everything had been auctioned except the dog.

For our long trip from Marvin to Minneapolis Dad bought a more elegant and roomier car—a Paige. It had jump seats in the back, and there was a little seat you could fold out from the back of the front seat where you'd fit two more passengers. The Paige was a very fine car; it had side curtains, running boards, and a tool box between the front and the back doors. On each side of the car was a place for spare tires. It was well equipped.

A 1913 Paige touring car similar to this one took my mother and father, grandfather, two Swedish maids, and seven children all the way from Marvin, South Dakota, to Minneapolis.

In the morning we took off in the Paige car bound for Minneapolis, with baskets of food. My grandfather and father were in the front seat. My grandfather would usually crank the car to start it, and my father would work the spark and gas levers to get the car started. One of the boys sat in the front seat with my grandfather, and my father was driving. In back of the front seat, in the jumper seats, were the other boys. And in the back seat were my mother, the two Swedish maids, and the girls, who were practically babies, in their laps. So we had a mob in there plus the dog. I remember my father saying we had three flat tires along the way, which delayed us about four hours getting into Minneapolis. On the first stop, the dog abandoned us; he just took off and went back to Marvin, which was probably 15 miles away. I think my father went to the first farm-house he could find to call a neighbor to take care of the dog.

And so we went on the gravel road. This was not just a ride from Marvin to Minneapolis; it was an expedition. The service stations, which were actually general stores in little towns, had gas pumps, and above them were big glass bowls, which were reservoirs, marked with lines indicating how many gallons we'd pumped. We'd get the hose, fill up, and watch the gas go down. When it got to a certain marking you could turn it off or get another tank. The toilet facilities were very bad; we generally had to use outhouses behind the general stores. It was at least five miles between houses, but because the country was open, you could stop the car, do your business, and nobody would ever see you. You'd seldom ever see a car coming.

We arrived in Minneapolis at night, and I remember none of us had ever seen bright lights before. Minneapolis had electricity, but it was just getting to the country. We went down Hennepin Avenue with all its bright lights. Marvin didn't have one city light on Main Street, and we come to this brilliant street all lit up. My mother would recall my being scared to death and crying and yelling—afraid of the big electrical lights. Our house was on 42nd Street, which would be 42 blocks from the center of town. Today, it's practically downtown.

When we arrived at the house, Dad had to go in first to light all the kerosene lamps. Then we unloaded the car. I don't remember much about the details. The house had two and a half stories, with an attic that had great big rooms. The boys slept up there. There were four bedrooms on the second floor for my grandfather, my mother and father, the maids, and my sisters. It was a roomy house, but we felt like we were in a different world.

CHAPTER 4

Life in Minneapolis and the Texas Oil Boom

The Clara Barton Grammar School, named after the famous nurse, was right across the street from our house in Minneapolis. The big brick building is still there. When we began school in Minneapolis we had a problem with communication. Our dialect was different from the kids in the city, and they would laugh at us. For example, we pronounced the word "yours," as "your-un." If we were to ask somebody, "Is this yours?" we would say, "Is this your-un?" At first a lot of fights emanated from misunderstandings. But the fights didn't last too long because being farm boys we were strong compared to city boys. If Clyde and Lyle, my younger brothers, got into a hassle at school, they would say, "You better watch out or I'll tell my brother on you." That ended it; the other younger kids didn't want any part of me!

In the beginning we also dressed differently from the other kids. Most of our clothes had been homemade by Mother or by a dressmaker, whereas the other kids' clothes were city-bought clothes. When they learned that we came from the Indian country, the kids would always ask, "Did you ever see any Indians?" They had never seen any except in the movies, but we had. They wanted to hear

Our family's house at 4224 Colfax Avenue,
Minneapolis, Minnesota. This is a recent photo.
The only difference from when I lived there
is that the porch has been enclosed.
Also, there used to be a bracket for a flag—
my grandfather would hang a U.S. flag out
every day when we were at war with Germany.

more, and they wanted to know if we'd seen cowboys, too. We had—they used to come into Marvin with their pistols and outfits just like you see in the movies. As kids, we had experiences that the city kids didn't have, and they were curious.

Our house became popular because we were right across the street from the school, and after school all the kids would come over to play in our yard. I think that because we were a curiosity to the kids, we became sort of popular.

When it was 18 below zero we didn't have to go to school: instead of going to school we would play, go ice skating or tobogganing, play football or throw snowballs. We often played football in the snow; if you fell you hit a cushion of snow, so you didn't get hurt much. I was one of the better football players of our gang—the game just came naturally to me. My father could afford to buy us good equipment; for instance, we always had a good toboggan, skis, and other sports gear. A lot of the kids didn't have any, so we would loan some to our friends. I had a bicycle that everybody envied, a special bike called a Pierce Arrow. It was the only bike in our territory that had springs on the forks, so if you hit a bump, it was very soft. A certain group of the boys all had bikes, and in the summer we'd go on long safaris down to the Mississippi River to a place called Minnehaha Falls. It was named after an Indian girl, Minnehaha. Our maids would fix up a good lunch for us, so we could have a picnic at the falls. It had a good swimming hole.

I remember I once had a fight with a bully about my brother Kenneth. Kenneth had a rough time because he was retarded. I was smaller, but I was solid as a rock and I beat the hell out of the big bully. From then on I was popular. I'm sure it helped that I was good in winter sports.

I palled around with a very popular boy who lived down the

street. His father had been in France during World War I. When he came home, he had a suitcase full of souvenirs. Among the souvenirs was a whole stack of French postcards, showing nude women and sexual scenes. The boy took me up to his father's bedroom and opened up a case—I'd never seen anything like those pictures. I talked the boy into letting me have a picture of a nude woman, and the word got around the school that I might be convinced to let some of the guys have a peep at the picture. Later my friend's father caught on, and he told my father. My father then asked me, "Do you have a postcard that belongs to [so-and-so] in this house?" And I said, "Yeah, here it is." My father looked at the naked picture and couldn't believe it. He had never seen such a thing. But it was little incidents like that that helped us become acquainted with the kids in Minneapolis.

There was a movie theater on Lake Street, which today is a big boulevard downtown. We could get to the theater on a streetcar. The fare was five cents and we got a transfer coming back. So, it cost us five cents to go to the theater and back and 10 cents to see the movie. A group of us always liked to go on Saturday when we could. The movies were silent then. The Mack Sennett comedies and Westerns were popular. Of course, we didn't care too much for dramas— we wanted the adventure, the cowboys, and comedies. One cowboy actor was William S. Hart. Later in life I became acquainted with him. He was a neighbor of mine in California.

One of the things I remember distinctly was the first job I ever had. I was about 13 years old. Two friends I palled around with on bicycles had gotten jobs with a lady living on Lake Calhoun, one of the five lakes in Minneapolis. Lake Calhoun joined Lake Harriet, which was just a few blocks from our home. In order to stay with my buddies, one day I went with them to the job. The woman made a product that would seal inner tubes of tires. With a lit match held to the end of the product (it was about the size and shape of a pack of chewing gum), you'd burn enough to melt it. You would drip it onto a cut or nail hole in an inner tube, and it would theoretically seal the hole. The boys were paid about 25 cents for each one hundred packages they wrapped, so I went along to help them increase their income. I worked very slowly and very meticulously, wrapping the packages I had with what we then called "tinfoil"—today it's known as aluminum foil. I made my little wrappings very neat. My buddies were in a hurry because they were being paid by volume rather than by the hour. The lady was so impressed with my work that she fired my two buddies and hired me.

I worked alone for about ten days. I would use most of my income to buy a pie for lunch at a bakery nearby. Then the police came to the lady's home claiming that users of her product found that the only time the inner tube would hold was while the car was parked; on the highway, the product, in the heat of the summer, would become liquid. If you had the car parked a certain way, the liquid would run to the bottom of the tire and the air would run out. When I told my father about it, he thought I should quit, so I wouldn't get involved with the police. So I did. I was so proud of the money I had earned, even though I had an allowance from my father and didn't really save it.

Lake Harriet was a beautiful, round lake in an affluent residential section of Minneapolis. The lake was well protected from winds and storms, so it was good for canoeing, fishing, and swimming. In the wintertime, we would ice skate along the shore. But one day we had great excitement at Lake Harriet. My younger brother Clyde, the youngest son in our family, had fallen off the end of the dock. Our house was only three or four blocks from the lake, and someone called my mother, who called my father, and we all went to the lake. A policeman had dragged Clyde from the lake, draped him upside down over a canoe, and he was pumping Clyde's back, forcing the water out of his stomach. Clyde had almost drowned, but the policeman saved his life. As a reward, my father gave the policeman $500 cash, which was a lot of money then. And from then on we were very popular with the police around the lake.

One of my friends, Earl Metling, lived near our home. We were buddies all the time I lived in Minneapolis. Back then nobody ever locked their doors. Earl and I found an empty house and thought we would go in and snoop around and see what we could see. The front door was open, so we merrily walked in. We found a woman lying on the living room floor in a pool of blood. We wasted no time running to the local drugstore, where we told the druggist about it. He called the police, the police came up, word spread, and a crowd eventually congregated around the house. A policeman interviewed us and we told him exactly what happened, and that night they came to my home and interviewed me a second time in the presence of my father. I don't think we were ever suspects, but one of the embarrassing questions was "What were you doing in the house?" Turns out it was a murder; she was stabbed. That created a lot of concern in our neighborhood, and, as I remember, the police put on extra patrols. I don't remember if they ever caught the murderer.

The day we moved to Minneapolis was the first time that my mother had actually seen our home. My father had taken her on a few occasions to see the city and show her around, but she had no friends that I know of in the beginning. Her social life was restricted to me and my brothers and sisters. My father was away most of the time in Texas and in Marvin with his real estate and oil business. Being ambitious, he entertained clients more than he did friends.

Mother kept busy seeing that we were dressed well and fed well, and that we traveled with the right boys in the right neighborhoods. Her life generally centered on my sisters, Evelyn, Dorothy, and Florence. They were at an age where they needed care and guidance. She gradually became acquainted with a few of the neighbors and began to attend a church that was within walking distance of our home—she seldom missed a chance to go to church. There she became friends with several women. So her whole contact with the outside world eventually came through the church and not through my father's activities.

I had a cat in Minneapolis, which had a black moustache, black whiskers, and a white face. When I came home one day from school, my older sister, Evelyn, and my younger sister, Florence, had the cat on the floor by the fireplace and had just clipped his whiskers off so that he looked sort of like Groucho Marx. That started a confrontation. I jumped on my sisters about the poor cat—he was so ashamed he was hiding. I raised a lot of hell with my sisters; for a couple years after that, I think they were afraid of me.

My sisters were pretty well chaperoned by my mother and the Swedish maids, and we boys gravitated to my grandfather's side. If we came home with some lesson from school that we didn't understand, my grandfather would help us with it. When he got through with us, we understood it pretty well. We got pretty good grades because Grandfather helped with most of our homework.

My grandfather had a lot of friends in Minneapolis from the days when he worked for the big department store there. They were mostly retired, and they liked to congregate in one of the saloons downtown. Sometimes my grandfather would come home on the streetcar pretty well loaded, which didn't go over too well with my father. Dad was more of a puritan. He didn't smoke or drink, and he thought my grandfather would be a bad influence on us because he occasionally smoked a cigar and would join his friends at the saloon. My grandfather also liked politics. When Woodrow Wilson came to town after the war, there was a big parade down Hennepin Avenue. Wearing a stove-pipe hat, Wilson sat in the back seat of a car. My grandfather and I were standing on the curb along with the crowd, and my grandfather lifted me up on his shoulders so that I could see the president. He made me stay up there until the whole procession was over.

During this time, my dad was selling farmland and was sort of a promoter of oil deals. Texas was getting a lot of attention because of the oil gushers that were coming in, and the farmers who had made money were always after my dad: "Hubert, can you get me in on an oil deal?" The oil wells in Texas were shallow—around 500 feet in Liberty County. That was before the big boom came and they went deeper. At one time you could get good wells at 500 feet. I later had a book about Texas oil that was full of the names of famous people in the oil business. I'd ask Dad, "Did you ever meet him? Did you ever see him?" He'd say, "Yeah, I knew him." There was a sort of fraternity of oil men who hung around the oil fields.

People would come to my father and say, "I understand you've got oil interests in Texas." Dad would reply, "Well, I do have an oil lease that we're going to drill, and we've got one or two working interests open and are asking $2,500 for an eighth interest," or something like that. And they'd either hit or get dry holes. But the boom was on; practically everybody who got into oil in Texas was making money just on the lease. If you had an interest, somebody would want to buy your share. People didn't lose much because they could sell enough of their interest to protect themselves in case there was a dry hole. But there weren't many dry holes; everybody was hitting oil.

The only problem that caused them to lose money came from John D. Rockefeller. He tied up all the railroads transporting oil—that's where he made his money. All the oil wells were put on an allotment basis—you could send out only so many barrels a day. That law is still in effect in Texas. If you strike oil in Texas today, after you get your costs back you may be limited to producing 20 barrels a day. (They did it to me on a well.) There was really more quick money to be made on the sale of leases. For instance, you could lease up to 5,000 acres and then break the parcel up and sell small parcels. You'd get big money for a lease, especially if you could see oil wells in the distance. The boom was on; everybody wanted to get into oil. Prosperity was practically forced on my father—he didn't have to look for customers because they all came to him. Most of these people were farmers who had sold their farms for a high price on a cash deal. They had good prospects for making millions of dollars investing in oil in Texas.

CHAPTER 5

Our Move to California, the Train Ride to San Fernando, and the Southern California Land Boom

In the summer of 1921, my family moved to San Fernando, California. After one of my father's trips to Texas, he told my mother and grandfather excitedly about some men he had met from California and, in particular, a man by the name of Brand, a multimillionaire. He was very excited about the prospect of moving to California, particularly because of a big land boom there. I remember how my father kept encouraging us with talk of the wonderful climate and the men he met from California and the stories they told about it and that he could make a fortune in real estate. My father once told me that the earth has only so many acres of land, and more people are coming all the time, so the principle of making money with real estate was to have it and sell it to other people. In the land of golden streets, orange trees, and wonderful climate, he would get away from the one thing that had been a constant hassle in his life—the very cold winters of South Dakota and Minnesota.

The prospect of moving to California did not appeal to my mother or my grandfather at first because both had friends in Minneapolis.

My grandfather had old friends, and my mother had acquired friends at the Presbyterian church. In addition, the boys had made acquaintances at school. I think it took a lot of courage for my father to override the wishes of my grandfather and my mother. The children really didn't know anything about California or the West; the only thing we knew about the West was cowboys and Indians. If divorces had been popular in those days, I think my mother probably would have divorced my father. Riding on a train so far seemed like a great expedition and an adventure, which appealed to me (I was fourteen then) more than it did to any other member of the family.

Finally, my father won out. The decision to go to California excited many of the neighbors and our friends because in 1921 not many people were pulling up their roots and taking off. The day that we were scheduled to board the train, my father had two large taxicabs or rented cars come to our house. He had two clotheslines, one for each car. In one car was my grandfather and the four boys. Grandfather's responsibility was to look after us at the railroad depot. The second car was occupied by my father, my mother, the maids, and my sisters, who sat on the adults' laps. After we reached the depot the first thing my father did was to tie us boys to my grandfather in tandem so that we had to walk Indian-style, one after the other. There was no way we could get lost. And the same thing was done with my mother, father, and the maids (I think the girls were carried).

It was fortunate that we *were* tied together because the depot was crowded. I don't think any of us ever saw so many people together at one time. And the trains looked so big! I think my father must have rented half of one Pullman car; it seemed like we had a lot of extra seats in our area. My dad positioned us so that the boys would be on one side of the aisle and the girls would be on the other, and we'd all be well chaperoned and protected.

The first night out was probably the most trying for my mother because she had to decide who would sleep in the lower bunks and who would sleep in the upper bunks. Pullmans were very luxurious then. There was a way of taking the back of your seat and forming it with the seat you sat on to make a double bed, so you could sleep two in the lower bed and one on the upper bed. The maids and my grandfather slept in the upper bunks because my parents feared that the children would fall and be hurt. My father and mother were in a lower bunk. We eventually settled on a routine for going to bed, so we all slept very well.

The train stopped often (which disturbed our sleep at first) to take on milk, eggs, vittles, and water. Water was, of course, crucial for the steam engines. Practically every little crossroads had a wooden water tower at which the trains could fill up their water tanks. It took us about two or three days to get fully settled on the train. We had an agreement with the conductors that they would advise us when the train was coming into a town so we could have a meal. Then we would all be lashed together with the clotheslines. The depots had restaurants known as Harvey Houses, which had wonderful waitresses known as Harvey Girls. We would eat at tables tied together. The steam engine would whistle several times to warn passengers that they had so many more minutes to eat. After the second whistle, there were still two to three minutes to board the train. My father insisted that we eat fast and be ready to leave by the second warning signal. We'd parade back to our train, and when the Harvey House was cleared out and everybody was aboard to the satisfaction of the conductor, the train would leave.

The South Dakota territory was familiar to us, so the trip wasn't too exciting for us until we were farther west. The farther west you went the more primitive it became. We would see straggler herds of buffalo—I don't think any of us, except my father and grandfather, had ever seen buffalo in Marvin. A man aboard the train told stories about the Indians and tried to frighten us, so we kept guard at the windows looking for an Indian attack, which of course never came.

At the beginning of the trip, my grandfather circulated from car to car. He met several Germans he conversed with. My mother and the maids stayed mostly in our Pullman car. The beds were converted back into seats in the daytime, except when my mother wanted to sleep in the afternoon. The porters would leave her seat with the upper bunk made up during the day, so anybody who wanted to take a nap could do so.

My brothers and I were naturally curious and sat near the windows, watching the terrain. As we got closer to the western part of South Dakota, I think part of the train was uncoupled and went south with another train to avoid going over the high part of the Rocky Mountains. At one point we were in Albuquerque, New Mexico, and we were running parallel to the super colossal mountains.

I remember one exciting time when the train ran parallel to a cattle drive; we waved at the cowboys and they waved back at us. There were cows as far as you could see. Once we got to Arizona, Indian women would be sitting at the depots in little groups, and each one would have trinkets and blankets for sale. We liked the idea that finally we could get close enough to Indians to see what they were really like. The Navajos and the Zunis were very friendly, and they depended on selling their goods to people on the trains. A lot of people bought them, too. (We did not, as my father didn't allow us.)

The desolation was very discouraging to my mother and our Swedish maids. It seemed to them that the farther west we went, the worse it got. We were simply on our way to hell—it was so hot.

We eventually got to a little town called Needles near the Nevada-California border. It had a hotel, a restaurant, and a place that sold ice cream. I think the train laid over an extra five minutes so everybody could have ice cream—we hadn't seen any up to that time except in Minneapolis. We all ordered ice cream cones, but by the time I got to the train I had a cone full of milk. That's how hot it was—around 120 degrees! The hot desert of Needles, California, was a new experience for our family. That was the point at which I thought my mother was going to commit suicide—she was crying. Even my father had been wondering if he'd made a bad move. Crossing the desert was the worst part of our whole long journey. It was so hot and desolate—just sand, dust, and heat.

All that changed the minute we got to San Bernardino. The air was different, the climate was beautiful, and as far as your eye could see were gorgeous orange trees and nice homes. By the time we got to Los Angeles, we had seen beautiful homes and a different world, and Dad convinced us that San Fernando would be the same as Los Angeles. In Los Angeles we changed trains to another line that took us to San Fernando.

San Fernando had a depot then; 20 years later it didn't—buses took over. We were taken to the Porter Hotel, about the only building in town that wasn't Spanish style. We stayed there one night, and I think on the second day we moved into a home that Dad had never even seen. He bought it like a pig in a poke through a friend he had met in Texas. The friend owned the newspaper in San Fernando, and my dad later went into partnership with him, creating Munn and Poppelman Realtors.

Our new house had a tremendous yard—over five acres—and about half of it was planted with orange trees. When we realized that you could go out and pick an orange off the tree, we were very excited. The house only had three bedrooms, though; we had to set up beds in the living room. My father immediately set a builder to work on a second house, and he added a big breakfast room to the original house. So there was a lot of activity at our home when we moved in.

My father immediately started investing in orange groves upon the advice of his first partner, a Mr. Brand, whose home is now a museum in Glendale. Dad started his real estate company with Mr. Munn by converting an orange grove into a subdivision. It was interesting how they sold the lots: They would take possibly ten acres in town and put stakes at the corner of each lot. Each stake would have a number on it and would be tall enough to hold a flag. At the entrance to the subdivision would be a temporary platform with a stand that would hold a band. The head salesman would have a megaphone, and as buses full of potential buyers came from the depots, he would make his pitch. (In San Bernardino, which was probably 50 miles outside of Los Angeles, a salesman would get on the train. By the time the train got to Los Angeles he'd have several busloads of customers ready to go from the train to the bus to the subdivision.) The lots would be sold between 10:00 in the morning and 5:00 in the afternoon. In some instances, the customers were advised to buy two lots because before the day was over they could sell one of them at a higher price, which would almost pay for the first one. The promotion was tremendous—free watermelons, free Mexican food, a Mexican band up on the stand; it was almost like a Mexican holiday.

Dad and the other developers always sold the lots when the oranges were nice and golden on the tree. People would look at the groves and wouldn't be able to resist. The price was ridiculously low, about $300 or $400 per lot. My grandfather bought an orange grove on 7th Street—ten acres of oranges, which took up almost a city block. He probably paid $600 or $700 an acre.

The San Fernando Valley was sparsely settled. The main road from San Fernando to Hollywood was two lanes. There were very few houses along Lankershim Boulevard, and the north end of the valley had big groves owned by Sunkist Oranges, with big packing houses in San Fernando. It eventually all became subdivisions. I think at one time my father must have owned close to 1,000 acres of the property of the big Sunkist Ranch.

There was no air pollution in the valley in those days; the San Fernando Valley was a paradise. It was a perfect climate with no smog, no freeways. There were several separate towns (Van Nuys, Chatsworth, Glendale—and Burbank, which is now a big hustling city). In our athletic league we would play teams from those towns. We practiced against Glendale one time when John Wayne was on the Glendale team. Like today, there were gangs. My gang included Peppe Herram, who was a Spaniard. (Peppe was a great athlete, too, and a nice guy. He was like a brother to me.) We had two to three Mexican boys. And the Utzman boys, Kenneth, Stanley, and Willis, would run around with us.

The area wasn't all orange groves; there were farms also. Japanese people couldn't own land, but they could lease it. Practically all the farm fields—strawberries, lettuce, carrots—were operated by the Japanese. My father leased some of his land to a Japanese farmer whose wife lived in Japan; his name was Emi. Emi kept our house supplied with vegetables; he was almost a member of the family. One day Emi came to my dad and said, "I want a little party at your house to celebrate."

My dad said, "Emi, what do you want to celebrate?"

He said, "A child."

And my father said, "How can you have a child when your wife is in Japan?"

He said, "Oh, me have good friend."

So we had the party. Of course, years later when World War II broke out, Emi left our family. It was just like a family member leaving. He was a nice guy.

Hollywood was sending all its movie stars out in the San Fernando Valley and beyond to tape movies, so there was a lot of interesting action going on in the valley between movie companies, farming industries, and the historical missions.

When Jack Dempsey came to San Fernando, he came out with his manager, Doc Kerns, I think they called him. They came to check on buying an orange grove. My father told me, "Raymond, tomorrow get cleaned up, put your best clothes on, and you come down to the office in the morning about 10:00. I want you to meet somebody." And that's when I met Jack Dempsey. He was at the height of his career. They had a big parade for him in Hollywood, and the crowd just moved in on him, which stopped the whole parade. He was very popular. I probably didn't appreciate meeting him then so much. He was a quiet-spoken guy, as I remember him. Dad told him that I was a good football player and bragged about me. Of course, comparing me as an athlete to Jack Dempsey was ridiculous, but I realize now it was a big day for me.

I worked one summer with the irrigation system at my grandfather's grove. There was a slight rise in the land as it went to the east, and a nearby concrete reservoir was used as a swimming pool. Water from the reservoir drained down toward the orange trees. Between each grove of orange trees was about an 18-inch piece of concrete culvert that projected up in the air. Between each tree would be six rows that carried water down between the trees. The pipe that extended out of the ground had six outlets, which could be controlled by sliding a piece of metal up and down with the amount of water to come. So the water went through each row in the whole orchard, watering all the trees. The first year we were there, I was trained to adjust the water; I worked all summer on my grandfather's orchard. Kenneth and I would walk up and down the ditches with hoes to remove the debris and leaves so the water would flow down and irrigate the trees.

The following year, Dad subdivided the property, and it was the same routine: free Mexican food (mostly tamales that could be wrapped and would stay warm), a Mexican band, a man with a horn, the master of ceremonies dealing out instructions to everybody, buses coming, and lots going like hotcakes. He would be sold out in a day.

Dad worked with three different building contractors, and they furnished the salesmen with maps and catalogs. Buyers would contract to buy a stock home from a catalog; prefabricated houses became quite popular. A truck loaded with lumber would arrive, and every piece of lumber on the truck was for the house. The truck would be unloaded and the houses would spring up. There was plenty of labor then, especially plenty of carpenters because many were moving to California. Mexicans provided a lot of labor. During the time I lived in San Fernando, from 1921 through 1925, the population was about 3 to 5 percent Mexicans. In 1991, the Mexican population was about 97 percent; the ratio has reversed.

My grandfather wanted to learn to speak Spanish, and every day he would walk about four miles, I think, from our home on 4th Street to the Mexican part of town to get a shave from a Mexican

My father, "Bert," and me at my father's home
in San Fernando, California, 1950.
So far as I know, this is the only photograph
I have of just the two of us.

barber. He wasn't particularly interested in the shave so much as practicing the language. In English, he'd ask the barber, "How do you say [this or that or the other thing]?" and the barber would tell him. My grandfather was soon a great help to my dad; when Dad had any occasion to use Spanish, he'd put my grandfather in the car and take him with him as an interpreter.

During our first year in San Fernando I attended a small grammar school. In 1922 I was eligible for San Fernando High School, one of the few high schools in the whole San Fernando Valley. San Fernando had a population in 1920 of about 5,000 people within the city limits. Just outside the city limits, which would be in Los Angeles, was the famous San Fernando Mission, built in about 1790. My father and Mr. Brand bought about 25 acres near the mission and gave it to the San Fernando Mission for a park. It was a great tourist attraction at the time I lived there and still is. The railroad station was practically on Main Street, which had stores on one side of the street. The other side, between the depot and the railroad track, was barren ground. On one of the corners of San Fernando Road was the Porter Hotel, owned by the prominent Porter family, where we had stayed our first night. Only one black person lived in San Fernando, and he was permitted to live there by a special vote of the City Council because he was the shoeshine boy at the Porter Hotel.

San Fernando was endowed and blessed with deep-water wells. Los Angeles, through old Spanish laws, claimed all the other water in the San Fernando area. There was a 24-year court battle commencing in the 1950s between San Fernando and Los Angeles over water rights. Later, the man who married my youngest sister, a prominent attorney, won the suit for San Fernando against Los Angeles, preserving San Fernando's water rights. His name was Neville R. Lewis.

The real estate firm of Munn and Poppelman lasted about two or three years. Mr. Munn died and the newspaper part was taken over by his family, none of whom were realtors. My father wanted to go on his own, so he started the Hubert J. Poppelman Real Estate Company.

CHAPTER 6

High School Years, Motorcycling around California, and Joining the Marine Corps

When my father went into real estate by himself, his main office was in San Fernando, but he covered an area that went all the way to Del Mar. At the height of his operations, he had almost 30 branch offices. He was an original developer of an area called Big Bear, a mountain resort. Today it's a big operation. He also developed a part of Del Mar, an affluent area north of San Diego. When my dad developed a subdivision, he would name the streets after his salesmen. San Fernando probably has 20 streets that were named after my father's salesmen.

In conjunction with selling land, which was my dad's main occupation, he was associated with builders who would construct the houses. During my high school days, Dad would always get me a summer job with one of those contractors. One summer I worked with a construction company that did mostly concrete work—building swimming pools— so I learned the concrete business. Other summers I worked with a carpenter, framing houses. I also worked with a plumber and with the Los Angeles Bureau of Power and Light, installing telephone lines and power lines. And part of that summer

I also worked on the San Francisquito Dam up at Saugus, California. The dam collapsed two years after it was opened, and hundreds of people drowned. So, although my school years were spent in typical high school classes, my summer months were spent in the heat, doing rugged work for contractors. I did not know then that I'd be a builder someday and make good use of the training I got.

At the same time, my father had a summer home in Venice, California—a big recreation and tourist area today. When we first lived there, Jackie Cooper, a child movie star, and his family lived next door. One Sunday my dad took our family for a ride to San Diego. We came home late, about 10:00 at night, to find our beds occupied by a bunch of professional wrestlers. They had leased Jackie Cooper's parents' home, but in those days people didn't lock their houses; our door was always open. The wrestlers were in the wrong house! (Our house looked just like the Cooper house.) Dad got them straightened out, and they moved on to where they were supposed to be.

As a result, I became acquainted with that group of professional wrestlers who were passing through Los Angeles. They taught me how to wrestle, and I had a lot of fun with them, which probably helped me in my football days. And believe it or not—this is a true story—out of that group of wrestlers, there was one wrestler I could sometimes pin down. And at the end of the summer, he said, "Hey, Ray, I got some free tickets to go to the wrestling matches. Guess what? I'm on the main event."

So we went to the wrestling match. Of course, all the matches were faked. My friend was the big winner, slamming the other guy down under his feet—and he was the same man I could sometimes pin down. The wrestlers showed me how to defend myself and how to walk up to a man, shake hands, and within five seconds have him on his back yelling for help. When I was working out in their gymnasium on the beach, they would rehearse before they'd go to Los Angeles for the big Saturday night matches. I learned little things like bending your opponent's wrist back, which would really make a wrestler howl. (They would never use any moves that would harm each other. They'd use holds and grimace to make it appear a guy was going to break a leg off, but they really didn't hurt each other too much.) As a result of that training, I became quite prominent in athletics in San Fernando High School. In my senior year I was captain of four teams: football, baseball, basketball, and track.

George Marshall, the world champion, was one of the wrestlers next door. When he was dressed up, he looked like he could have been a salesman in a department store selling children's clothes. He looked so gentle. Joe Savolde from Notre Dame was a rough, tough guy. He had some movie parts—some of the wrestlers were employed by the movie industry. Londos, another in the group (he was also a world champion), was a gorgeous human being. He wrestled the old-fashioned way (Greco-Roman style); the wrestlers would get tangled up with each other and maybe be on the floor for an hour. But most people didn't want to see that sort of thing; they wanted action. That's what wrestling turned into and why it is what it is today—an exhibition. If you slam a man down hard, it excites the crowd much more than it would if you got a leg hold around your opponent's stomach or in a scissors hold and made him squeal. Savolde once got a scissors hold around my leg, and I squealed for my life. I thought he was going to kill me, it hurt so much. He had tremendous strength.

In high school I was about 5 feet 10 inches tall and weighed 165 pounds. I was very muscular, and I was a natural athlete. I was the star of the football team because I was a shifty runner. I didn't like baseball, but I played—second base—because the coach wanted me

CONGRATULATIONS

Raymond Poppelman
1925 Team

On behalf of the City of Los Angeles, I would like to congratulate you on being inducted to the San Fernando High School Football Alumni Association Hall of Fame.

Congratulations and best wishes in all your future endeavors.

RICHARD ALARCÓN
Councilmember
District 7

December 7, 1994

This award was given to me in 1994 by the City of Los Angeles, congratulating me on being inducted into the San Fernando High School Football Alumni Association Hall of Fame. It was a great honor.

to. If the pitcher threw me a fast ball, I could hit it—my eyes were good—but I had trouble hitting a curve. I was not a great pole vaulter because my top height wasn't extremely high (that was with the old bamboo poles). I was also on the swimming team; I used to swim the 50-yard and the 100-yard, but it was not an official team; it was a haphazard group that got together. Later, when I was in the Marine Corps, I was on the swimming team. But I think that my early training when I was a boy on the farm—clearing rocks off the field, and the chores I had working in the barn, getting hay down to the cows and horses, splitting wood—built me up so the hardships of athletics in high school didn't bother me much. I was just naturally a strong guy.

Because I liked football and I was good at it, I was on many of the all-valley teams and had offers to go to several universities. I had thought I would go to the University of Southern California (USC) because my coach had come from there. But during my high school days, one prominent student athlete went to the U.S. Naval Academy. After he graduated he came back to our high school to make a speech. He spoke well and told us about the training and some of the trips they'd take sailing boats. I was practically hypnotized by him, and he looked so handsome in his uniform. I met him after the speech and he said, "Ray, you should go to the Naval Academy." And I decided, "By God, I'm going to go."

I put aside a lot of the offers I had—from schools like Stanford, the University of California at Berkeley, and USC—because I wanted to concentrate on Annapolis and be a naval officer. My father was enthusiastic; he had worked with our congressman on a land deal as the broker, selling a big chunk of land adjoining San Fernando to the U.S. government for a hospital. He and the congressman made a deal to have me appointed to the Naval Academy. But the congressman wanted a kickback from my father, which my father wouldn't consider since it was illegal. (My father made a good commission on the deal.) Because my father would not give in to the congressman for that kickback, my chances of being appointed evaporated. I began to reconsider the offers I was getting through my coach to attend one of the other schools.

Just before graduation, our basketball team was getting ready for a championship game against Van Nuys High School in the San Fernando Valley. As a preliminary buildup for the championship basketball game, our gang decided that we'd go down and play a prank. We were going to paint "SF High School" on some big pillars on the main administration building of Van Nuys High School. The question was, Where would we get the paint? My father had a contractor named Bowles. We went over to his house, went through his garage, and found a can of black asphalt paint we decided to use. In two automobiles about 12 of us went to Van Nuys High School, which was 12 miles from San Fernando. We set lookouts to warn the guys who were going to do the painting of approaching cars. I was one of the lookouts. Willis Utzman, who had graduated from San Fernando High School, had gone into the navy, and had come back after he was discharged, had two brothers who went to San Fernando High School. He decided he would do the painting, but instead of painting small letters, maybe a foot or 18 inches high, he made six-foot-tall letters.

Of course all hell broke loose. Investigators tried to find out who painted the letters and who owned the paint. Bowles had mentioned to his daughter, Ruth, that he was missing a can of black paint. Ruth decided to be the heroine. She went to the principal of the school and told her that Ray Poppelman had taken the paint. I was called into the principal's office. I said, "Yes, I was in on it, but I was just a

My high school graduation
portrait, 1925.

lookout. I had no idea it was going to be such a big job." The principal said, "Do you mind telling me who was with you?" And I said,
"No, I can't tell you." We had an honor system in our gang.

The manuals training teacher, the coach, and everybody else set
to work trying to get me to tell on my buddies so that we'd all go
down and apologize to Van Nuys High School. They eventually decided that as part of my punishment, I had to make a speech to our
student body. I was seated on the stage of our large auditorium with
the principal and a couple of teachers. I got up and said, "If there's
anybody in this room that was involved in the painting of Van Nuys
High School, just keep your mouth shut and don't say anything because they don't know who you are and I'm not going to tell them."

The school administrators then took me to Van Nuys High School

Some high school friends and me (center)
clowning around before graduation in 1925.
On one particular day everybody dressed
in odd clothes and had a lot of fun taking pictures.

and made me apologize to the students. I told them, "I didn't paint
your high school, but I was with the gang that did. I'm honor-bound
not to tell their names, so I will take full responsibility. I will pay for
getting the paint cleaned off your school. I assume all responsibility
and have come here to apologize to you."

So my name became known all over the valley. I was blamed for
the prank—which I didn't do—because I was the only one caught.
My father was upset because he was a prominent businessman. Then
the principal decided I should be expelled and said I would not receive my diploma. After my father heard that, he put me in the car
one evening and drove us to the principal's house. He read her the
riot act—so she reconsidered.

At about this time, I was interested in and had some experience
with motorcycles. I had borrowed $90 from my grandfather to buy a
used Harley-Davidson racing motorcycle. When my father found

out I had the bike, he told me I had to get rid of it. So I told him I would, but I lied; I hid it with Kenneth Utzman, a buddy of mine. One day in 1926, not long after I had graduated from high school, Dad bought a new Stutz car—it was very low slung, was black with red wheels, and had a big long hood. You won't believe the coincidence: Dad was driving through San Fernando at Main Street, and I was driving the motorbike that I had supposedly gotten rid of. I had been behind a bunch of dump trucks hauling wet gravel, and I came out from behind the trucks, moving along at a pretty good clip. Who should come up Main Street in San Fernando to the intersection I was crossing? Of course it was my father in his big super Stutz automobile with the long hood. And because the road was gravelly and wet, I slid into his car, hitting the right front wheel. I was thrown on top of his car and hit the hood and put a big dent in it. My father jumped out. I was a bit stunned, and he was concerned that I was hurt. But I wasn't. I was in pretty good shape. My dad grounded me.

Then I decided that I wanted to go to visit Stanford and a couple of other colleges up north. I went on a motorcycle safari up north for two months with my buddies Kenneth Utzman and Peppe Herram. When we ran out of money, we got jobs as gardeners and carpenters. We worked in San Jose, California, where the widow of the Winchester Arms Company was building a big mansion. She had a mill on the property and she kept adding to it, and everything she put in it was crazy. For instance, she would have stairs going up to a landing, and when you'd open the doors at the top, there was nothing there—you'd fall to the ground if you walked out. And in another spot, you could pull a lever and all the stairs would fold into a slide, so that anyone who went up there, like a burglar, would slide back down. She had many such tricks in this house.

(It's famous for that reason, and is now a museum.) But we picked up a little money there as carpenters as we traveled up toward Sacramento.

We'd been up to the University of Oregon, I think, and were on our way back, rolling along one night just after dark, when we saw an automobile with headlights shining straight up in the air. When we got to the car, we realized it had gone down about a seven- or eight-foot embankment and was upside-down in a foot of water. There were two occupants in it, a woman and a man, and there was very little traffic on the road. We pulled them out of the car and up onto the highway. We flagged down a couple of cars and had them take the couple to a hospital in Sacramento. Before we left, the man was just awake enough that he could talk. He said, "Who are you boys?"

And I said, "Oh, we're just bumming around looking for jobs."

He said, "Follow me to the hospital. I want to talk to you." So we did, and he introduced himself. He turned out to be in charge of the underworld in Sacramento—prostitution, jobs, everything. We visited him the following day and he said, "What can I do for you boys? You did save my life."

He gave Kenneth a job at the employment agency hauling loggers up to logging camps. Peppe didn't want to stay, so he went back to where we'd had jobs as gardeners on the estate of the president of the Union Pacific Railroad. I got the prize job—I was the bagman for the prostitutes. I went around with my motorcycle to different addresses and rang the doorbell, and I'd be handed an envelope with money. After I collected the envelopes, they'd say, "You know you're entitled to a freebie." I'd say, "I'm not interested."

I lasted about ten days. I was amazed at how young the girls were and at the nicer addresses some of them had. Most of them were quite nice looking, too. They were always kidding with me: "You're a cute little fellow. Why don't you come in?" I was a novelty to them. I would turn the money in to the big boss—the guy we had rescued—and was paid well. Finally I decided it was time to get back to San Fernando, so I thanked the big boss, who asked, "What do you think you're going to do now?"

I said, "I guess I'll go to school." And I told him that I wanted to go to the Naval Academy.

He said, "Naval Academy? Go to the marine recruiting office in Sacramento and see [so-and-so] and talk to him."

I went down there and told the guy I wanted to go to the Naval Academy, and he said, "Hell, if you would join the marines and become a corporal, you'd be eligible to take our examination." So my whole future brightened up. I hooked up with my friends Kenneth and Peppe again, and we raced like hell toward San Fernando. I was going to talk to my dad about going to San Diego and getting in the Marine Corps.

In San Francisco, Kenneth broke a chain on his bike, so he parked his bike and drove double with me and Pep to the motorcycle agency in San Francisco. We went to the back door where the mechanics were working. Kenneth borrowed a set of coveralls and some tools, making the mechanic think we had trouble with my bike. Then he walked into the showroom where they had the bicycles on display, acting like he worked for the shop. He took the chain off a new bike, and out we went.

When we reached San Luis Obispo we were short of money. We found a little hotel we thought we could run out on. We checked into it and were sneaking out early in the morning when we got caught. Between the police department and the owner of the hotel, someone called my father. He was surprised as hell at the whole thing because he hadn't seen me in six weeks—and he didn't even know we were traveling by motorcycle!

My dad promised he would send some money to pay for our hotel room and other expenses. When I finally got home, I had my father to contend with. I told him some of what I'd done, but I didn't tell him I'd been running around as a bagman for a bunch of whores. I told him that if I joined the Marine Corps and become a corporal, I could take the officers' examination. Dad was concerned about my activities with motorbikes and thought the Marine Corps would be good for me. So Kenneth Utzman and I decided we would join, but we hadn't gotten around to doing it when we had an incident that was the stimulus for enlisting.

Here's the story. The city of San Fernando had hired a motorcycle cop, a pudgy sort of fellow. His motorcycle was a stock Harley-Davidson with big fenders and spotlights. Kenneth and I were cruising up a street by Main Street right opposite where the policeman was parked. We tried to tease him a little bit by slipping the clutch and racing the engine right in front of him. He accepted our challenge and started chasing us, with his warning siren going, so we went up to 4th Street, which crossed an old riverbed, and had gravel with a high bank on each side. We used to practice jumping up the bank with our bikes. You'd go like hell, jump, and if you leaned forward over your handlebars you could make a good landing. If you just hit the bank, you'd fall over. We raced across the riverbed and made the jump. The cop followed on his stock motorcycle. He didn't lean forward, and he went up and made a U-turn in the air and landed on the riverbed. He took quite a jolt, but he had enough fat on him to give him a cushion, I think.

That night, Kenneth and I were both put in jail—not the good jail uptown, but an old abandoned jail that was nothing but a cement building with bars on it. I told Kenneth, "Don't worry about it. My dad will get us out. He knows the chief of police real well." But my father told the chief of police to leave us in there for a couple of days.

It got worse. We had to go to court, and the judge, by the name of Decker, gave us an option of going into jail or joining the marines. (Father had told him that I wanted to go into the Marine Corps. I think my father was cooperating with the judge, or the judge was cooperating with my father.) That was just what I wanted to hear. So Kenneth and I were given a reprieve: We could join the marines and we wouldn't have to go to back to jail.

PART 2

China Marine and Football Years (1927-1934)

CHAPTER 7

Boot Camp, Meeting Lon Chaney, and Playing Football for the Marines

On December 14, 1926, I, along with Kenneth Utzman, and John Scott, another friend, traveled to San Diego by train. Then we took a bus to the marine base, which was located on Rosencrans Avenue. The base extended from Rosencrans all the way to the San Diego Bay—it was quite a large training area. A lone arcaded sidewalk connected all the buildings. It was in a Spanish style and very beautiful. The recruiting depot was inside the marine base and independent of the Fourth Regiment Base. It was a long two-story building, part of the arcade complex, and the instructors all lived upstairs in private rooms. The lower floors were used for classrooms for the training of marines. I was assigned to the 42nd Platoon, which was composed of about 50 recruits.

Upon arriving at the base, we were interviewed by one of the officers connected with the recruit depot. Of special interest to him was my account of my athletics at San Fernando High School. My statement that I had been captain of four teams in my senior year caused him to be a bit suspicious, so he wrote a letter to the high school checking on what I had said.

We were assigned to what we called a squad room, a very large room with bunks lined up on both sides just a few feet apart. Approximately 50 of us slept in that room. The first activity was to have our hair cut. I had long, curly hair and I was almost in revolt when they took clippers and cut it all off. They cut our hair to see if any of us had infections on our scalp, and, I think, to deflate any ego we might have. When I looked into the mirror, I thought very much of running out the door and going back home.

Our usual routine was to get up promptly at reveille. A bugle would blow and the sergeant would come charging into our room, yelling at us to get out of our bunks. We would then proceed to what we called the head, which was our bathroom. And then we assembled at the parade ground for calisthenics. At 7:00 we'd have breakfast. By 8:00 we would begin training for the day. We were taught how to use bayonets and how to kill people with them. It was not very pleasant, but it was a requisite. We were taught how to crawl close to the ground. We had a very good space for that because our parade ground extended into natural cover that ran all the way to the bay. The area that we used to train in is now part of San Diego Airport. The parade ground was nice, flat, level ground and we used to drill for about two hours every morning there. Each recruit would take his turn directing the platoon.

In the afternoon we had classes after a very fine lunch. About 4:00 we would assemble at the wash rack and wash our own clothes. Each man had a bucket, and after the clothes were washed and hung on clotheslines that extended to the top of the pole, we had fights using boxing gloves. Any marine who had a reason to want to fight would tell his sergeant that he was mad at a certain fellow for what he said about his girlfriend or whatever. Just a slight infraction would be reason enough to have a fight.

I had one fight with sort of a bully, a giant of a man who for some reason always had some remark to make to me. We fought for about 15 minutes and were both bleeding badly from the nose. Because I was expected to get beat up badly but held my own with this bully, I gained respect from the other marines. It was a fight that I dreaded because I thought I'd get killed by this big brute of a fellow, but I was very lucky. They stopped the fight as a draw.

The discipline was very severe. Of course, they don't do it now, but if for any reason you turned your eyes the wrong way or were not standing properly in your ranks, one of the instructors would come up and give you a slap on the face. And if that didn't work, he'd take his fist and hit you. Another punishment we had was to scrub the whole head (the whole bathroom) with a toothbrush, crawling on the floor. For more serious infractions a marine was sometimes taken to the parade ground and forced to roll a marble the length of the parade ground with his nose. It was very severe discipline; years later, those punishments were given up. But at the time I was there, if you had an infraction on the field, you could be expected to be hit right on the face with the fist of an instructor, and consequently our discipline was very good.

In fact, the training changed me. When I went home for the first time, my grandfather and father remarked to each other how nice I was, and how subdued I was; my rambunctious attitude had gone away. I didn't tell them about our treatment, but they seemed to be very happy about my attitude.

One of the delightful episodes of the training for our platoon was being in the movie *Tell It to the Marines* with Lon Chaney. The actors wore pink hats and pink belts with their marine uniforms, and we used to whistle at them until one day, when the actor William Haines explained (he had been whistled at and lost his temper),

This photo was taken the year I joined the Marine Corps, in 1926, in San Diego, California.

"We wear pink hats because the pink looks whiter than white in the black-and-white movies, and if any of you son-of-a-bitches want to fight, I'll take you on." And the marines all stared at him. Lon Chaney was the star of the movie; he was cast as a tough drill sergeant. Each time he completed a scene, the director would yell, "OK, great." We never had to do a retake with Lon Chaney. With Eleanor Boardman, the lady star of the movie, and William Haines, and others, sometimes we would have to do the scenes up to ten times to get it perfect. The director was very tough. We enjoyed being in the movie because we avoided a lot of disagreeable training out in the field, and we felt quite important being in a movie with cameras all around us.

Our platoon was given a break after the movie—about a week

or two-week furlough. Kenneth and I decided we'd go fishing at the lakes around Mt. McKinley near Bishop, California. I had given up my bike, but Dad loaned us a car and gave me a little money to go on this vacation. We had a cowboy pack us up to one lake, and Kenneth and I fished for about two days. We were using salmon eggs out of a jar for bait and were doing real well. We ran out of salmon eggs and substituted live grasshoppers. We'd put a grasshopper on our hook, cast it out into the lake, and WHAM! the big ones hit. Across the lake a lone man was fishing. He wasn't doing so well, so he came over to see what we were doing to haul those big trout in. (We were hauling trout in 18 inches long.) Lo and behold, it was Lon Chaney.

We showed him how to catch grasshoppers, and we fished with him for about three days more, camping in the pine trees there. He was all by himself, not a living soul with him. He said he wanted to get away from people for a while. He was curious about us, and we talked about the movie we'd filmed together. He was a man of few words. He was a very likable guy and so accommodating. He insisted that all our tents and packs and fish be carried back down on the mules that were coming up to get him. (A couple of years later, I was at a football game in a coliseum in Los Angeles. We were sitting on the 50-yard line and here's a guy poking me in the back. I turned around and there was Lon Chaney right behind me.)

The first real furlough I had was when I got notice that my grandfather had died. That was in late 1926. I was hit pretty hard because I had been with my grandfather all my life. He was 75 years old, and the doctors said he died from natural causes.

While I was home, I learned that the San Francisquito Canyon dam that I had worked at one summer had washed away, leaving only a monument in the center part of the dam. A large number of

My family in San Fernando, California, 1926.
Back row, my mother and father.
Front row, from left, my brothers Clyde, Lyle,
and Kenneth; sisters Dorothy, Evelyn (holding
the cat), and Florence; and me. The dog was
the son of movie star Rin Tin Tin.
My father wanted a family photo because
the year before, my grandfather, who had
been living with us for many years, had died,
and my father regretted that he hadn't had
a photograph made with Grandfather
and the family. So he called me home from
the Marine Corps and got us all together.
I put on civilian clothes and we had
the picture taken.

people had been killed and washed to the sea. I got permission from the Marine Corps to extend my leave a couple days so I could go see the site. It was a traumatic experience for me to go back to the dam where I had worked so hard and see it all washed away.

I thought I would be going to Hawaii with the 42nd Platoon, but I had a great disappointment. While I was aboard ship, on the day we were to depart, within an hour of the time they were going to cast the lines overboard and pull away, a jeep came racing down the dock. The driver said, "Stop the ship. We want Poppelman!" That was because my coach in high school, in responding to the recruiter's inquiry about my athletics, had padded up the report so I was, the way he talked, the second coming of Jesus. He told them I had offers from all the big colleges on the West Coast and that I was the greatest prospect they ever had at the high school. He built me up to the point where the marines figured they had to have me for their 1926 team. So the ship was held up until they rounded up my sea bag, put up a boarding ladder, and got me off the ship. As I rode back to San Diego, it was as if I was going to the guillotine. I was so disappointed. All my friends were going to Hawaii. I returned to the marine base and was immediately inducted into the 4th Regiment and assigned a tryout with the football squad.

The 4th Regiment Marine Corps Expeditionary Force, known as "San Diego's Own," was originally organized at Mare Island, California, in 1914 for service on the west coast of Mexico. When not fighting overseas in places such as Santo Domingo, China, and Mexico, the 4th Regiment honed its football skills. The game had been of special importance to the regiment since 1917, the year the marines had the best football team in the United States, defeating the University of California in two games, 28–0 and 27–0; Oregon University, 28–0; and the University of Southern California, 34–0;

and, later, winning the Tournament of Roses game in Pasadena, California. In 1925, the regiment won the West Coast Service Championship. Hopes were understandably high for the 1926 team with head coach Lieutenant Elmer E. Hall (who had played on the legendary 1917 Marine Corps team).

That was the beginning of a new era in my life. One of the drill instructors in our boot camp weighed about 245 pounds, all muscle, and I had heard he was only on the third team. So I had visions of the first team being a team of giants. I requested to be reassigned to the 42nd tour in Hawaii, but that was denied. I was put with 100 other marines on the football field, all training for the San Diego base team. I started out being on the sixth team, but as we progressed with our training, I worked myself up to the third team.

After the season started, I gained momentum and began to like the players and was moved on the second team. By the middle of the season I had worked my way up to the first team. The championship game was our team against a submarine football team, for the first time I was in a big game. That was a lucky day for me. At the end of the game, I intercepted a pass and made a touchdown. The general of our marine base, Smedley D. Butler, was proud of his football team. I had never met him, but after the game he came charging into the dressing room, wanting to know where Poppelman was. I was half undressed, but when he approached me I jumped to attention. He said, "Private Poppelman?"

I said, "Yes, sir!"

He said, "Wrong! *Corporal* Poppelman."

With less than six months' service, such a promotion was incredible. It usually took four years of service to become a corporal if you were lucky.

From then on I was somewhat of a pet of his. I learned that he had had a big bet on the game with some admiral, and my touch-down helped him win big money. Some people said it was much as $5,000, which was a lot of money then. I didn't believe that, nor did I ever ask the general.

In those days they did not have separate defensive and offensive teams. You played both offense and defense. I was a running back, a shifty, fast runner, and if I got any kind of interference I could usually make long gains. I had ability. On defense I played back where I would be a defensive end against the passing game. As I said, I won the championship game by intercepting a long pass. A big lineman by the name of McHenry, who later became an officer, ran up beside me and said, "Pop, grab onto my pants and let's go." So we went down the field together, and he was slugging at players, which was illegal, and really paving the way for me. I just hung on the back of his pants and flew along with him until I got within 30 yards of the goal and had to dodge a couple of players to get to the goal line.

At that time, each marine base had a football team called the post team. The two best post teams were in San Diego and Paris Island, South Carolina. The Marine Corps also had an All-Marine Team, which played in the college leagues, not in the service games, except for the final game of the season. The All-Marine Team consisted of the best of the players from the post teams plus college players, mostly all-Americans who were given commissions to be in the Marine Corps. So we had a mixed bag of enlisted men, officers, and young commissioned lieutenants mostly from the colleges.

The post teams included teams from ships and submarines; I would say that throughout the United States there were close to 30 teams representing ships and marine bases. They had quite a field of players to pick from. In San Diego, we had over 100 players, and they all played very rough. In those days, the linemen would coat their arms, wrists, and elbows with plaster of Paris and let it get hard, so when they whacked you behind the head in the line, it was like a hammer hitting you. Most of the linemen on our team in San Diego chewed tobacco, which they would spit across the line into the other linemen's eyes. It was a bitter experience to get an eyeful of tobacco juice about the time you received the ball to run.

We wore shoulder pads but did not have face masks. Our helmets were leather, quite soft. For running purposes I did not wear hip pads. We were trained so hard that we really didn't need the kind of equipment they have today. In one game, a fellow named Wigmore, a lineman, was taken off to the bench. The coach said, "Wigmore, what the hell's wrong with you?"

Wigmore said, "I think I've broken my ankle."

The coach said, "What the hell's wrong with the other one?"

They were a tough bunch. When we were training in San Diego once, a big tall lineman and I got to fighting because I thought he whacked me in the back of the head too hard. I went up to him and I said, "You son of a bitch, don't you ever do that again, or I'll knock your goddamned teeth out."

Another lineman ran over and pulled me away. He said, "Jesus Christ, don't fight with him. He used to be a heavyweight fighter." So I backed off.

CHAPTER 8

China Marine

M y duties in the 4th Regiment, consisting of 1,200 marines and officers, were vastly more exciting than those in the recruit depot. I was no longer a "boot," but a marine of the real Marine Corps. My fellow marines in the regiment were experienced and seasoned, including old sergeants who had seen service in all parts of the world. I was learning to appreciate the spirit of the real Marine Corps.

Brigadier-General Butler, only 45 years old, small at 140 pounds but epitomizing the ideal soldier's general, always took part in the enlisted ranks. He believed in surrounding himself with good officers, and leadership was his strong point. He had served in the Philippines in 1899, in China in 1900, and in Puerto Rico and Panama. He had been awarded two Medals of Honor prior to World War I; during that war, he commanded the 13th Regiment of Marines in France. On his return to the States in 1919, he became the commanding general of the marine barracks at Quantico, Virginia. (In 1928, at the age of 48, he was promoted to major-general, the youngest

An earlier version of this chapter appeared under the title "A China Marine: The Adventures of Ray Poppelman," in the June 1992 issue of Leatherneck Magazine, *a publication of the Marine Corps Association.*

marine to ever hold that rank.) His father, Thomas S. Butler, was a congressman and chairman of the House Naval Affairs Committee, and a great help to the marines. During General Butler's lifetime, the U.S. Marine Corps grew from an auxiliary arm of the U.S. Navy into an important expeditionary force around the world.

On October 18, 1926, the federal government called upon the U.S. Marine Corps to set up a mail guard system to combat a rash of violent gang-style robberies in mail cars on trains throughout the United States. General Butler was assigned to command the Western Mail Guard with 15 officers and 630 enlisted men. Marines equipped with .45-caliber Colt pistols and 12-gauge repeater shotguns rode the mail cars and protected major post offices.

I was posted to the Los Angeles–Fresno mail route, riding with the mailmen along the way and back, and staying at YMCAs in each city. These rides were usually boring and lonely, depending on whether the mailman, sorting mail in the car, would talk or not. I would stack the mail bags into a fort at the far end of the mail car, putting the so-called red bags, carrying cash and valuables, on the bottom of the pile. The mailman sorting mail at the opposite end of the car had a .45-caliber pistol hanging on the wall. When the train stopped at a station, the mailman would cautiously open the door from the inside only after hearing a familiar voice from the outside. If someone attempted to open the door without authority, we marines were empowered to shoot to kill. In one instance, a marine officer, attempting to test our system, lost his hat with a blast from a diligent marine guard.

Although General Butler's headquarters were in San Francisco, he moved around a lot. I had the pleasure of meeting him several times at the Los Angeles station. He told me there were no attempted robberies anywhere in the United States since the marines had been

This photo was taken during my assignment to the Marine Corps's mail guard in 1926. We stopped all the train robberies that were occurring in Southern California then. I am on the right; Harold J. Scott is on the left.

guarding the trains, and that he expected we would return to San Diego after Christmas 1926. In January 1927, his prediction came true.

On January 8, 1927, we found, upon returning to our marine base, great excitement at the prospect of going to Nicaragua to chase down the bandit Sandino. Hasty preparations were made, and we were put into a standby status. Within a week, our orders were changed for an immediate departure to China. We heard no solid reason for going there, except to fight the Chinese. Actually, China was in the midst of a civil war.

In 1900, with the approval of the Dowager Empress of China, a Chinese militia called the Ho Chuan, or Righteous Harmony Fists— hence "Boxers"—undertook their motto, "Protect the country, destroy the foreigners!" Their duty was to kill westerners and Chinese Christians. The United States had responded by stationing marines in Shanghai, Peking, and elsewhere, and formed the U.S. Navy Yangtze River Patrol. In 1911, Dr. Sun Yat-sen's democratic and ill-articulated revolutionaries brought down the old empire and China was plunged into chaos.

The Russians, following their resounding defeat in the Russian-Japanese War of 1905, had for all practical purposes turned over their interests in China to Japan. Furthermore, the Versailles Treaty, which had set the terms of peace between the Western Allies and the Germans and Austro-Hungarians at the end of World War I, had also given the Japanese rights over the Shantung Province of China.

In 1927, the United States lacked a definite policy in China, which was torn by a bitter civil war between the Nationalists under Chiang Kai-shek, strong in Southern China, and the bickering warlords in northern China, led principally by Chang Tso-lin, who occupied Shanghai when we arrived. In the complex game of politics, Chiang Kai-shek was not all-powerful. He faced an ever-shifting field of regional warlords and power brokers. Alliances kept changing. The warlords feared that if Chiang grew too powerful, their revenues from opium might be lost. They did not wish to see either Chiang Kai-shek or the Communists become too strong. Some welcomed the Communists' patriotic appeal for a united front against Japan, which was anxious to control all of North China, particularly Manchuria.

The British, guided by their own political and commercial interests, had designs on the Yangtze Valley area. The reality of the situation in 1927 was that the lines were beginning to be drawn for World War II. It was no secret that Japan's ultimate ambition was to take as much of China as it could into the "Greater Japanese Co-Prosperity Sphere." It was also no secret that they intended to expel the British, French, and Americans when the time was ripe.

China had 18 major provinces governed by warlords profiteering in opium, the bloom of evil. A mishmash of politics, double crosses, and intrigues prevailed. As Chiang Kai-shek's forces, the Nationalists, fought their way north from Southern China and battles broke out between that army and Chang Tso-lin's Northerners, panic swept foreign residents in the north. American missionaries and businessmen appealed to Washington for protection.

President Calvin Coolidge felt that to send a large force of the regular army would probably provoke war. Marines are international troops, and no one objects to them visiting countries under international law. That is not so with the army. President Coolidge felt that our presence in China was needed, and on January 10, 1927, General Butler was appointed to lead a new expeditionary force, the 3rd Brigade, composed of 4,074 enlisted men and 261 officers (including the 4th Regiment's 1,200 enlisted men and 50 officers), into Shanghai and Tientsin.

Our 4th Regiment embarked for Shanghai on the USS *Chaumont*, a navy transport, while the remaining 2,874 enlisted men and 211 officers embarked for Tientsin in northern China on the transport USS *Henderson*. General Butler would divide his time between Shanghai and Tientsin. The War Department warned Butler to be extremely prudent in anything he did or said; the smallest error of judgment on his part might have disastrous consequences in the highly volatile situation.

(Our naval transport ship, the USS *Chaumont,* was built in 1920 for the purpose of carrying expeditionary supplies. She was named after Ron De Chaumont, a French citizen who made a major contribution to the American Revolution by outfitting American ships during the revolution. After Pearl Harbor, she served our navy in the South Pacific and Alaska. She was decommissioned March 1, 1944, renamed *Samaritan,* and converted to a hospital ship. On February 20, 1945, she carried 606 patients from Iwo Jima to Saipan.)

Prior to our departure on February 3, 1927, when there was still some speculation that we were going to Nicaragua, supplies, ammunition, weapons, and bulk potatoes were hastily loaded aboard the *Chaumont* at the Broadway Pier in San Diego Harbor. Part of the marines' quarters, just below the main deck, were used for a temporary potato bin built of heavy planks from floor to ceiling. Tons of potatoes were dumped through a deck hatch and fell ten feet onto a steel floor, damaging many. Opposite the potato bin, marine bunks were equally spaced from deck to ceiling five feet high. I had one of the bottom bunks. A six-foot aisle separated our bunks from the potatoes.

By sunset of February 3, we were at sea. Within a few days, we saw flying fish, allaying any further speculation that we were going to Nicaragua. We were nearing Hawaii, according to old hands. The *Chaumont* laid over one night in Honolulu—just long enough to load additional supplies. Artillery guns were loaded through a deck hatch into a hold adjoining the potatoes. Thus, we had potatoes and artillery guns positioned side-by-side in separate areas.

Civilian crews worked all night completing every contingency needed while we had one night of liberty in Honolulu. On February 9, we sailed west toward the East China Sea. The *Chaumont* was overcrowded and hot. Time quickly passed between guard duty in the ammunition holds, calisthenics, penny gambling, reading, sack time, cleaning gear and clothes, and holding classes on Chinese culture. We ate, standing, from 12-inch-wide counters suspended between steel posts. The smell of potatoes, some of which were going bad, required the installation of canvas ventilators. In the evenings, just after dark, we enjoyed movies on the afterdeck [stern]. As we approached the East China Sea, the waves became colossal in size. Many of us became seasick.

About 300 miles east of the mouth of the Yangtze River, where cyclonic storms develop, we were on deck watching a movie and were caught by a typhoon. Although we had radio weather reports daily, this one hit us by surprise. A blast of wind tore our movie screen loose from a two-inch steel frame, sending it overboard. We were all hustled below deck. As huge waves lifted the stern of our ship out of the water, the propeller, running loose and exposed, would accelerate, causing violent vibrations. The seas would break over our bow, crashing onto the bridge deck. Later in the night, rivets from the steel deck beams above our bunks began to break and ricochet like bullets. The seas built up commensurate with the screaming wind. Our skipper headed the ship into the wind at slow speed. As the bow plunged into an oncoming wave, the whole ship shuddered. At the climax of the storm, the artillery guns, stowed next to the potatoes, broke loose from their moorings and crashed through the wooden partitions, causing an avalanche of potatoes to smother the marines in the lower bunks, one of which was mine.

Our mess sergeant, an old sea dog riding an upper bunk, didn't help us any by relating a story about the sister ship of the *Chaumont*, which had broken in half in a storm off Cape Hatteras, North Carolina, and said if anybody had any religion, now was a "hell of a good time to use it." With our canvas ventilators torn away, we suffered not only from a wild sea but from the stench of spoiled potatoes.

Our ship's sick bay was equipped for only a limited number of patients: I was one of them. For several days and nights, I lay tied to my bunk on my back, in agony, wanting to vomit, but I couldn't. When I did, only blood appeared.

After the storm, most of our potatoes were thrown overboard. Canvas ventilators were reinstalled. Morale appeared better. According to our mess sergeant, our refrigeration system had been damaged, hence the blue chicken we were served. I remained in sick bay with seasickness until we reached the mouth of the mighty Yangtze River. In spite of the storm, and losing a day in Pearl Harbor, the *Chaumont* made a record run from San Diego to Shanghai in 20 days. She was not only seaworthy, but fast. She was a world within a world in a strange, vast land.

As we headed south into the Whangpoo River, soldiers of the Northern Army could be seen. Shanghai was only 14 miles away. On February 24, 1927, we dropped anchor opposite Standard Oil's tank farm compound, just a few miles from the Bund in Shanghai. We lay at anchor in almost freezing weather for several days, while all hands were eager to get ashore. Chinese sampans swarmed around our garbage chute. With a bowl of rice and scraps of our garbage, salvaged from the muddy river, a Chinese family living aboard a 25-foot sampan could eat sumptuously by their standards.

Shanghai in 1927 was the major international *entrepôt* and industrial center on the China Coast, and one of the great cities, with a population exceeding four million people, including 80,000 rickshaw coolies. Shanghai's location, only 14 miles south of the intersection of the Whangpoo and Yangtze Rivers, two important waterways of China, made it a leading industrial city. The latitude is the same as

New Orleans, with winters at 13°F and summers at 90°F. Shanghai had been a small trading town until the 1800s. In 1842, Great Britain forced China to open the city to foreign trade: tea, raw silk, tung oil, and pig bristles. People from France, Great Britain, the United States, and other countries settled in Shanghai.

The city had three main parts: (1) the old foreign section in the north (Chapei), (2) the original Chinese settlement in the south ("Old Shanghai" or "Chinese City"), and (3) three suburban areas around these two sections. Shanghai suburbs, unlike American suburbs, formed part of the city. The International Settlement and the French Concession, expanded to 2,000 acres after 1912, were the two major foreign settlements. The International Settlement was made up of British and American sectors in 1863. The Hangchow-American settlement grew up on the northern side of Soochow Creek. In 1927, England, Italy, Holland, Japan, Germany, Russia, Portugal, and the United States all had sectors within the International Settlement, each with separate military forces to protect its respective areas. These included the Chinese headquarters of more than 100 U.S. firms, the largest American school overseas, and imposing European and Japanese banks, trading houses, and factories. The Americans had properties scattered throughout Shanghai, making patrol duties difficult and hazardous. It is no wonder that the Chinese were angry, with foreigners taking their land and making their own laws since 1800.

When we arrived, the anchorage off the Bund, the central industrial and banking center on the western bank of the Whangpoo River, was crowded with over 150 warships of different nations, including the flagship USS *Pittsburgh* of the U.S. Asiatic Fleet. The most modern and beautifully designed ships were those of the Japanese Fleet. Even their foot patrols wore medical face masks for protection against airborne diseases.

The tallest buildings along the Bund were only six stories high because of sedimentary problems—the subsoil could not support more. The beautiful public gardens, endowed with magnolias, at the intersection of Soochow Creek and the Whangpoo River in the International Settlement for foreigners, had a sign that read "No dogs or Chinese allowed."

Chang Tso-lin, a warlord commanding the Northern Army, controlled Shanghai. However, as we arrived, the Northern troops appeared to be evacuating Shanghai. The people in the Foreign Settlement were in near panic, anticipating the approach of Chiang Kai-shek's Nationalist KMT Army following its rampage in Nanking.

About 30,000 foreign troops, which made up the Shanghai Defense Force, including Britain, the United States, Japan, Italy, France, and others, were assembled in Shanghai by March 22, 1927, and stood by to man barricades and patrol the international concessions. The United States deliberately held back, in keeping with its "protect Americans only" policy of reticence, using only 1,200 marines. We remained crowded aboard the *Chaumont* or confined to tents on the Standard Oil complex so that we would not appear warlike or aggressive.

I began to feel better in quiet waters, although my stomach was still sore from the seasickness epic. I was placed on light duty by my company commander, Lieutenant Elmer E. Hall, and the exercising from drilling ashore helped me to regain my strength.

When Chiang Kai-shek's vanguard reached the perimeter of Shanghai, the *Chaumont* pulled anchor and tied up at the Standard Oil pier. Finally, liberty was granted, providing at least 12 marines stayed together and wore bayonets and .45-caliber Colt pistols. A 130-foot work boat shuttled us across the Whangpoo River to the Bund and to the ferry jetty near the Astor House Hotel at Whangpoo

On one of my first
liberties in Shanghai.

Road and Broadway. In a city known for its center of gangsterism, gambling, beggars, prostitutes, and sleazy nightclubs, marines had to be careful about other dangers besides bullets.

Generally, the coolies pulling the rickshaws were polite and honest, and they liked marines. The fare was about two cents (American money) per mile. With an American cigarette for *cumsha* (tip), a coolie would be ecstatic! But there were exceptions. At night a coolie, sensing his passenger was drowsy, might drop the shafts of his rickshaw on a cobblestone street, causing his passenger to fly headfirst onto the street. If the ploy failed, the coolie would claim that he stumbled and expected a better tip accordingly, for assisting the passenger back into the rickshaw. If a coolie, day or night, was not given specific instructions of where to go, he would always run to one of his allied cat houses (bordellos). When marines missed their liberty boats on scheduled runs back to the *Chaumont*, sampans, propelled only by a hand oar fishtailing from the stern, came to the rescue. The fare cost about five cents plus an American cigarette for a tip.

On February 19, a strike by the Labor Union, instigated by the Communists, became citywide. A week later, the laborers, fearing that Chiang Kai-shek's Nationalists would soon be in power, returned to their jobs. At the same time, the Northerners were heading out of the city, north through Chapei.

It is a strange coincidence that General Butler, commanding all marines in China, and Chiang Kai-shek, commanding the Nationalist Army, arrived in Shanghai generally at the same time, between March 21 and March 25.

Soldiers thought to be Nationalists coming into Shanghai were really labor Communists taking orders from Hangchow and Moscow. The Settlement and the Foreign Concession were not overrun by the Communists (in workers' clothes) because of the Shanghai Defense Force. It is my opinion that had not the U.S. Marines arrived in Shanghai when they did, the Communists would have taken over the city. They eventually did anyway, but we saved thousands of American lives. It was not until 1949 that U.S. businesses were forced to leave China, and by then they had time to liquidate their holdings and leave in a relatively organized fashion.

Each day we would have drill exercises on Standard Oil Company premises, and we gave special attention to our weapons. We were on and off the *Chaumont* all day long, between meals and duties.

While we were drilling one morning near the pier where the

Chaumont was docked, the Northern troops stole a large Standard Oil tugboat right out from under our noses in their desperation to evacuate Shanghai and started steaming down the Whangpoo River toward the Yangtze River. Lt. Colonel Kilgore, our regimental executive officer in charge, together with Captain Tighe, commanding the 22nd company of our 3rd Battalion, commandeered another Standard Oil boat and gave chase with a detail of marines armed with 1903 Springfield rifles, Browning Automatic Rifles (BAR), and Thompson submachine guns. We finally overtook the fleeing Chinese. They surrendered without a struggle. We returned the soldiers in sampans towed behind the Standard Oil boats—a unique sight—and held them captive until they were transferred to Chiang Kai-shek. We never learned of their fate.

With a bit of action, our esprit de corps escalated. On March 5, about 11 days after we dropped anchor in Shanghai and before we had gained our strength from the hectic voyage across the China Sea, we had our first parade. We needed exercise, and it was necessary to show our strength to the Cantonese army, the vanguard of the Communist forces that were closing in on Shanghai. With our marching band, we paraded from the Bund along Nanking Road to the racetrack for an inspection by Captain Leroy P. Hunt, our 3rd Battalion commander. Then it was more marching back to our point of origin at the Bund.

We began to hear guns firing across the river from the Chapei (Chinese) district. While we were living aboard the *Chaumont*, billets (marine quarters) were being constructed for us throughout the western area, which included the best residential section of the city and a strip of the mill district along Soochow Creek. The latter constituted the north boundary of the International Settlement, which was a critical area and had been assigned to our 3rd Battalion.

By the time Butler arrived in Shanghai on March 21, 1927, tensions were running high. Chinese troops had attacked several con-
sulates at Nanking, a city near Shanghai, killing many foreigners
and looting and burning the city. American businessmen and missionaries had escaped on gunboats to Shanghai, whose port was
now swarming with ships. Never before in history had the war ves-
sels of so many different nations anchored together in one harbor.
Barbed-wire entanglements had been erected, and the International
Settlement was under martial law. All legations had ordered their
nationals from the interior of China, from which there were daily
reports of murders and outrages. A more violent version of the Boxer
Rebellion appeared in the making, and the concession settlements
were desperately apprehensive.

In honor of General Butler's arrival, the 4th Regiment, under
Colonel "Jumbo" Hill, commanding, held a parade, headed by Chinese and Indian Sikh municipal police on horses. (The Shanghai
Municipal Police consisted of Chinese police and Indian Sikhs. The
Sikhs accounted for 50 percent of India's armed forces and half of
the athletes on the country's Olympic teams. In stature, they were
taller and stronger than the Chinese police. With their turbans, ful-
some beards, and fierce eyes when serious, they made ideal police
and great allies for marines on liberty. They were very friendly to
the U.S. Marines, who considered them with great respect.)

We were transported from the *Chaumont* across the Whangpoo
River to the customs jetty, adjacent to the business district near
Nanking Road, in Dollar Steamship Line tugboats. As we marched
up Nanking Road, one of Shanghai's main streets, Cantonese
Communist flags were flying over stores where the colors of Chang
Tso-lin's Northern Army formerly waved. At the racetrack on
Nanking Road, we assembled for an inspection party headed by

Bamboo officers' quarters and offices
in Shanghai, China, 1927.
Lieutenant Harry Liversedge, who later
became commander of the 28th Regiment,
which put the flag up on Iwo Jima,
is seated on the right. On the left is
Elmer Hall, who was commander
of our company and my football coach
in San Diego.

Captain Leroy P. Hunt. Our weary regiment then returned, dead tired, to our jetty and to our ship. Only the support of our band made our return trip possible. There is a certain drive that marching music can do for morale and sore feet.

Within 15 minutes after we reached our ship, we could hear firing in the outskirts of the city, and orders came to pack up. We were going ashore to our assigned quarters. The Communists had arrived

Our winter barracks in Shanghai. We slept on canvas cots and kept warm by a kerosene stove.

and were infiltrating the International Settlement! We then began the long march with full packs, toward rifle and machine-gun fire, in the direction of our new home, Billet No. 6. Billet No. 6 was a small compound of officers' and enlisted men's barracks, made of bamboo framing and woven mats. We also had a mess hall made of wood framing covered with six-inch tongue-and-grooved siding. All the buildings had wooden floors. Each barrack, approximately 16 feet by 30 feet (about 10 in all), was heated by kerosene stoves, which made them very comfortable. Foot patrols and outposts were immediately established within the western sector along Soochow Creek against the depredations of Chinese mobs in case of an attack.

It was a case of our 4th Regiment of only 1,200 marines poised against 80,000 Chinese (with more to come) who, according to our officers, could without weapons stomp us to death! Our situation was precarious. President Coolidge's policy precluded the participation of any action against the Chinese—we could protect American interests only. The perimeter defense of the city was in the hands of the British and other allied troops.

The British Durham Light Infantry held the front line along Soochow Creek adjacent to the area patrolled by our 3rd Battalion. It was this front line that the marines of our battalion were to support. The western area was undergoing considerable fire from machine guns, trench mortars, and four-inch Howitzers during the nights of March 21 and 22. On March 22, the British Coldstream Guards, England's finest soldiers, arrived in Shanghai and immediately relieved the Durham Light Infantry in the Soochow Creek area. We expected to see the Coldstream Guards, the pride of the British Army, appear in their beautiful uniforms of black bearskin helmets and red jackets, as they are shown on guard at Buckingham Palace, but they arrived in combat khaki uniforms. They never leave England except to go on active duty, and this expedition was the first time the Coldstream Guards had ever been east of the Suez. Lord Marsham commanded the company guarding the Markham Road bridge connecting the International Settlement with the Chinese Chapei district of the city. In the event the British needed support from our marines, they would send up rockets as a signal that help was needed.

On the night of March 22, the Chinese blew up the Standard Oil

Company's oil tanks in the Chapei area. The marines took the flames as a signal for help. We left our bunks in the middle of the night and raced to the Markham Bridge. Although it was a false alarm, history was made. It was the first time the U.S. Marines had fought alongside the Coldstream Guards. The Shanghai press made news with headlines about the two crack outfits fighting shoulder to shoulder. In the weeks to follow, there were many calls for marine support. Our paths crossed several times.

The air of tenseness continued to prevail, and shells from both the Communists (Cantonese) and Chang Tso-lin's Northerners continued to fall in the Settlement. Although some shots were wild and were undoubtedly directed at one or the other, they were destructive when they landed in our territory.

Chiang Kai-shek, commanding the Nationalist Army of the Republic of China, arrived in Shanghai on March 25, 1927, and held a parade soon after in honor of General Butler. The parade was several miles long. Butler received enough gifts to fill the *Chaumont*'s ammunition hold. Of special interest was a lace dining room set made in Canton. It took the eyes of three generations of one family to make it all. (General Butler told this to me himself.)

The general's first piece of business was to surround himself with efficient and trusted officers. Major Alexander A. Vandegrift joined his staff after putting our 3rd Battalion into top form. (He later became commandant of the Marine Corps during World War II.) Captain Leroy P. Hunt, assistant coach of our San Diego football team and very much liked by General Butler, took over our 3rd Battalion. Because Captain Hunt thought I needed some light duty after my "potato episode," he assigned me as his driver, and since I was no stranger to General Butler, Captain Hunt loaned me to him during his time spent in Shanghai. Lieutenant Elmer E. Hall, head coach of

I took this photo of General Smedley D. Butler, allied commanding general of all the armies in China, in 1927. I was very fortunate to be his chauffeur. The car in the background is an old Packard. I used that plus an old Buick to drive the general around.

our football team, was my commander, and he also was a close friend of General Butler.

Admiral Clarence S. Williams, commander of our Asiatic Fleet, turned General Butler's proposals for more troops sour at their first meeting. Admiral Williams wanted our troops to stand by for emergency purposes behind lines manned by the British. After all, Shanghai was basically a British colony. General Butler under no circumstances would allow our marines to come under the command of foreign commanders or associate themselves with the defense of foreign concessions. Our American Minister, John. W.A. Murray, in Peking, recommended an army brigade from the Philippines supercede the marines if the Chinese poured into the International Settlement.

General Butler had our 4th Regiment out for a parade and inspection at the racetrack honoring Admiral Clarence S. Williams at their second meeting. After the parade, I drove Butler and the admiral from the racetrack along Nanking Road toward the Bund in a 1925 Packard touring car, one of our staff cars. Of course, we always flew the American flag while underway. I overheard a plan being devised in the back seat between the two of them that in the event our defense forces were overrun by the invading Cantonese, our flagship and other gunboats would blast a protected escape route through the city for both marines and American residents.

Butler didn't like the idea of Chiang Kai-shek getting cozy with the Japanese. Admiral Williams wanted Butler to stay close to and watch Chiang Kai-shek, who had chased Chang Tso-lin and his Northerners out of the city and was waging mass executions with the Communists who had been captured infiltrating the city.

At a moment when tensions were high, our left rear tire blew wide open, with the decibel rating of a mortar shell. I stopped the car, examined the tire, and said, "General, we have a flat tire. It will take me a few minutes to change it." The general barked, "If the damned wheel is still on, let's get going!" With the Packard listing badly, we dodged and wove our way through a mass of humanity to a jetty at the Bund, where two of the highest-ranking officers of the United States forces in the Orient shook hands and parted. At this point Butler didn't like Williams, but later they became good friends.

When Admiral Williams refused to grant more troops, General Butler decided to equip the marines with greater firepower. Through the influence of his father, Congressman Thomas S. Butler, Chairman of the House Naval Affairs Committee, and his friend Major-General John A. Lejeune, Commandant of the Marine Corps, a fast destroyer brought a shipment of Thompson .45-caliber submachine guns with 50-round drums to our 4th Regiment in record time. The general advised me one time, "When you want something, go to the highest authority you can possibly get to. Beware of the underlings."

Patrolling continued for over a month, and we were frequently pulled from our bunks in the middle of the night to answer a riot call from some remote point or to support some of the troops occupying the front along Soochow creek.

Whereas the British patrolled on foot with a full platoon with rifles, we patrolled on foot with three marines: one carried the Thompson submachine gun while two marines carried rifles and ammunition for all guns. With only 1,200 marines, we patrolled the whole western sector of Shanghai. The British had 14,000 troops and patrolled less territory. At this point, the weapons carried by the marines were Springfield rifles, model 1903; Thompson submachine guns, caliber .45, with 50-round drum magazines; Colt Model 1911 A1 .45-caliber pistols with an extra magazine; and bayonets.

Since American interests were scattered but vulnerable, and our marines were dangerously limited and the nature of our skirmishes were sporadic, our staff, under General Butler and particularly Lieutenant Evans F. Carlson, our intelligence officer, developed the mobile patrol. A windshield-less truck chassis with hard rubber tires, a wooden floor, and longitudinal back-to-back seats running the length of the truck bed accommodated six marines on each side armed with rifles and Thompson machine guns. I was one of the charter member drivers, and usually Lieutenant Carlson sat up front with me, checking maps.

This photo shows a motor patrol devised by
our intelligence officer, Lieutenant Carlson,
to quell riots in Shanghai. He designed
a special truck that had marines facing out
in two directions. In addition to that, we
started carrying Thompson submachine guns.
Whenever a riot would occur, we would
race to the site in these trucks, jump off,
and take cover wherever we could.

We soon became known as the "Carlson Raiders," a name that
was later carried into the Pacific Theater of World War II. (Japanese
atoll strongholds were attacked by the raiders from submarines, who
landed in rubber rafts. In Richmond, Virginia, there is the Raider
Museum dedicated to these special marines.)

General Butler joined us on one mission into an outlying village
north of Chapai, where troublesome "Red Bandits" (Communists)

were reported to be hiding. We struck just before daybreak, smashing into one-story buildings without warning. General Butler was giving orders to marines up and down the street. Our team in truck No. 3, with Lieutenant Carlson in charge, rammed the front door of one building with a post. The stench almost asphyxiated us all. There were over 30 Chinese sleeping in one room without ventilation; but no soldiers! Our plans had leaked out the night before. We found evidence that the soldiers had been there, and that was all. As we were leaving the scene, the British Coldstream Guards came charging down the street in their sharp-nosed riot tanks. They were too late. Again, the press gave a glowing account of how the Marines and the Coldstream Guards had fought "shoulder-to-shoulder" against the Red Bandits.

General Butler was always concerned about the welfare of his enlisted men. One day, in our Buick staff car, as we approached a certain billet, Butler suggested, "It's about chow time, Pop. Let's see what the boys are eating at Clement's billet." We were early, but a few marines were waiting for the chow line to open. We entered, and the marines jumped to attention. After Butler put everybody at ease, he decided to sample a stew cooking in a large cauldron. Picking up a ladle, he stirred the stew. The one in a million chance of Murphy's Law came to pass. Reposing in the cup-shaped ladle was a small rat! I expected Butler's nostrils to spout fire. The mess sergeant stood by in shock. I adroitly attempted to lower the general's boiling point by suggesting, "Sir, you saved the day! Suppose you hadn't found the rat!" The general remained cool, much to my surprise. Turning to me in the car, he asked, "How do you suppose that rat got into the stew?"

I replied, "He couldn't have crawled in—the pot was too tall. I think he fell off a bamboo rafter."

"That's good officer thinking," he quietly replied. I never could figure that one out. I was just a private at a salary of $20.80 per month plus a horse blanket, and I wasn't supposed to know what officers are supposed to think.

General Butler was eager to know what was going on with the Chinese armies outside of the Settlement. Rumors weren't reliable, and he didn't trust reports from our allies. He preferred to depend on our own intelligence facilities, namely those of Lieutenant Evans F. Carlson, our intelligence officer, and what he could actually see for himself with on-site sorties.

Our "snooping party" was usually composed of an interpreter, one or two marines with Thompson submachine guns, the general seated in the front passenger seat, and me. If Lieutenant Carlson was in the party, only one marine accompanied us. On some missions, only Butler and I would go out. That was usually when the general would warn me, "Pop, get some sack time this afternoon, we're going out tonight." We investigated both at night and in the daytime in the Chapei and Hangchow districts and along the north bank of the Whangpoo River on the Yangtzepoo Road in the vicinity of the Northern army of Chang Tso-lin. We also surveyed the area south of the French Concessions, estimating the strength of the Communist camps near the Shanghai Hangchow Ninpo Railway.

Returning from the Chapei district about 9:00 one night in March, we found a crowd blocking the street in a wild, yelling melee. We were forced to stop. Butler went to see what the commotion was all about. After a few minutes, at the suggestion of our interpreter, I took our submachine gun and went to see what was happening. Two Chinese boys about eight years old were fighting as though they were in a cock fight, holding steel cleavers about four inches square in each hand while striking at each other. Both boys were bleeding badly when Butler charged into the arena, stopped the fight, and took the bloody cleavers away from them. The crowd started jeering at Butler. I turned loose with the machine gun, firing a few rounds over the heads of the most violent protesters. The crowd dispersed when they saw we meant business. The boys were hustled away by their parents. The interpreter said it was a "death fight" and that spectators bet on the boys. The parents were paid for surrendering their children to this sport. In later research, I couldn't find any information on what we had witnessed. It apparently was a locally contrived form of recreation. Life in China was very cheap.

In another instance, when we were returning from a night sortie, several Chinese spotted our American flag, stepped in front of our car, and warned us to stop while yelling "Moline! Moline!" Butler and the interpreter waited while I followed the excited Chinese up a flight of stairs into a luxurious waiting room of a cat house. A marine had been stabbed in the back and was being attended by several prostitutes attempting to administer first aid. I ran back to our car to fetch General Butler. We carried the marine, who was helpless, down the stairs to our trusty Packard and raced to a hospital nearby.

The first time I drove General Butler to the Russian Consulate, north of Soochow Creek, two Russian sentries guarding the gate stepped in our path with fixed bayonets. I left the car, explaining who we were and who we wanted to see, at the same time pointing to our American flag off the right fender. The soldiers remained fixed, shaking their heads no. General Butler came from the car, grabbed one rifle with the fixed bayonet from one sentry, and motioned me to bring our car through the gate, which I did. Returning the rifle, Butler climbed aboard as if there had been no problem. The Russians backed off when the general called their bluff.

The U.S. Marines were actually a vanguard for Chiang Kai-shek, who subscribed to the theory that you didn't have to know how to fight the enemy so long as you knew how to surround him. At a press interview, he expressed displeasure at the defense of the International Settlement and the French Concession. Although the Northerners were gone, the national unity for which Chiang was striving was jeopardized by the increasing strength of the Cantonese, or the Communists, who daily were adding thousands of laborers and civilians to their masses. Chiang was ready to kill every Communist in order to gain power for himself. On April 12, he executed a bloody coup against Communist labor unions in the old Chinese City of Shanghai. Although Chiang also had problems in the northern provinces, they were remote to the residents of Shanghai.

While Chiang's Nationalists and the Communists were struggling for power, the Japanese, who were preparing for a full-scale invasion of China, began showing their strength by parading along North Szechwan Road. The British Royal Marines paraded through the International Settlement for the same reason.

As for the U.S. Marines, the plot thickened. Colonel Hill, commanding our 4th Regiment, committed suicide. The press contended the colonel had a mental illness. Rumors varied. Personally, I liked the colonel very much and found him to be a friend and a loyal officer to us all.

Colonel Henry Davis, who replaced Colonel Hill, had little respect for Chiang Kai-shek. While General Butler was at his alternate headquarters in Tientsin, Colonel Davis had dinner with Chiang Kai-shek and wrote to General Butler as follows: "How in the name of God he ever exercised control over those people to the extent he did is a mystery to me. Usually, a man of strong character will demonstrate it in some way without ever speaking a word. This bird has nothing of that kind as far as I could see, and looked and acted like a love-sick boob, his fiancee, Miss Meiling Sun (her father was Sun Yat-sen), also being present at dinner. Of all the stupid boobs I ever met, he is it. I don't believe he ever was the brains behind the movement of last summer [killing Communists in Nanking]. He looks like a stupid rickshaw coolie and grunts like a pig when spoken to." (Chiang Kai-shek married Meiling Sun in December 1927 in the Majestic Hotel before 1,500 guests.) Actually, Chiang Kai-shek didn't have to do much thinking for himself. He had good German advisers.

An interesting item about Chiang Kai-shek was the fact that his Nationalist Army, beginning in 1926, marched along with Chou En-lai, age 29, leading the Communist Party from Canton to Shanghai as allies. Chiang displayed his treachery by turning on the Communists. On April 12, Chiang put a price of $80,000 on Chou's head. This worried Butler: Would Chiang Kai-shek turn on the United States? The Communist underground in Shanghai fell apart under the blows of Chiang's secret police. He was on a rampage to rid Shanghai of all Communists, and there were rumors of wholesale executions being held north of the city. Two trucks loaded with executioners were seen crossing the Markham Road Bridge toward Chapei.

Early one morning I drove General Butler and two other officers, one of whom I believe was Lieutenant Carlson, along Yangtzepoo Road on the north bank of the Whangpoo River. When we could no longer drive because of the terrain, I stayed with the car while the officers, with binoculars, made their way as close as possible to the river, where executions were taking place. I could hear shooting but couldn't see the action. The procedure, as best I could determine from overhearing conversations later, was that the victim Communists were marched to the river's edge, shot in the back of the head from a kneeling position, and then shoved off the bank into the Whangpoo River. Their bodies eventually floated into the Yangtze River and on into the China Sea. It was reported that 3,000 Communist soldiers had been executed that day. One officer said, "It could happen to us." Since enlisted men only speak when they are spoken to, and I wasn't spoken to, all I could do was drive and keep my mouth shut.

From a Chinese coolie's perspective, life is dear, but actually his intrinsic value is worthless. When driving in the crowded sections of Shanghai, it was sometimes necessary to push into crowds with your bumper, bulldozing a path. On one occasion, a pedestrian fell under our Buick staff car. When I backed off his body, my left front wheel was resting on the Chinaman's Adam's apple. I yelled for a Chinese cop, who in turn summoned a Sikh policeman of higher authority. The victim's death cost the Marine Corps $8, which was probably more than this family had ever seen at one time.

General Butler believed we could not settle disputes between the belligerent Chinese armies by promiscuously shooting innocent Chinese coolies. The Chinese must decide among themselves their own form of government and their own rules. But we could set examples with spit-and-polish parades and sports events. Butler liked things flashy—he even had our helmets nickel-plated. Frequent inspections, strict discipline, and sports, he thought, would allay the venereal problem, which was reaching an alarming rate.

Our 4th Regiment entered Shanghai's university basketball tournament. I played forward on our team. The Chinese newspapers, particularly the *China Press*, gave us great coverage. We knew the Chinese liked us, but we wondered why they never cheered for us. Finally we learned that we were winning too many games. It was a custom for the spectators to only cheer for the losing team. Second

Lieutenant Randolph McCall Pate coached our team. In 1956, he became the twenty-first commandant of the U.S. Marine Corps. During World War II, he was the deputy chief of staff for the 5th Amphibious Corps and as such was in on the planning of Pelilu, Guadalcanal, Iwo Jima, and the Okinawa campaigns.

The Chinese players were very friendly and hospitable to us. We were invited to their homes, and since most of them came from affluent families, we experienced a taste of Chinese culture and elegance. In one home there was a beautifully carved table that would seat 48 guests. Ivory, jade, Ming urns, rose quartz vases, deep-piled rugs, and crystal stemware were just part of the museum-quality furnishings. There must have been over 50 servants in one home we visited. The homes were well protected by ten-foot walls capped with jagged pieces of broken plate glass set upright in concrete.

The sports writers were equally as hospitable. One writer arranged to take us into Old Shanghai (Chinese City) to witness civil executions. Since this part of Shanghai was out of bounds for marines in military uniform, we were required to wear civilian clothes. Within the city were beautiful pagodas, temples, narrow cobble-stoned streets, opium dens, and craft shops. One particular street was of special interest to me —I call it the "street of listeners." About every five feet down the street were small confessional windows. Outside each window was a stool. Beneath the window sat a professional "listener," usually a venerable old man with a Fu Manchu–style beard. For a few coppers (the Chinese penny), a customer would pour out his troubles, the fee depending upon the time involved. The listener didn't engage in any conversation; he merely listened, changing facial expressions as the monologue continued. Any one of the listeners could have won an Oscar in Hollywood. They had sympathetic expressions that would make you cry.

China resorted to a very severe penalty to control drug trafficking and stealing: beheading. There was a park in old Shanghai where each day a group of criminals would be beheaded. The executioners received medals for their actions—if they made a good clean cut, and the victim didn't suffer, they were rewarded. (In some places in China, if the swordsman made a bad cut he, himself, would be beheaded.) Each person's crime was written on a long notice shaped like a white feather, which would be held up for the crowd to see.

The Communists later stopped public beheadings. I purchased this photo from a photographic shop in Shanghai in 1927.

In a park within Old Shanghai, executions were held daily for such crimes as stealing, homicide, disloyalty, law-breaking, and perjury. The accused or condemned victims would be escorted, in single file, to the execution area with their hands tied behind their back, holding feather-shaped placards listing their crimes. Several uniformed executioners were on hand. The ones wearing red scarves were the honored ones. They also wore medals. After the sentence was read, the victim, with the placard removed, would kneel with his head forward over a basket. The executor held a sword in both hands, over his head, and would swing downward with great force. Blood from the jugular vein would spurt out as the victim's head fell into the basket. The head would then be tied to the limb of a tree by the victim's pigtail (queue) as a warning to the relatives and spectators on hand. Heads from previous executions hung from most of the trees. First-time spectators vomited. When the Communists took over Shanghai in 1949, this type of execution ceased. Bullets replaced the swords.

In late March, General Butler and Chiang Kai-shek had several high-priority meetings. On one occasion, after I had been waiting outside of Butler's headquarters for several hours quite late at night, General Butler came out, escorting Chiang Kai-shek to our Packard touring car, and said to me, "Pop, will you take Chiang to the Majestic Hotel?" Chiang and an aide got into the back seat. Chiang's car went away first in a different direction. I realized it was a security ploy. The ride was uneventful. Of course, I was nervous, but all went well.

On another occasion, I drove Chiang to his residence in the French Concession. It was raining, so Chiang sat up front with me. (An open touring car without side curtains isn't the ideal way for most generals to travel.) Evidently, General Butler had told Chiang that I was a

This photo was taken after I had been out all night driving General Butler and Lieutenant Carlson along the outskirts of Shanghai. We would drive in the mud along the railroad tracks looking for boxcars, which we would climb onto so that we could then scan the horizon for campfires. We figured that for each fire there'd be at least ten Chinese soldiers trying to keep warm. Behind me is the old 1923 Buick.

football player. Chiang liked the game, so the ice was broken for me. In the back seat an interpreter and a marine with a Thompson submachine gun seemed to get along OK. I mentioned to Chiang that he was very young to head up the whole damned Chinese army. He laughed and said there were many armies, he only commanded one. When we parted, he gave me a first-issue Chinese silver dollar of the Republic of China with Dr. Sun Yat-sen's face on one side of the coin and thanked me for the ride. It was difficult for me to accept that he was a reckless executioner and a powerful general. He looked so young and innocent. He was then 41 years of age and a world figure. I drove for him a third time, but General Butler was with

Our summer barracks were tents with wood floors. Two marines were housed in each tent. For 50 cents a month from each of the marines in each tent, a Chinese boy would keep the lawns cut, the floor scrubbed, and all our clothes cleaned. The barracks were on a parade ground near a big house occupied by the officers, and we would play football there when we weren't on duty.

him and we didn't have a chance to talk. I never saw him again after that.

By the first of May, when the "emergency" pressures had eased, our 3rd Battalion moved from our bamboo shacks at Billet No. 6 to the premises of a former Chinese warlord at Avenue Foch and Moulmein Road designated Billet No. 10. The main two-story mansion accommodated our officers. With 30 or more servants, who were dressed in white, our officers under Captain Hunt lived like members of royalty. A large building in the rear at one time housed over 300 concubines. Our enlisted men, including myself, lived across the street in tents. We had an adjoining parade ground for games and drill exercises. We had Chinese boy servants who cleaned our tents, cut the grass, washed and pressed our clothes, made our bunks, shined our shoes, polished all brass eyelets on our leggings and belts, and ran errands. The cost was 50 cents per marine per month. Nothing was ever stolen.

We were entering the spit-and-polish era, competing with other nations for being the best-looking military servicemen in China. The Coldstream Guards were our keen competitor.

By this time, General Butler had leased a red English Sunbeam touring car. Officers kept me busy taking them to social events, the famous French gambling and country club, shopping, and to a very beautiful apartment house on Wei-Hei-Wei Road. Of the 15,000 Russian girls in Shanghai, I think the most beautiful girls lived here, at our officers' expense.

Because of the excess amount of nickel-plating on the Sunbeam, the general liked this car best, but he admitted that the old Buick (1923) and Packard (1925) were workhorses and served us well. He even talked about shipping them to Quantico, Virginia, for safekeeping until we created a museum there.

By June, General Butler was mired down most of the time in Tientsin. The last time I saw him, he thought I would have my corporal stripes within a few months. (That December his prediction came true. Major-General Lejeune commissioned me a corporal for playing on the 1927 All-Marine undefeated football team. I played again in 1928 and was made a sergeant.)

Shanghai was a paradise for the marines once the hostilities settled down to perfunctory patrol and sentry duty. Marines who attended church services were invited to Sunday dinners at the homes of missionaries and civilians. We were the first marines most of them had ever seen. One beautiful home, owned by a missionary family, had about 40 servants, including gardeners. For a time I was dating a beautiful daughter of the family, who helped me buy a Cantonese shawl and cloisonné vases, boxes, and varied items.

In China there is a certain protocol to use in shopping—be patient! Buy only after several visits to a shop. Each visit to the shop reduces the price of the item. My Cantonese shawl, 60 inches square and made of the finest silk, was originally priced at $80, the price expected from a tourist off the Dollar Steamship Line. After three months, it was mine for $8. The medium of exchange was based on the Mexican dollar, $2.50 "Mex" for one U.S. dollar; a Mexican dollar had great purchasing power. Of course, the Chinese always wanted American dollars.

The Chinese tailors made clothes of the finest chino khaki for marines cheaper than our quartermaster could buy from American manufacturers. Shirts were available for 60 cents (U.S.), trousers for 90 cents, and ties at five cents each; camel's hair bathrobes with decorative dragon designs were $8; silk civilian suits were $12. Most of the marines wore tailor-made silk underwear. And all could be purchased by using the "chit" credit system.

Credit was very loose and almost unlimited, though residents couldn't leave the settlement until all their bills were paid. The same courtesy was extended to the marines. Because there was so much paper money from different provinces, and most of it was bad, merchants preferred IOUs (chits—just a slip of paper signed with anyone's name). Some money was accepted if stamped by the Wing On's Department Store, a wonderland of new and old treasures. One floor was filled with intricately carved ivory. One item particularly intrigued me: as many as 10 ivory balls, one inside the next, each carved with delicate filigreed designs. Each ball could rotate in any direction, free of all the others. An outside ball with a diameter of four inches might have eight balls, with the innermost ball about the size of a golf ball. Another floor of Wing On's store would have all jade items, another floor all lace and silk. The store was five or six stories high, filled with items of every craft dating from ancient to current times.

There was no need for marines to unfurl their wallets in Shanghai. Jack Dempsey's name on a chit was used with magic in the finest shops, restaurants, bars, nightclubs, or tailoring shops. (When I left Shanghai for the United States, I had five beautifully tailored civilian suits, camel's hair robes, silk underwear, silk shirts, socks, handkerchiefs, and many beautiful chino khaki uniforms, all made by Shanghai's finest tailoring shop and purchased with chits signed with Jack Dempsey's name.) Later the Marine Corps paid for all chits incurred by the marines in order to maintain goodwill. The merchants actually weren't too unhappy, anyway. After all, the U.S. Marines came to their rescue.

General Butler insisted that marines not drink water while on liberty and condoned modest drinking of beer and champagne instead. So the chit system became a way of life for us, even with champagne! (At our billets the water was so loaded with chlorine it looked like milk.) Johnny Walker Scotch was priced at less than $1 per quart, gin at 65 cents per bottle, and the finest German beer at 8 cents per quart-sized bottle. The rate for a rickshaw was about 2 cents a mile when we first arrived in Shanghai. Butler suggested we pay 5 cents in order to build up goodwill. With cigarettes at only 5 cents a pack, even those of us who didn't smoke carried them for *cumshaw* (tip) purposes. One cigarette would put a rickshaw boy into ecstasy with gratitude.

However, rickshaw boys operated under a peculiar philosophy: If a passenger tipped too much, such as tourists do, they knew they were not "streetwise" and would slam coins onto the pavement while yelling for the police and raising a protest in general. The passengers eagerly added coins until the fussing stopped. In one instance, when I was the victim of such a circumstance, a Chinese policeman ran to the scene, followed by a Sikh cop. The Sikh sided with me and whacked the Chinese cop on the head with his three-foot-long billy club. I rewarded the Sikh with two American cigarettes and made his day. The German language was the common denominator—most rickshaw boys could speak a few German words.

Captain Hunt preferred that we patronize such places as the Astor House, the Cathay Hotel, and the elegant Majestic Hotel, which was my favorite bit of paradise, thanks to the chit system. Among the most unique eating places in Shanghai was a German market and restaurant. In the market area downstairs, you were given a numbered basket. You filled it with whatever food you desired. The loaded basket was placed on a line with a hook hanging from a hole in the ceiling. An attendant gave the line a yank and up would go your meal to the upstairs kitchen. On the second floor was a large cocktail area where you would wait until your 18-course Mandarin dinner was ready. The price for the entire meal was less than 50 cents U.S. Regardless of what you selected in the market, additional surprise dishes were added. Usually there would be one waiter per customer. They moved so silently you didn't know they were around.

The French Concession became a haven for the White Russians from Manchuria following the Revolution of 1917 that overthrew Nicholas II. Licensed prostitution, gambling, and ignored narcotic empires flourished. Avenue Joffre and its arteries became known as "Little Moscow," well laced with sleazy bars pandering to servicemen. For many Russian women, the only recourse was prostitution. The Circle Sportif Francais, "French Club," in the French

Concession was the most popular social club in Shanghai. The beautiful gambling casino became a hangout for some of our officers.

Also in the French Concession was a nightclub known to every old-time soldier in the world—St. Georges. Although very sophisticated in its French decor, it was not a place you would want to take your sister. A spacious vestibule opened into an enormous two-story combination of lobby, barroom, and hotel rooms, somewhat like the saloons in Western movies, except grandiose in decor. The elegant European-style bar was furnished with beveled glass mirrors, marble pilasters, and rosewood fixtures. The oval-shaped ballroom, as I remember it, was softly lighted with crystal chandeliers. Circling the dance floor were tables, and from the entrance were stairs leading to an upstairs promenade with a railing on one side and rooms on the other side. From any point of the promenade, you could overlook the whole downstairs scene of dancing, brawling, fighting, and all the action that usually occurs when sailors and marines from different nations mix girls with booze—particularly Chinese *samshu*, which to me tasted like kerosene mixed with carbolic acids. The girls from all nationalities, mostly Russians, were both taxi dancers (you had to pay them to dance with you) and prostitutes, whichever was required of them first. The fee was usually 50 cents for the girl but slightly more for the room, depending on how long you wanted to use it.

Captain Hunt put an "out-of-bounds" status on St. Georges after it became too notorious and wild. However, marines still sneaked in. On one occasion the captain heard that his marines were at the nightclub and had me drive him to the scene. He took one look inside and said, "You go! Get the marines out of there!" What a sight! Everybody was fighting. German sailors teamed with our marines against the French, Italian, and Russian sailors, whacking each other with bottles, chairs, and fists. I don't know where the British "limeys" were—probably upstairs. One by one, I hustled the marines out, about 18 in all. But I had to fight the girls to do it, and I lost a lot of hair. In a procession of rickshaws, led by our Packard touring car and directed by our young officer of the day, we finally returned to our billet. Our sick bay treated the cuts and bruises and gave each marine a preventive prophylaxis against venereal disease. (In 1929, while I was a student at the University of Maryland, a Russian professor in our public speaking class who once lived in Shanghai asked me to give a talk on Shanghai and the infamous St. Georges. It was so well received that I had to give a repeat performance for the entire student body.)

On liberty, we were always intercepting funeral processions. The wealthier the deceased person was, the longer the procession. Paid professional mourners, sometimes up to 50, would throw themselves into a frenzy, the wailing and lamenting both spontaneous and genuine. They were followed by brass band musicians, relatives, mourners, and, sometimes, a group of chanting monks carrying incense. Behind them were attendants carrying the coffin. Sometimes a large framed photo of the deceased was carried in the procession, too.

The Cathay and Grand Theaters were the best ones in Shanghai. However, I enjoyed the native ones despite the language barrier. In the summer, when the temperature was 90 degrees, the humidity in Shanghai was about the same as in New Orleans. Lacking air conditioning, the Chinese substituted hot towels. After you entered a theater and found a seat, an attendant or usher would furnish you with a bowl of hot water and a towel, which you would soak in the water and then place over your face. When you removed the hot towel, after a minute or so you actually felt cool.

Since I liked boats, I sometimes browsed among the sampans

and old junks made of the naturally oiled teak that could last hundreds of years without paint. Silk sails, patched occasionally, would last almost forever. Some junks had painted eyes on the bows as an "aid" to navigation.

To Orientals, the new year is a time to settle accounts. Debts are not carried over into the new year; they are simply washed off the books. During the first few days of the new year, there is considerable gambling surrounding the game mahjong, a fascinating game to watch. The tiles are moved so swiftly that it is difficult to follow them.

A popular haunt of the marines was a very elegant massage parlor. I liked to go there. (It was not a place to find sex.) Upon entering a red-carpeted lobby, you would be assisted by a Chinese girl into a private dressing room to remove your clothes. A robe was furnished. The girl then would escort you to a very large marble steam room with marble tables. Once on the table, two husky male masseurs scrubbed you with soap and water and gave you a preliminary rubdown. You were next taken to a very hot sauna room. After about 20 minutes, you were scrubbed down again in preparation for a complete massage by six female masseurs in a large, beautifully decorated room with a massage table. At this point, I would be so debilitated from the steam room that I wouldn't have been interested in Marilyn Monroe. One girl would massage my toes and feet at one end of the table while another worked on my neck, ears, face, and scalp. The other four women would massage my calves, thighs, arms, back, and shoulders. Massage finished, a girl would assist me in dressing. My bill was about 50 cents U.S., and I added ten cents for a tip to be divided by all hands, who as a group bid me a friendly goodbye.

Prostitution was rampant in Shanghai. The modern-dressed girls on Nanking Road, with Clara Bow hairstyles, high heels, and dresses (*cheongsons*) split up the thigh, were the most expensive and most appealing, and they usually wanted a date for the evening for drinks and 50 cents U.S. In the traditional cat houses, which were usually upstairs and off the street, it was like entering the freshman class of a private school, the girls were so young (from 14 to 17 years of age). Girls above that age were usually sold off as private mistresses or maids. They all wore traditional dresses. The average bordello housed about 30 girls. The cost of the average girl was about 15 to 40 cents, though some commanded a price as high as 80 cents. Most of the marines that I knew said a bar of toilet soap—even Fels Naptha (an American laundry soap)—would induce any girl in the trade. The venereal disease hazard scared me so much that I stayed away.

Concerned about the rate of venereal diseases among all allied servicemen (in some outfits, the rate was to be as high as 75 percent), General Butler required all marines to receive a prophylaxis treatment at the gates of our billets when returning from liberty. Treatments were given even if you only went out for ice cream. The general proposed to his congressman father that the U.S. government send medically supervised girls from the United States to Shanghai as a solution. His proposition was denied. Strict discipline, plus an alliance with raven-haired Russian beauties, became the answer. The Russian women weren't exactly whores, but they needed the money. Each marine eventually found a steady girlfriend or two.

During much of my time in Shanghai I was performing courier service using one of the staff cars. I sold the idea to Captain Hunt that I could travel faster in traffic on a motorcycle when messages to legations and allied headquarters needed to be expedited. He took me up on my offer and requisitioned a bike, which I used both for official business and on liberty.

When a shipload of marines, afflicted with the mumps, arrived from Guam in early summer and were immediately put under quarantine, I met disaster. My commanding officer needed someone to carry a message by hand to the captain of the quarantined ship. I volunteered. It was an excuse to use the motorcycle. My mission was accomplished, but in a few days I was in a huge tent, with yellow flags flying high, in the boondocks of Shanghai with 200 boys from Guam—I had caught the mumps! I stayed there for 19 days with Chinese doctors and nurses, and no visitors. Chinese attendants could be bribed to smuggle beer into our circus tent, and a "circus" it was!

At times, General Butler was somewhat of an enigma. When you least expected it, he would come up with a surprise. On one of our excursions, with just the two of us in our red Sunbeam, he opened up the conversation: "You remember, I promised you corporal stripes. I have written to General Lejeune. You'll get them in time. Why don't you give up the idea of becoming a naval officer? I'll recommend you for the Marine Corps Officers' School in Washington, D.C. You'll like that better."

Bubbling Well Road is a continuation of Nanking Road and was named after a real bubbling well, its water charged with carbonic acid, located at the ancient Zing Ang Sze Temple (Temple of the King of the City). It was still bubbling when I was there. Although photographs of the interior are illegal, I smuggled my camera into the temple for some nice shots of the ten-foot golden Buddha and rare altars. I also took photos outside. Many of the Chinese had never seen a camera before and were timid about my taking their pictures for fear I would steal their spirit identities.

Each day I found new sights and adventures, although there was a level of fear when browsing within the city. One of the most primitive construction devices I saw was a hand-powered pile driver. About a dozen men or more, standing on a circular scaffold, each holding a rope tied to a large reinforced bag (probably silk) filled with something durable and heavy, would lift and drop the bag in cadence with a singsong chant. The wooden piling would penetrate the ground about a half-inch each time it was pelted.

On a certain excursion, I encountered a large group of men and women building a street. Stones were laid by hand, with the larger stones on the bottom, fitted into the spaces. Smaller stones were laid on top in layers, graduating in size. The final layer of stones was composed of pea-sized stones. The workers, mostly women (nearly 1,000 from my count), were on their knees in groups, and each group worked with a certain size stone. The thickness of all the layered stones was about 16 to 20 inches. After the stones were laid, a roller, pulled by hand, completed the job.

Beggars sometimes became a nuisance. We solved the problem by carrying Chinese pennies, which were about the size of a U.S. half-dollar, made of copper (hence the nickname "coppers"). With our exchange rate, we would get almost three coppers for a U.S. penny. When beggars (and sometimes lepers) approached us in Chinese City, we would throw a handful of coppers onto the street, and while the beggars were scrambling for the coins our rickshaws would escape.

The food served in our billets was mostly shipped in from San Francisco. Since the Chinese farmers use human waste taken to the country from Shanghai in "honey barges," their vegetables were taboo with us. Most of the better hotels and restaurants also imported their food. Sometimes, on patrols, we would buy hard-boiled eggs for two cents a dozen. At our sandbag outposts along Soochow Creek, hard-boiled eggs were always available for passing patrols.

The 4th Regiment Air Force used Curtiss Hawks and so-called Hell Divers with double wings and Wasp and Hornet engines made by Pratt and Whitney of East Hartford, Connecticut. The airplanes were made by the Curtiss Aeroplane Company and brought to Shanghai in April 1927. It was the first time aircraft squadrons accompanied an expeditionary force. In May 1927, when Charles Lindbergh flew solo from New York to Paris, the Chinese declared a holiday. You would have thought from all the wild excitement that Lindbergh was Chinese. Our air force was used mostly for observation work to keep up to date on the Chinese Communists' movements.

In early September, orders from Washington, D.C., were received at our headquarters in Tientsin for me to be sent to Quantico, Virginia, for the All-Marine Football Team on the next available transportation. Not liking the "tub of a ship" available for the ride home, Butler held up my orders until a better ship was available. Luck followed. Two other marines, Private Lincoln Hart, Jr., of Los Angeles and Private Charles H. Von Frank of Chicago joined me for the return on the Dollar Steamship Line's beautiful *President Taft*. We enjoyed first-class cabins through the Inland Sea of Japan to Kobe, where our ship was quarantined because of cholera patients in the steerage hold of the ship—all Chinese. A certain senator from Kentucky arranged to have the first-class passengers leave the ship and travel by train through Japan; ten days later, we arrived in Yokohama and caught our boat to Seattle (barely—the boat was almost at sea when we arrived to board, and so we chartered a speedboat and climbed aboard a rope ladder to the cheers of the passengers). This was followed by a train ride to Washington, D.C. Shanghai became just a sentimental journey.

Epilogue

On October 16, 1934, Mao Tse-tung and his followers took to the road under the banner of the Long March from Jiangxi at the Yudu River in north-central China, covering a distance of over 3,000 miles while adding to their Red Bandit Army as they progressed. Mao was no dummy, making the long march in a sedan chair. Eventually Mao and his army defeated Chiang Kai-shek despite Russian and American support. Chiang fled to the island of Formosa, now Taiwan.

Today, Shanghai may be the world's largest city, with over 44 million people, its limits extending to the Yangtze River. All British statues have been removed. A beautiful park has been established along the Bund replacing the sampan villages. A large sports center replaced the racetrack where the marines drilled, paraded, and participated in sports. The "No Dogs or Chinese" sign has been removed from the beautiful public gardens of what was the International Settlement. Shanghai, a city of people friendly to the marines in 1927, no longer exists.

Officers of the 3rd Battalion, 4th Regiment

Colonel "Jumbo" Hill, Commanding Officer, 4th Regiment

Colonel Henry Davis (replaced Colonel Hill)

Major Alexander Vandegrift, Commanding 3rd Battalion (later Commandant of Marine Corps)

Captain Leroy P. Hunt (replaced Major Vandegrift as Commanding Officer of 3rd Battalion, later Commandant of Marine Corps)

Captain R. R. Robinson, 21st Company

Captain T. A. Tighe, 22nd Company

Captain W. T. Clement, 19th Company

Lieutenant Elmer E. Hall, Commanding B-N-2 (World War II Quartermaster General)

Lieutenant Evans F. Carlson, B-N-3 (in World War II, Colonel of Carlson's Raiders)

Lieutenant D. G. Oblesby, B-N-1

Lieutenant Irving Odgers, B-N-4

Lieutenant Dean Blanchard, 22nd Company

Lieutenant Dewit Hubbard (M.C.)

Lieutenant J. O. Brauer, 19th Company

Lieutenant H. E. Dunnelberger, 19th Company

Lieutenant Harry Liversedge, 21st Company (in World War II, Colonel, Commanding Officer of 28th Regiment, 5th Division. His E Company put the flag up on Mount Suribachi, Iwo Jima)

Lieutenant W. D. Bassett, 22nd Company

Lieutenant William Ulrich, 24th Company

Lieutenant R. McCall Pate, 24th Company (later Commandant of the U.S. Marine Corps; my basketball coach of the 4th Regiment)

Lieutenant W. E. Lee, 24th Company

Lieutenant L. R. Kline, 24th Company

Lieutenant Andrew Mathiesen, 24th Company

Gunner W. A. Allen, 24th Company

CHAPTER 9

The All-Marine Football Team

When I got to Quantico I learned that the All-Marine football squad had been temporarily moved to the University of Maryland so that the two teams could scrimmage against each other. I joined the marine team at the University of Maryland and lived in the dormitory. Every day we would work out against the Maryland team.

At the beginning of the 1927–1928 season, we were presented with a sort of threat: If we lost a game, we'd all be shipped into the jungles of Nicaragua. Of course we didn't want that, and so the threat helped us achieve our undefeated season. At the end of the season, when we beat the navy's team, we all got to meet President Calvin Coolidge. The commandant introduced each player as he came up. We were cautioned not to squeeze the president's hands too hard because he had tender hands and our strong hands might break his fingers! I was very cautious when I shook hands with the president. The commandant of the Marine Corps, General Lejeune, told the president, "Ray Poppelman has just recently returned from China. He was working very closely with Smedley Butler."

General Butler and the president were close friends. So the president asked me a few questions and then asked, "In your travels, did you run into any starving missionaries?"

I said, "I only knew one family, but they weren't exactly starving—they had about 40 servants in the family. They were living very well."

Calvin Coolidge turned to the commandant and said, "Hell, that's more than I've got on my whole damn staff." So the president was relieved to know that the missionaries really weren't starving.

At the end of the season, General Lejeune promoted me to corporal. I was a private until that football season, 1927, when I got on the big team. As a reward for making the big team, and thanks to General Butler's earlier recommendation, they gave me what they called a headquarters warrant. It was a warrant by the commandant of the Marine Corps that I could not be busted except by an Act of Congress or by the commandant himself. So it was a special assignment.

In those days, you had to be a good marine for almost eight years before they'd consider you for corporal. In a lot of ways the promotion was a handicap to me because when I was assigned back to the San Diego regiment, all the other corporals, who were practically old enough to be my father, resented the fact that I was promoted to corporal ahead of a lot of people. In fact, it was so bad that when I was made a sergeant, none of the sergeants in San Diego would even speak to me. They practically ignored me. The sergeants had special tables to eat at, four at a table. Nobody would ever sit with me. I got fed up with it and thought, "Jesus Christ, this being a sergeant's really rugged." So I asked permission from the officer in charge of the dining room to make a talk. So I did. I said, "I would like to have you gentlemen sign a petition, which I want to give to General Lejeune. I want to resign as a sergeant. I would rather be your friend and be a corporal than be a sergeant and not be able to speak to you." I left the dining room, and shortly after, a committee of about

In late 1928 I was appointed corporal, thanks to General Butler and the Marine Corps football team.

three sergeants came to see me. They told me that they had remembered me when I played in San Diego, and they were sorry. We got along pretty well after that.

The football players at the University of Maryland had a trick that they played on the marines. Near where we scrimmaged and played football there was a tennis court, and girls would usually be playing there. A University of Maryland player would go up to a new marine and say, "You see those two girls playing tennis?"

He'd say, "Yeah."

"Well, the one with the red hair, she lives near a little white house." (There was a little house by the tennis court, I guess for some employees to live in.) He'd say, "That girl's husband is out of town, and she's a hot number, and maybe tonight you'd like to go over there." They'd get this marine all steamed up, and he would go down after dark and knock on the door and call, "May? May?" Her name was May. So the door would wheel open, and there would stand a big man the marine thought was her husband—but actually it was one of the Maryland players or a coach, only the marine wouldn't know that.

"So you're the son-of-a-bitch who's been screwing my wife?"

The "husband" would have a pistol. The marine would run, and the "husband" would shoot the pistol. The marine would run back up to the dormitory. The others would cool the marine down and say, "O.K., we're going to pull the same trick on Joe," or whoever hadn't been in on the joke. The marine who had run like hell from the "husband" got to be the husband this time. On one occasion, the new guy was in on the joke. He had a big cream pie with him, and as the irate "husband," played by the marine, said, "So, you're the son-of-a-bitch who's been fooling around with my wife?" the guy with the pie said, "Yeah, and what the hell are you going to do about it?" as he slammed the pie in the marine's face. They tricked about ten guys this way. I was lucky because I was tipped off about the joke.

One guy ran off and didn't go back to the dormitory; he went on down the highway toward Hyattsville, and they had to get a police car to get him. Another fellow ran about 25 feet when the "husband" started shooting at him. Then he turned around and yelled, "You dumb son-of-a-bitch, you can't even shoot your goddamn gun. I got a notion to come over there and take it and use it on you." He wasn't even afraid; we couldn't believe it. They pulled the same trick on a pair of auditors from Baltimore during the summer. One of the auditors fell off the stoop, broke his leg or something, and that stopped the whole thing. But during all the years the marines went up there, they played the trick. All the newcomers were taken to May, beautiful May.

Two of the guys on the team, Bob McCracken [Sr.] and Fred Kimball, were food nuts. Kimball knew a company that canned

U·S·MARINE PICTORIAL SERVICE

THREE BROTHERS WIN GRID LAURELS

The three Poppelman brothers were outstanding grid aces with the San Fernando (Calif.) High School before they joined the Marines. This year they wore Marine Corps moleskins and were mainstays of sea soldier backfields. L. H. and C. M. Poppelman (left) played with the Marine eleven at San Diego, Calif., while their brother Raymond (right) was the brilliant fullback of the East Coast eleven.

United States Marine Corps Recruiting Station
MARINE BARRACKS, BLDG. NO. A-1, SAN DIEGO, CALIF.

A 1928 Marine Corps recruiting advertisement featuring me and my brothers Clyde (left) and Lyle (center). Lyle joined the Marines after I did on my parents' advice; then Clyde figured he was missing something, so he joined too. Somebody got the bright idea to take this photo, but I was back East while Lyle and Clyde were in San Diego, so they made a composite out of two separate photos—that's why I look smaller in the photo. It hung in all the post offices throughout the country that year.

whole kernels of wheat. He was buying the stuff by the case and giving it to the football players, claiming it would give them extra strength and so forth. McCracken got in with Kimball, and he was eating that damn wheat. Finally, the coaches found out about it and they raised hell with Kimball, because Kimball's theory was, you

My brother Clyde was a running back on the all-marine championship team in 1928. He also was selected to the all-time best U.S. Marine football team, which included the best players from 1917 to 1933.

don't eat the regular dinner, you just eat the can of wheat. Well, one thing the football coaches didn't want was to starve their football players. They had good chefs and good food.

We had a big game in New Orleans in 1928. We were playing Loyola College of New Orleans, a Catholic school, a perfect team with a famous all-American by the name of Ducky Swan. People would bet on the games (New Orleans was a gambling town), and we had one officer who was assigned to handle bets for the players or anybody who wanted to bet on the marine team. He had a window in the dressing room, and the civilians who wanted to bet against the marines would line up outside. They figured with Ducky Swan they couldn't lose. There were about 25,000 people, and everybody wanted to bet.

In our dressing room, there were seabags full of money from the bets. As players, we could borrow money from the officer taking the cash in. I decided, "We're going to win this damn game. We got Allen Chapley, an All-American from the Naval Academy; and an All-American back from Nebraska, Frank Daly; and me in the backfield"—we had a big heavy line, and we had backups. We didn't have to have cash; we just told the officer that we wanted to put some money on the game. I wanted to bet, so I got bold and said, "I want to borrow $1,500."

The officer looked at me and said, "Jesus Christ, you must feel pretty confident."

I said, "Yeah, we're going to win." So he took my bet for $1,500 and covered it. It was really a knockdown, drag-out game. We won six to nothing. So here I was money ahead and I didn't have to put up a nickel, just talk big.

One of the universities, perhaps Tulane, hosted a dance after the game. There I met a girl, and I practically blew my whole $1,500 on her. We got free hotel rent for a month with our meals as a reward. So I used up my furlough in New Orleans with my winnings and the free room and the free food. I almost fell in love with that girl. I'd called my father about something and told him that I was thinking of getting married. He said, "You forget that damn girl and get on the train and get home." So I went back to my home in San Fernando, enjoying a furlough.

CHAPTER 10

On Enrolling at the University of Maryland, Playing Football for the Pacific Coast League, and Getting Married

After my second year with the big team, in 1929, I had a deal to go to the University of Southern California (USC) when I got out of the marines. There was a rule among the Pacific Coast schools that any athlete who had played against colleges in a certain year would lose a year of eligibility. For example, a player who played two years with San Diego State and then wanted to go to USC could only play two years with USC. So I was only eligible for one year at USC, and at that time the University of Maryland was putting pressure on me to attend Maryland. Because I was scrimmaging there, the Maryland coach, Curly Bird, had seen me in action. He came to me in 1927 and said, "How would you like to go to Maryland?"

I said, "Hell, I wouldn't go to this cow college if you gave it to me."

But in 1928, he said, "I have a proposition for you, Ray." (By then I knew that I only had two years at USC at the best, maybe only one.) He'd worked out a way to get me enrolled at the University of

Maryland in 1929 and have all my expenses paid. So I called Howard Jones at USC and told him about the offer, and he said, "Hell, grab it." The commandant of the Marine Corps, Lejeune, had Senator Tidings, who was the senior senator from Maryland, and the governor and the president of the University of Maryland all sign an agreement that they would pay my expenses for four years in college whether or not I ever played football. On that basis, the commandant released me from the Marine Corps. So in 1929, at the beginning of my third season in Quantico, an officer came out to the field in an automobile and told me, "Poppelman, you have been discharged from the Marine Corps; they want you up at the University of Maryland to watch their game this Saturday, and you've got an order to get up there. You have to catch a train by 2:00."

I rushed like hell, got cleared out of everything you have to do when you're discharged, and got on the train from Quantico to Washington, D.C. I wasn't on the train 15 minutes before a man sat beside me and said, "My name is Beatty. I'm from North Carolina State. I have a check for you for $5,000. You come down and play for North Carolina State." And he said, "We have a room where you can dive out the window into a swimming pool, you'll have an insurance company that will buy you a car, and [So-and-so] will give you clothes."

And I said, "Hell, I've got a contract here. I've got an agreement with the University of Maryland—they got me out of the Marine Corps."

He said, "Here's my card. If you change your mind, call me at Hotel Willard." Five thousand dollars then would be like $100,000 now. I thought, "Jesus Christ, what kind of team are they going to put together?" Anyway, what a day I had. I went to the depot from the train and got on a bus to Maryland. They were playing North

Carolina University. I had to fight with the gatekeeper to get in and see the game, and Maryland got beat 40 to 6.

When I got to the campus a freshman told me he knew where to take me. We went to Sylvester Hall, and he took me to a room and said, "This is where you're supposed to stay, I think. You're supposed to be with Shorty Chalmers." (Chalmers, who later became a baseball player in the big leagues, was playing on the Maryland team.) We opened the door, and there were about 40 pigeons in the room. There was nothing in there but some furniture and all those damn pigeons.

The freshman said, "It sure is a mess here; you're going to have clean these pigeons out of here, I guess."

I said, "No, I tell you, buddy, what I'm going to do. You know somebody who can get me down to the highway?" It was about two city blocks from Sylvester Hall to the Baltimore-Washington highway, and the freshman found somebody who had a car and took me down to the highway where the bus stopped. While I was standing in my blues with a seabag, waiting for the bus, some students in a beat-up old Dodge touring car stopped in front of me. They said, "Hi, Marine, you want a ride?"

I said, "Yeah, where are you going?"

He said, "To Washington to see a movie. You want to go?"

I said, "Yeah, I want to go to the depot."

I was going down to the hotel to meet that guy with the $5,000 who wanted me to go to North Carolina. I figured, the hell with Maryland. If they're treating me that way—a lousy reception and they want me to sleep with a bunch of pigeons. So I got in the car with the Sigma Nu fraternity guys going to Washington. There were four of us—three students and me, a marine. We got to a little town called Hyattsville, which is near College Park, Maryland, where the university was. One of the students said, "Do you like beer?" (This was during Prohibition.)

I said, "Yeah, I like beer."

He said, "Well, they got a speakeasy in Hyattsville. Why don't we go and have a beer before we go the movie?"

I said, "Well, if that's what you boys want, but all I want to do is get to Washington."

We went to an old lady who was making beer in a bathtub or somewhere; it was awful stuff. They said, "Only drink one bottle; two of them will kill you."

So we each had a bottle of beer and got in the car and started off toward Washington. Soon a police car pulled up beside us and wanted the driver's license. He had followed us from the beer joint. There was a racket going on, as we found out. The policeman took us all up to a judge's house. The judge, who was in bed, came out in a nightgown and a nightcap, and the policeman told him that he got a man for driving erratically through Main Street and the boys had been at a certain beer joint. Of course the judge knew about the place. He said, "OK, boys, start emptying your pockets." The students had just a few dollars apiece with them, about enough to get to the movie. But I had $39. I said, "Judge, this is all the money I have, I'm going to the University of Maryland. I need this at the University of Maryland."

He said, "All you got to do, Mr. Marine, is put that money on the dining room table." We were standing up around the table and the students had emptied their pockets. I said, "Judge, I want an attorney. I'm going to the University of Maryland, I want to call Maryland and get somebody to come down here and get me."

He said, "All you got to do is put your $39 on the table and you can go to the university. If not, you go to jail."

I said, "OK, take me to jail." And goddamn if they didn't. The students drove back to the university and found one of the assistant coaches. The coach came down and got me out. I think he told the judge that I had come to play football. After the assistant coach got me out of jail, we started driving toward the campus. I said, "Wait a minute, we're going the wrong way."

He said, "What do you mean?"

I said, "I want to go to Washington. I don't want to go to your goddamn lousy college and have to sleep with a bunch of pigeons."

He said, "Well, tell you what. You have an agreement with the coach. The coach is out of town, but why don't you come back? I'll get you a good room, and Monday morning, you go in and see the coach; he'll get things straightened out. You at least owe it to the coach to tell him that. You're honor-bound." So he took me back and got me a nice room, and on Monday morning I went to see the coach. He said, "We're going to do something about that judge." He told me that near Hyattsville there was a wooded area where students would go to neck in their cars. The police would come out and pounce on them and take them up the judge's house and that was the routine—just empty your pockets. So he informed Senator Tidings about the judge and got the judge removed.

Anyway, they smoothed things over and told me that Shorty Chalmers had moved in with another guy in a bigger corner room, and I was suppose to join them. Shorty Chalmers's hobby was raising pigeons. He'd bring them down from Delaware and release them, and then his mother would record when they arrived home. He'd take a squab that he'd blindfolded all the way down from Delaware through Baltimore to College Park. He'd turn the squab loose at a certain time, and the squab would go up, make three circles, and head for home. When the bird landed at home, Shorty's mother would record the time.

I was in the room about one day when Scotty, the other guy, got back and asked me if I had a car.

I said, "No."

He said, "Now you do—I'm going to give you one." His dad was a millionaire, and so he just gave me an automobile, about four years old, an old Franklin. But Curly Bird made me give it back to Scotty because it looked like the school had bought the car for me.

Anyway, 1929 was my freshman year at Maryland. I had made the right decision to go there and not depend on USC, because October 1929 was Black Friday, when we had the tremendous bust in the stock market and the Depression started. So from then on money got tight, and schools had to slow down on bringing players into colleges. However, I was protected by General Lejeune's contract, so I was very lucky. In my freshman year, I was sitting very nicely because we had an undefeated freshman team. Curly Bird had brought players and two of our assistant coaches from Pennsylvania. So we had a hell of a squad at Maryland my freshman year: two former Marines, Al Woods and myself from the Quantico team, and some guys out of Pennsylvania. We were undefeated; we knocked off everybody we played—the freshman teams we played against seemed like a bunch of kids to us. Our team in 1929 was the best freshman team they ever had at the University of Maryland, and Al Woods and I were stars. Al was a good blocking man and I give him a lot of credit for making me look good.

At the end of the football season, I was practically adopted by my roommate Scotty's family. His family, the Scotts, owned the largest printing company in the United States. That year I played on the

Me in the standard
running back pose,
on the University of
Maryland team, 1930.

freshman basketball team, and in the spring I started playing lacrosse. The coaches thought that lacrosse would help my running
and wanted me to forget basketball and have just two sports—football and lacrosse. (I was inducted into the State of Maryland's Hall
of Fame for lacrosse and Hall of Fame for football.)

When summer came, I got a job helping bricklayers on some
new big buildings on campus. The federal money had been obtained
by Senator Tidings. The football players got jobs working on these
construction projects on the campus in the summertime. But I wasn't
there long. A professor named Brown, who came from the University of Southern California and was dean of our school of econom-

ics, wanted to drive back to California. When he found out that I was from California, he came down, found me on the job, and said, "Would you like to drive me to California? You'll get the same money that you're getting here. I've talked with the coach and the president of the school, and they are willing to let you go if you'll promise to come back." So Brown and I took off for California.

He was writing a book about the secret societies of black people in the South, so we made quite a few stops in the South. Because it was during the Depression, we were getting rooms for a dollar a person a night in homes. There were no motels then. When you'd go through a city or a town, you'd see great big homes with signs that read, ROOM ONE DOLLAR. I drove the professor to California and he changed my life. He was telling me about the All-Americans that were made at Southern California. They didn't study because they didn't have to, and when they got out they were not qualified to get good jobs. He said, "You should take advantage of your opportunities at Maryland and study hard." My grades from my freshman year were very poor—I didn't think I had to study. I was there for football. I had the wrong attitude, but after touring all the way to California and back with this professor I was convinced I should study. He taught me how to study, and my grades zoomed up into B pluses and A minuses. I was in the arts and sciences school, studying mostly business administration.

Brown liked cactus plants and was interested in them. So, on the way back from California to College Park we contacted several companies that were growing cactus plants. The professor made a conditional deal with me. He said, "Ray, if you can talk the school into letting you have a greenhouse to work in, I'll buy the plants and we'll go into partnership and maybe we can make some money." When I got to school I went to our coach and said, "Coach, I've got a chance to make some extra money if we can get a greenhouse." So he got us a greenhouse and we planted our plants, and Brown took the initiative in selling them. He made a deal with the department stores in Washington and Baltimore. In my first year I made $3,000. The department stores sold them because they were a novelty. Professor Brown, who was an adviser to a stock market firm in Washington, invested our money from the cactus sales into certain stocks and bonds.

After I graduated, Brown decided to quit teaching. He told me he had land in Palm Springs, California, and he asked me, "Ray, why don't you join me? We'll go out and sell my land, get a boat and sail around the world." I should have done that, but I didn't.

I was an All-American at Maryland. I was on the Associated Press's Honorable Mention list, but I was on the *Baltimore Sun*'s All-American team, and the *Washington Post*'s—a lot of newspapers. Being an All-American is too much pressure. The fans expect too much from you—it's great if you win, but hell if you lose. I came to Maryland from the Marine Corps and had played against colleges for three years, when suddenly I was back on the freshman team. Maryland had the number-one rated freshman team in the United States that year, above USC, so I got a lot of publicity. When we started playing different colleges, when I went to the varsity, it was OK as long as I had a big line ahead of me. But in my senior year, our line had all graduated and I was with a bunch of freshmen and sophomore linemen who weren't sufficient to back me up. Every team we played wanted to get me out—in fact, the Naval Academy had my name painted on their tackling dummy. I was on the navy's all-time opposition team!

On campus, everyone I met knew me. When I first came to Maryland, before I got tipped off about not being a snob, I'd just walk by, because in the Marine Corps you never said "Hi" to anyone—you just went where you were going. I couldn't do that in college. If I was walking on the sidewalk and some students approached, I'd have to look at them and say "Hi," or I'd get a bad reputation.

I'm often asked what was the secret to being an All-American running back, aside from natural ability. The answer is, you had to have a smart coach. And newspaper reporters had to like you. For instance, when we were practicing, reporters from the sports departments of the *Washington Post* or the *Washington Herald* would come out to the campus to watch us skirmish and play. I'd be introduced to them, and I'd take the opportunity to make a fuss about them. For example, if they had written up a good report on a previous game or something, I'd mention it. Shirley Povich was a famous sports reporter for the *Washington Post*. He came up to me one time to interview me, and I said, "Mr. Povich, I sure appreciate the write-up you gave about me. I'm not saying you shouldn't exaggerate, but I wasn't that good."

He said, "I'll do the writing." But we later became friends, and I know it helped to have him and the other writers in my corner.

I'm often also asked what made me a good running back. I was a good open-field runner. I could change directions. I wasn't too fast but I was big and bully—I was really a fullback in a good running position. I could shift and dodge. I set a yardage record for Maryland that lasted 42 years. Not too long ago a coach at Western Maryland University was a guest speaker somewhere—I think it was at the Touchdown Club in Washington, D.C. He was talking about players and said, "The greatest running back this state has ever seen was Ray Poppelman." I was a good runner. I was on the All-South Team for three years in a row and was captain in my third year. Nationally I was second—I think there was a player from USC who held first place for yardage in a particular year. But I was a good running back and my advantage in college was that I had already played three years against colleges on the marine team before I had a chance to play against the colleges on the collegiate circuit. It was a break for me that I could play football, because during the Depression I got that good offer from Maryland. Other schools had to drop their big offers to players—they just didn't have the funds.

So I took the punishment of football for seven years. I think what helped me was my second sport—lacrosse. There's a lot of running in lacrosse, and all that running helped me in football. Conditioning was very important. I used to work out all the time. Just because the season was over didn't mean I could relax and do nothing. I *had* to be in good condition because when you get a reputation, the other team's laying for you. In one game, Duke University kicked off to us, and we had two men on the backfield to receive the ball. Shorty Chalmers was on my right, and a horde of guys came to get me. The ball was coming down high and Shorty caught it, but not a damn soul worried about Shorty—they all piled on me. When I went up against big linemen who weighed 250 pounds and could run fast, I might sidestep one, but still I've got another one to worry about. One of them is going to get me. The trick I learned was that if I was going to get hit, I should get off my feet and ride with it. I didn't make a solid stance and then let them hit me.

By the time a season's half over, if you go into a dressing room of a football squad you'll see a whole mob of mummies: They've got so much tape on them. You can have a charley horse, and by the time the assistants get through steaming it, and massaging it down, and putting extra padding on, with the pressure of the game, you forget about it once you get on the field.

I remember when I played in the Marine Corps, we had an

All-American from the Naval Academy named Shapley, a lieutenant. He and I had the same build and we both had curly hair.
We were playing Loyola Chicago or some team in Chicago at Soldiers Field Stadium. There was a big crowd, and Shapley had been
given an awful lot of publicity to build the crowd up: "Rich All-
American from the Naval Academy will be playing Saturday at
Soldiers Field." Our publicity department would always build up
players. We had an All-American from Nebraska and a couple of
other All-Americans. They always got a lot of publicity before we
hit a town. In Chicago, Shapley was injured. Tom Keating, our coach,
came to me and said, "Poppelman, now switch jerseys with Shapley.
I hope you won't mind. We've got so much publicity about Shapley
that he's got to make an appearance, and I don't want him to get
hurt again because we're going to need him some other time."

So Shapley was sitting on the bench with my jersey and I was
out on the field, getting luckier than hell with one of my best games.
"Shapley does this, Shapley does that," the announcer called. After
the game, we went into the dressing room and Shapley patted me
on the back. He said, "Ray, thank you for the best game I ever
played." I couldn't do anything wrong. On defense I'd be standing
there flat-footed, and Christ, they'd throw a pass in my hands.

After college, I played pro football in Los Angeles on Sundays.
There were five teams owned by a Jewish syndicate, and the players
all trained together. We had games at Gilmore Stadium. Our deal
was $200 a game, except we'd get a bonus if the crowd went beyond
17,000 spectators. I was playing the backfield, and one Sunday the
coach sent me from the bench. He said, "Ray, you go out, take a flat
pass, run a few steps, fall down and fumble the ball. I want the other
team to have the ball." I thought he was being facetious. I ran out,
dodged two men, and ran for a touchdown. He called me to the

bench and said, "Goddamn you, I told you to fumble that ball. You sit on the bench here." After the game I talked to one of the lineman. I said, "What the hell is he fussing about?"

He said, "Hell, don't you know what they're doing? Why do you think they're shuffling us every week on different teams?"

I said, "I don't know."

He said, "They're betting on their own teams up in Las Vegas. We're supposed to lose every once in a while."

The teams were all with the Pacific Coast League. I played mostly on the Rams, and another was called the Shamrocks. A lot of players from the Stanford team were on their squads. Wednesday nights we got together, not to scrimmage against each other, but to work out plays on the blackboard in one big room. They'd say, "Poppelman, this week you're going to be playing with [so-and-so] team." They made up the teams so the scores would be a certain way because they were betting on them in Las Vegas. One of the big linemen once said to me, "What the hell, we're playing for money, not glory."

Once, we went to San Diego to play, and the trucker who was supposed to bring our uniforms got mixed up and went somewhere else. The game was to begin in four hours, and we had no uniforms. The coach said to me, "You used to play for the Marine Corps, didn't you?"

I said, "Yeah."

He said, "You think you know the coach out there?"

I said, "I know who he is. His name is Bill Bluett—he used to be with the University of California."

He said, "Let's go out and see if we can borrow some Marine Corps uniforms." The Marine Corps agreed to loan us uniforms on one condition: that we let the marines in free to the game. So that was the deal. I forget what the score was at halftime, but the coach came to me and said, "Now, we've got to satisfy these marines. You're an ex-marine and they've come to see you play. We're going to kick off to you and you're going to run for a touchdown."

So I did, and I looked over at the marine section, and hats were flying in the air.

Near the end of the season, one of the Los Angeles newspapers got wind of what was going on. They got the state in on it, and all the teams were disbanded. And that was the end of our football. (At that point the National Football League came in. A lot of the teams that had played on our Pacific Coast League later became teams of the National Football League. The team I mostly played on became the Los Angeles Rams. So I'm a pioneer of the Los Angeles Rams.)

While I was in college, I married Doris Evans. Doris still holds a scholastic record at Maryland—she had straight A's from her freshman year through her senior year. She was a brilliant girl, and I think that was probably one reason I married her. A professor told me, "Ray, with your drive and that Doris Evans, you could own the world." Doris's father, who was the leading attorney for the Internal Revenue Service at the time, had a friend named Charles Hamel with whom he had gone to school in North Dakota. Hamel was now a leading tax attorney in Washington, D.C. Hamel liked me and had no children of his own, so when I married Doris Evans, he sprung a big wedding for us. He lived in a prestigious part of Washington on Albermarle Street in a great big home built of stone—the roof was all slate, and he had the whole roof covered with roses. It cost him a fortune. He invited all the prominent attorneys in Washington to the big party. Here I was a nobody—being married in his home.

We received some small presents, not too valuable, and about only $50 in cash. So Doris and I headed for California with less than

$120 in our pockets. The first night we stayed in Fredericksburg, Virginia. My former roommate Scotty, the wealthy boy whose father owned the biggest printing company in America, decided to spring a surprise party for me. He said, "I'll take care of your room and where you stay the first night. Just let me handle everything." So we stayed at a fine country inn in Fredericksburg. Our room was quite large, and it had double doors opening to another great big room. I think at one time or the other they used it for a small convention area upstairs. Well, Scotty really pulled a good one on me. He got the University of Maryland crowd, a lot of whom had been to the wedding, and they all ran out to this inn and packed in the room behind the double doors. Doris and I went upstairs, got into the bed, and about that time, BOOM! the doors opened and everybody ran in. So they had a big party there.

We got a late start the following morning going west in an old Ford A-Coupe that I had bought for $75 and had fixed up a bit. We headed for California and stopped at the Grand Canyon. Five miles from San Fernando, the damn car broke down and had to be towed. Imagine that, going 3,000 miles and then being towed the last five! We were lucky.

CHAPTER 11

Creating the French Village, and My Move to Washington, D.C.

When I arrived in California in 1933, I joined my father's office long enough to see what was happening because of the Depression. Movie stars in Beverly Hills were selling their homes to get money to pay the stockbrokers. Everybody was buying stock on margin—they paid so much to get stock, and if the stock went down they had to put up so much money. In good times it worked, but when the stockbrokers started calling in more money, the rich people did the wrong thing. They liquidated real estate to protect the stock. The ones who were smart let the stock go and kept the land.

My father had a lot of land in the San Fernando Valley. In order to get jobs for people, the county projected streets, sewer, water, lamp-posts, and sidewalks right through all the open land there, no matter who owned it. And then they assessed the owners. The county wanted about a $2,000 assessment per lot for improvements my father didn't even want. He couldn't pay, and his estate of about $8 million vanished. My father also had a mortgage on a property called French Village, a complex of some cabins, a big dance hall, a garage, and a house. He let the property fall back to him because the man who owned it couldn't pay the interest on the mortgage my father held.

One day I was reading the newspaper and I saw a picture of an old high school friend named Hobbs, who had been put in jail in Los Angeles because he was selling booze in a nightclub illegally. I went to see him in the jail, and he told me that his arrest was a setup with the police to satisfy the churches. He owned the Plantation, the biggest nightclub in Beverly Hills. He said, "What are you doing, Ray?"

I said, "The best offer I've got is a job for Chrysler Motors for $18 a week in an office. I don't like that."

He said, "I tell you what. Beer and wine will be legal again next year. I'm in here just to satisfy the sheriff, so the churches think he's doing a good job cleaning up the booze and so forth. I just bought a shipload of German beer made in Japan. Why don't you find an old garage somewhere and start a beer joint? I'll furnish the beer to help you get started."

I said, "Hell, I got something better than that—my father owns the old French Village out in Newhall."

And he said, "Great." So in his cell he told me how to make money. He had bought a shipload of beer for, I think, a cent a bottle. Back then Japanese products could not be sold in America. Someone had tried to bring in this shipload of Japanese beer, but the government confiscated it and put it up for auction. My friend who owned the nightclub was high bidder and got it.

I went to my father and said, "Dad, what are you doing in the French Village?"

He said, "Some people have dances there on Wednesday and Saturday nights. And Noah Beery, a movie actor, sells some trout from his trout farm up in the mountains." (They had a stand on the highway where they were selling trout for ten cents apiece.)

I said, "Dad, I got a deal for you," and I told him about Hobbs and what he suggested.

My father said, "Oh, hell, I've got a reputation to live up to. I can't be running a beer joint."

I said, "Well, let me have it. We'll go 50-50." So he agreed to it, and he put the property title in my brother's name in case of lawsuits against me or my father. The state passed a law that you could sell beer if you sold it with food in a restaurant. So I had to build a restaurant on the front of the dance hall in order to sell beer. An orchestra by the name of Happy Liggams, which had been recording for Bing Crosby, was out of business. Hobbs arranged to get that orchestra to play for a percentage of the gate receipts. The musicians were all broke and looking for jobs, but there were just no jobs to be had. So I built, under very strange circumstances, an addition to the big dance hall with a stage; it looked like a big barn. We designed the addition to have a separate entrance into the dance place, and so we could also serve people in the dance hall from the restaurant. I needed $1,500 worth of lumber for the construction, and my father got credit for me at the lumberyard; he knew the owner.

I went over to the railroad tracks and put a sign up on the telephone post with an arrow: FREE FOOD AND LODGING FOR LABOR. Okies from Oklahoma were coming in on freight cars, which would be filled, and more guys were sitting on top. After I got the sign up and the first freight car came through, men would jump off the freight train that was going slowly through Newhall and would come over to my French Village. I had to get the police to handle the crowd. I interviewed all the guys in the line who were carpenters, and I took eight guys who looked pretty good to me. I put them in the eight cabins to live. I also hired a drunken painter who claimed he was a pretty good cook. He cooked in the kitchen in the house. With my

The exterior of the French Village, 1935.

carpenters and the $1,500 worth of lumber, and a foreman who had a pickup truck and some tools (he got board and room and $10 cash per week), we built the addition onto the French Village. When it was finished, we opened up with the Happy Liggams Orchestra and charged 50 cents admission to the dance hall.

Although slot machines were illegal, the sheriff who controlled the slot machine business came out to see me and said, "You can put slot machines in your place providing you put mine in."

East Side Brewery had been brewing "near beer," as they called it; then it went to 3 percent, and then finally they went into making 6 percent beer. They would furnish all my taps and barrels and equipment if I used their beer. So we had East Side Brewery's Beer and my Japanese beer, which we called "French Village Special." We took the labels off the Japanese bottles and put our own labels on them. Hobbes let me have the beer for a penny a bottle; with the labels it cost me about 3 cents a bottle, and I was selling it as fast as I could get it out for 25 cents a bottle.

The bar at the French Village,
about 1935, near Newhall, California.

When we got the Japanese beer, we had no place to put it. So we
stacked it in wooden boxes under olive trees out in the little valley
between the cabins we had. It was wonderful beer. When we ran
out of it, we got in trouble, because everybody wanted the French
Village Special, so we took East Side's 6 percent beer, soaked the
labels off it, and put our French Village Beer on it. Everybody thought
that it was the Japanese beer, but it wasn't.

We had kegs of 3.2 percent beer from East Side Brewery that we
would keep in reserve. After about 11:00 or 12:00 at night, we would
switch to that if a guy wanted a refill, so he wouldn't get so drunk.
For that reason, 3.2 percent beer was very popular.

When beer and wine first came back in California after Prohibi-
tion, it could be sold only with meals. Sandwiches were considered
a meal and it became a damn nuisance. When somebody ordered a

sandwich, he might have two or three beers and not touch the sandwich. It restricted sales to some extent. To get by the law, we had sandwiches wrapped in paper, which we put under the counter. When a man ordered a beer we would take the sandwich, put it up on top of the counter, and when he'd leave we would put it back.

One time a federal man ordered a beer, and when we gave him a wrapped sandwich he put an X on the bottom of it. We had to bribe him by giving him $20 to get out of that mess. Later, a salesman came in with a suitcase full of rubber sandwiches. He had a hamburger and a cheese sandwich—about four different sandwiches all made of rubber. From five feet away you couldn't tell them from the real thing. We never had a bit of trouble with our rubber sandwiches, and they were used all over Los Angeles. One night a drunk guy tried to eat one!

My father couldn't believe what was going on. He'd come up Sunday mornings, after our big Saturday nights. We'd dump the cash on the middle of the dance floor and make two piles. He'd take his pile back to Hollywood, and I'd take my pile to the bank. We were making about $3,000 a week after the first three months. We had to buy land next to us for additional parking. A lot of Western stars with ranches in the Newhall area would come on Saturday nights. We had big crowds—about 500 people on a Saturday night. We could get acts to go with our 18-piece band for about $5 or $10, just enough money for food. It was the Depression; it was terrible.

We were trying to find out how to get income on other nights beside Saturday. A fellow from Warner Brothers came out with a camera and said, "I know how you can make some money."

I said, "How?"

He said, "We'll have a chance [a raffle] to get into the movies on Wednesday nights. Happy Liggams will have his orchestra here, and

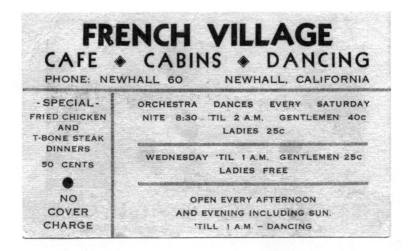

FRENCH VILLAGE
CAFE ◆ CABINS ◆ DANCING
PHONE: NEWHALL 60   NEWHALL, CALIFORNIA

-SPECIAL-	ORCHESTRA DANCES EVERY SATURDAY
FRIED CHICKEN AND T-BONE STEAK DINNERS	NITE 8:30 'TIL 2 A.M. GENTLEMEN 40c LADIES 25c
50 CENTS	WEDNESDAY 'TIL 1 A.M. GENTLEMEN 25c LADIES FREE
NO COVER CHARGE	OPEN EVERY AFTERNOON AND EVENING INCLUDING SUN. 'TILL 1 A.M. – DANCING

A business card from the
French Village, circa 1935.

I'll have my camera panning the crowd as they dance. The following Wednesday, we'll show the movies and announce who the studio wants to give a movie tryout to." After about six months of that we found one person who actually got a job, but that gimmick really worked.

We also had a William S. Hart Night. William S. Hart, the famous old silent movie star, had property that adjoined ours, and occasionally he'd come down to the French Village. We asked him if he could come on slow nights to help bring in business, and he agreed. He would tell stories, and everybody would flock around and get his autograph. He was an attraction. Since people seemed to like that cowboy, I got another guy, Harry Carey, who had a ranch nearby to come down, and two or three other cowboy stars also. We started to get the cowboy crowd coming into the French Village during the week and that helped.

Once I was closing up the French Village late, around 11:00 p.m.

I had the outside lights off, the parking lights off, and the cook had gone home. I was alone checking out the cash register with just a few lights along the counter. Much to my surprise, who should come in but Clark Gable, the actor. He was at the height of his career at that time. Along with him was his girlfriend Carole Lombard. At first I didn't recognize him; he had on a broad black hat and a dark shirt. I recognized his voice first, as he was coming in. He said, "Sorry, but we haven't had anything to eat today. We've been up in the desert. Is there anything at all you've got here?"

And I said, "No, I'm sorry. The cook's gone home, and I'm not a cook at all, I don't know how to cook anything. If you go down to San Fernando, they've got a little place in Mexican Town that should be open this time."

He said, "Haven't you got anything?"

I said, "My father and I have some special meat that we fix up for ourselves for hamburgers. We were taught how to do it by a Mexican cook—it's full of onions and peppers chopped up, and we use it only for ourselves because my father likes good meat. He buys T-bone steaks and puts it in our grinder. I know how to cook one of those."

And he said, "Hell, yes, let's go for it."

So they sat down at the counter. Both of them played the slot machine, which I think was a lousy penny machine. (We had penny machines in those days, and nickel machines. The penny slots made enough money for us to pay our light bill, which was about $90 a month.) While they were playing the slot machines, I went out and made them two hamburgers the way I would make one for myself. I had lettuce, tomatoes, cheese, and our good meat. I was a little nervous about it, but I brought it out to them, and Clark Gable took one bite and said, "You may not be a cook, but this is the best damn hamburger I've ever tasted in my life." And they each ate a hamburger. Then he said, "Do you have enough there to make a half of another one?"

I said, "Sure," so I made one more for Clark Gable. And when they left, he asked me a few questions about the village and I told him briefly my situation—that I was temporary, and I was a graduate of the University of Maryland but because of the Depression I couldn't get a job. He said he knew what I was talking about—the studios were besieged with people trying to get bit jobs for peanuts. "Anyway," he said, "how much do we owe you?" And he threw down quite a large bill; I think it was a $50 bill.

I said, "The cash register is closed, and I can't mess it up now by taking anything else." I pushed the money back. I said, "Besides, I owe you. With all the good movies of yours that have entertained me I could never charge you for anything."

And he said, "Well, I'll come back sometime; see you again." And they left. A couple years later, he did come back to the French Village when my brother was in charge, and he asked for me. I couldn't believe a famous movie star like Clark Gable would remember me.

I had heard about Gable's large ears, so when I could, I glanced at them. With the big broad hat he had on, his ears seemed small. Of course, I was giving some attention to Carole Lombard. She was attractive, but movie stars all look different in life than they do on the screen. I thought with all the beautiful girls they had in Hollywood that Clark could've done better as far as pure beauty is concerned. But she had a wonderful voice, and she was first-class, and I was impressed with her. I wanted to get an autograph, but I didn't have anything but the slips of paper that you use for bills. When he mentioned he'd come back, I figured maybe I could get a photograph autographed. But I was amazed how ordinary they were, just like regular people. You'd seen them on the screen in their finery, and how they act, and then you see them in real life, and they're really talking to you, it's entirely different. I was very impressed with them.

Then there was the miner who came in with gold. That was probably our biggest night in the history of the French Village. A miner came in dressed in corduroy clothes, with high boots, a Western-style hat, and a bandanna, and he plunked two sacks of gold nuggets on the counter. He said, "I'm celebrating. This is my night, and I want to pay for everything for the crowd." We'd never heard such talk. Fortunately, that night my father was there. We were a little undecided at first how we could handle the gold nuggets—we weren't sure of their value. I think at that time they were worth about $32 an ounce, so it was decided that we would take one sack of gold nuggets and keep it on sort of deposit, and when the man came back we would adjust with him. He passed one sack of gold nuggets to my father. When the crowd found that everything was going to be free, they started calling friends, and it wasn't long before we had at least 500 people in the French Village. Everybody was ordering drinks and every damn thing they could think of. It wasn't long before the miner decided he'd better leave us his second sack of gold nuggets too. Ordinarily we closed up about 2:00 in the morning; this time we didn't close up till daylight. The orchestra was paid an extra fee to hang on, and when the musicians went home we played a Nickelodeon piano that had been left there.

We had gotten the piano from a man who brought it in and said he would be back the next week to change the records. The piano was good for business because when the band left, the hangers-on would dance to music from the machine. All they had to do was put nickels into it. Well, three months passed and the man never showed up. The piano had so many nickels in it we couldn't get any more in. One Sunday I decided to dismantle a panel in the back and take out the part of the piano that held the nickels. I would count the nickels—it was a 50-50 deal. The man who owned the piano got half the nickels, and the house got the other half. I pushed the piano into the center of the floor and had a man help me get the back off. Just as we had started to count all the nickels in a big pile on the floor, lo and behold, who should come into the French Village but the guy who owned the piano. He looked at us and said, "How long has this been going on?" He had been sick, which is why he hadn't come back. The upshot was we divided the nickels with him. I think there was about $150. That's a lot of nickels. The man cleaned up the piano and gave us new records. We got tired of three months of the same records over and over, but the crowd would take anything after they'd been drinking and dancing.

At one point we wondered why our beer sales weren't doing so well. My father called a friend of his who was the manager of the Ambassador Hotel in Los Angeles, which had a first-class nightclub—the best in Los Angeles. He came out one day and was sitting at the bar, and he said, "Hubert, where did you get that goddamn paint?" (The bar part of our French Village, the front of the dance hall, was painted a ghastly green.)

My dad said, "We had a cook working here who used to be a good thief, and he stole it from someplace."

This fellow said, "Hubert, get rid of that damned paint. I can't even stand to look at it. I don't see how you sell any beer." He suggested, "Paint it white and put an amber wash over it, like the old Monterey antique on the houses that were stained with rainwater. Give it a little antique in here." We did that, and our beer sales tripled.

We sold beer by the pitcher; which was a trick that we learned from another place. You sell it by the pitcher, and while the people are dancing and there's maybe a third of the pitcher left, you take their pitcher away, and refill it. You don't pour the beer out; you refill it from one of your taps and bring it back to the table. Nobody ever suspected you cheated them because they figured the other couple drank the beer while they were dancing. So we were getting almost 30 percent more income from our beer by the waitresses bringing the pitchers back before they were empty.

We also sold wine. Our wine came from a man in the San Fernando Valley who was making his own wine and distilling it with a special process we had never heard of before—he filtered it through chicken feathers. We sold it for 25 cents a glass, and if you held it up to the light you could see tiny feathers floating around. We also sold a better grade to the Hollywood crowd—it was 35 cents a glass and had no feathers in it; it was clear. The Civilian Conservation Corps (CCC) boys who worked up in the camps—those of the proper age—would usually drink the 25-cent stuff we had.

The dance hall was quite large, close to 100 feet long and 40 feet wide. There was a large fireplace on one side of the hall. If it was cold and nippy at night, with the fireplace going for a few hours the temperature would be just about right. It's amazing how body heat from a lot of people causes a room to become warm. When they left, it would cool right down.

An old man who looked like a retired banker would walk around through the crowd and would sense where there might be some trouble coming. He would call one or the two of the boys together and say, "Boys, you're getting a little too rambunctious here; just back off a little bit." And he would smooth things over. If that didn't work, we had an ex-prizefighter, a heavyweight fighter, who was the bouncer. If there was real fighting, he would get between them, bump their heads together, and say, "Knock it off or you go."

We also had a policeman from the department at Newhall assigned to our place. He would hang around the front of the dance hall, and if necessary we would call him. He would take whoever was at fault—whoever got too drunk and was raising hell and wanted to fight—to the jail and leave him in there till about daylight, and then they would release him without a fine. That was our routine: You had the diplomat—the old man who would smooth things over—the bouncer, and the cops. So we were well protected; we never let a fight get out of hand.

Down the road about a mile and a half there was a man who had all kinds of wild animals that he leased out to the movie people. He was reasonable until he had a few drinks, then he'd get belligerent. This tough guy came in one Saturday night. The bar was crowded and he was at the counter. For some reason or another he was in a mood and he was picking on me. And finally he challenged me. I said to myself, "Here's where I get the hell beat out of me." But I had to save face, so I said, "You know what I'm going to do?"

He said, "What?"

I said, "I used to be a fighter back East. It's illegal for a fighter to hit another guy, but I'm going to break the law. I'm coming around to beat the hell out of you." So I came out from behind the bar and he ran like hell. So I became sort of the hero with the drinking crowd.

People from Hollywood who knew my father would come out, talk big, act big, and order every damn thing. When the chit came, they'd say, "I'm a good friend of Hubert's. I'll be out next week to care of it." They'd sign the bill and walk out. They had no money. It was hard to believe that the movie crowd didn't have money. We constantly had a cigar box full of chits signed by movie people. They were good spenders, and we figured about half of them came back and paid. So we lost 50 percent, but the profit we made on the other 50 percent balanced it out, so we weren't losing, and the movie crowd helped bring in other people.

We also had a garage for car repairs with two gas pumps in front. Our best gas was 17 cents a gallon. We hired a young fellow to run the garage on a percentage basis, 50-50. He had a trick that brought in more income than the gasoline did. When he lifted the hood to check the oil, he would cut the fan belt almost off with a very sharp knife, so that when the driver started up the engine, that fan belt would go. He'd go back to the owner and say, "You got a bad belt down here; you better change that." The man would look under the hood and see that the belt was about ready to break and would buy a new belt. He'd sell them for a dollar and a half or something like that. Practically everybody got the new fan belts. They didn't want a broken belt way out by Newhall. That was really out in the country, about 12 miles from San Fernando, compared to now.

One aspect of our business we didn't know about: There was a good-looking prostitute doing business in our parking area. One day she came in (after the cops caught her). She put down an envelope full of one-dollar bills and she said, "My fee has been $3 dollars, and you get $1 commission."

My wife, Doris, kept the books of the French Village; she was sort of the administrator, the brains. She would tell us where we were losing and where we were making money. She was really good. We lived in the little house on the property. Doris had one bedroom as her office. Except for dance nights and during the day, she seldom ever came over to the bar. When Doris's father came to Los Angeles with about 50 lawyers to make settlements with bankrupt corporations, he came out to the French Village to visit us. When he saw how we were living, he told his daughter, "Doris, you get away from this place. Mr. Hamel has a branch office in Beverly Hills. I'm going to talk to him about giving you a job there; I want you to get out of this beer joint."

Doris went to Beverly Hills and took an apartment, and worked in her uncle's branch office. She met a young actor from Texas and thought she was in love with him. We talked it over and decided that neither one of us was meant for each other. She was going to night school to study law. She passed the bar and became a lawyer with her uncle's income tax company.

At one time, we were using the French Village as campaign headquarters for a politician running for Congress. He really didn't want to run and didn't know anything about politics, but the American Legion wanted him. He was poet laureate for the state of California—a man named John C. McGroarty, a real gentlemen. He never thought he had the chance of being a congressman, but he agreed to let them use his name to support the American Legion. The French Village was the headquarters and we had certain nights where beer was free and we had labels on the bottles: VOTE FOR JOHN C. MCGROARTY, and he would make talks there. And lo and behold, much to everybody's surprise, he was elected. The night he was elected, they had a big meeting about 2:00 in the morning, with all the politicians who were fighting for the jobs they would get. For instance, the government was getting ready to build a dam in the San Fernando Valley, and the contractors that had contributed wanted John C. McGroarty to be sure to get them in on the contracts and so forth. McGroarty was heading for Washington to secure an office.

My mother became very sick and was close to death. At that time, my father met a woman (I don't know if it was in Minneapolis or Hollywood) who had money. She was in the Hollywood crowd, and she and my father fell in love and waited for my mother to die before they got married. So she got into the act and wanted to convert our French Village into more of a glitzy, sophisticated place and to get away from the working crowd. But it was the working crowd who had jobs that brought us our money, really. So my father and stepmother starting moving in, pushing me out more and more.

I had told my father that I would quit on a certain night at midnight and that I had agreed to go to Washington with John C. McGroarty to help him arrange jobs. Dad and I had made an agreement to trade my interest in the French Village for 80 acres of oil land that he had in Texas. If he ever sold the French Village, the money would go to our family, not to his new wife. That was the agreement. At midnight one night I was at the French Village, working as a bartender, and I took my apron off and said, "Dad, midnight's here, and here's where we part." I shook hands with my dad, told Anne, my stepmother, goodbye, and went to get the car. My pet black cat jumped on my stepmother's leg and dug his claws in, and the chef had to run in with a broom and kill the cat to get him off her leg. The cat knew I was leaving and that I had a feud with my stepmother.

After I sold the village to my father, he kept it for two years, and then he sold it to a popular Western star who had a band. He couldn't make a go of it, so it fell back to my father, who then sold it to the American Legion. The legion used it for its headquarters and did very well with it. Today only remnants of the French Village remain; I think the building is now an upholstery shop. The railroad tracks cross the highway a quarter of a mile or so north of where the French Village was. Today, if you went into the town and asked somebody, "You know where the old French Village building would be?" they wouldn't know. (Our old house at 519 4th Street was wrecked during an earthquake, and now that area is commercial.)

PART 3

Living in Washington and
Starting Out as a Developer
(1935–1942)

CHAPTER 12

Working for the Resettlement Administration, and Developing a Subdivision

After I left the French Village, I took a bus back East with McGroarty. We rode that bus through one of the famous dust bowl episodes in the Middle West. In little towns in Kansas it was so black you'd think it was night, and cars were running with their lights on. Restaurants that we stopped at were always jammed full of people waiting to get on the bus. People would wave money at us to buy our seat. The windows of the bus and the door were taped to keep the dust out. When passengers would need to get off the bus, the driver would untape the door so they could get in and out. It was a horrible experience. We never stayed in motels; we stayed on the bus all the way.

Once McGroarty and I got to Washington, we found out that Senator McAdoo had all the jobs lined up and that the people who had supported us during the election were out of luck. When we couldn't get the jobs out to California, McGroarty said, "Ray, let's see if we can get you a job in Washington." He went to the Democratic National Committee and said, "Ray Poppelman here was very helpful getting me elected in California. He was one of my managers and I want him to have a job." They sent me to the Resettlement Administration, which was a new boondoggling outfit to rehabilitate farmers. Those who were bankrupt and broke were given a new chance—a new type of farming, European-style. The participating families would live in little communities clustered together for social reasons, especially for the wives. When I began at the Resettlement Administration, it was just getting organized. The big boss, named Tugwell, was under Secretary Wallace of the Agriculture Department. Tugwell was the kind of guy who would come to the office in a formal outfit—striped pants, wing collar—like he'd just come from a social gathering, and have coffee with us.

The Resettlement Administration was located in a big commercial office building on F Street in downtown Washington. Because I was one of the first ones there, I was put in charge of a big section with 200 people auditing vouchers that were sent in for payment. After the vouchers were audited and approved, they were sent on to the General Accounting Office, where they got another audit, and then they were sent on to the Treasury for payment. The vouchers were coded so that the Republicans would never know how much money they were spending and how. I had more responsibility piled on me than I was equipped to handle, but because I was one of the first ones there and because of a recommendation from one of my former superior officers, I was given a big job.

I had a variety of clerks; a lot of them were well educated. There was an ex-mayor of Atlanta, Georgia, who came into a job at $1,440 a year as a file clerk. I had problems with him because when he was introduced to me, he said, "I do one thing that you might not like. I usually didn't get to my office in Atlanta until about 11:00, and if it's OK, I'll come at 11:00." I had to get in a fight with him, and finally his senator called me and said, "[So-and-so] is a good old boy. Just look after him."

I said, "Well, I've got him working on a file cabinet. We have more clerks than I need, and I have one set of clerks messing up the files and another clerk coming back to straighten them out."

I arranged to have him transferred.

When I took over the job, my boss took me into a room that must have had three stacks of vouchers, five feet high. He said, "You're going to have a lot of men coming in to help in the next few days." Soon clerks started coming in and occupying the desks.

One day a clerk came to me and said, "We've got a voucher here that's got a peculiar code on it. What can I do with it?" The code wasn't listed so I tried out the number on the phone, and who should I get on the end of the line but Eleanor Roosevelt! She was so friendly, and I told her, "I've got a telephone bill charged to your code, if it is your code. There are over 2,000 calls at 5 cents a call. Did they come from your office?"

And she said, "Yes." She asked me about my unit and our office and how things were going, and I found out that she was the big boss behind the whole damn organization. She said, "Well, Mr. Poppelman, if your office has any problems, you be sure to call me."

I said, "Thank you, that would be great. We really have some problems on appropriations. We're running out of money on one big project."

Then I went to my boss, Bob Fukes, and said, "Guess who I talked to? Eleanor Roosevelt."

He about jumped out of his chair, "Eleanor Roosevelt! Jesus Christ, what did you tell her?"

"I told her we had a great organization." So he took me up to

Tugwell, the guy who always had coffee in the morning. I told him I talked to Eleanor Roosevelt, and he said, "You did? What did you tell her?"

I said, "I was checking on the damn phone bill: 2,000 calls at 5 cents each. How the hell do people talk so damn much?"

He said, "That probably included all the employees in her office." I immediately gained status—I was the guy who had the contact with Eleanor Roosevelt, and so now they wanted to promote me to the bonding section.

Employees were bonded by different bonding corporations. If for some reason or other there was malfeasance and money was misappropriated or stolen, we could make a claim to the bonding section to get the money back. I got a case assigned to me right off the bat on one of our Alabama projects, where the project manager was taking money that was to be used for furniture. The houses built for destitute farmers were equipped with furniture, and the farmers were furnished everything, including seed and animals. Getting the money paid to the suppliers was part of offsetting the Depression. That was the battle cry in our office: "GET THE MONEY OUT. GET THOSE VOUCHERS OUT OF HERE!" We found that a manager had taken appropriations for furniture and bought the furniture, which was OK except it was all bedroom furniture, and it was shipped to a defunct hotel that the manager turned into a whorehouse. The government was charged for the furniture and for renting the building. I prepared the case for the Justice Department along with the accountant, who knew more about it than I did. We were ready to go when I got a call from Senator McClelland out of Alabama about the case. "Mr. Poppelman, do you like your job?"

I said, "No, not particularly. It's a hell of a job. I don't like this case."

He said, "Well, just sort of put that on the back burner. Just take it easy. [So-and-so] got us a lot of votes in that election. He's a nice fellow, and I'll see that he gets that furniture put where it belongs."

My boss of the bonding section didn't like that idea, and because he was going to retire, he wasn't worried about offending some senator. He took the case away from me and gave it to somebody else. They found out there was wholesale misuse of funds on that project.

Every once in a while a messenger would come around our office. He was an arm-wrestling champ, who was always looking for somebody to have an arm-wrestling contest with. At that time, I was pretty strong. Mr. Dorman, my boss, said, "Ray, why don't you try it with this guy?" One day I beat him, so I gained a lot of status with all the men who worked in my office. Mr. Dorman liked me for that, and one day he said to me, "Ray, I'm going to resign shortly, and if I recommend you for my job, do you think you can handle it or want it?"

I said, "Geez, I don't know. I'm not a lawyer."

He said, "Well, if you want it I'll recommend you for it." If I got that job, my salary would jump to about three times what it was. In those days, I was almost always broke and everybody in my group was broke; we would borrow quarters from each other to get lunch. A fellow by the name of Wiley Buchanan, from Texas, was a buddy of mine. We would often borrow money from each other and eat lunch together. One day we both needed money. I said to him, "Wiley, where can we borrow some money?"

He said, "I'll tell you what. My father is a good friend of Nance Garner, the vice president. How much money do you have?"

I told him, "A few coins."

"Well, that's enough for streetcar fare. Let's go up to Capitol Hill."

We went to see the vice president of the United States, and he said, "What can I do for you boys?"

Wiley said, "We came up to borrow $5 from you."

Garner had a brief chat with Wiley about his father and so forth. Then he said, "You boys had lunch yet?"

And we said, "No."

"Let me take you to lunch then," he offered. So he took us over to where the senators had lunch, and he treated us. We came back to his office, and Garner started asking us about our salaries and why we had so little money. He found out that Wiley was earning $1,400 a year and I was getting $1,600 a year although I was in charge of a whole room full of people. He started taking notes, and he said, "Let me check into this a little bit." He loaned us each $5—which I promised to pay back at a dollar a week or something like that.

The next thing I knew, four men from the Civil Service Commission came to our office. They checked over what I was doing, and one of them said, "Would you be satisfied with $1,800 a year?"

I shook my head and said, "No." At that time I knew I might go to the bonding section, so I had some leverage. Well, after I talked to the four men, they decided I should have $2,400 a year—a colossal raise. From then on, things were a little better. But the head of the bonding section wanted me to go to a position where I would get $3,600 a year. Then he said to me, "Ray, you know what I would do if I were you?"

I said, "What?"

He said, "Let me show you something." He pulled out some maps of Paris, London, and some other big cities. He said, "Look at this map." I looked at the map that showed Washington, which was a tiny place. "Some day Washington's going to be bigger than all of the others. If I were you, I would quit this job and I wouldn't take the bonding job. I would get out somehow and get into the business world in Washington. Anything you can get into is going to make some money."

And so I took his advice, although I wondered if I was committing suicide. But I decided to hell with this government job. Mr. Dorman had told me, "When you get my job, you're going as far as you're going to go for the next ten years. You'll be bucking up against politicians. If you want to live the rest of your life on $3,600 a year, you can have my job. If I were you, I wouldn't do it."

I was divorced from Doris, living on Connecticut Avenue just two blocks from the Mayflower Hotel. (Doris eventually married a fellow in the State Department and traveled around the world. She was a very good friend of the secretary of state. She retired in La Jolla, California, managing a bookstore. She loved books; she had a big collection of rare books. She died in about 1997 in Del Mar, California, where she had a home.) There were businesses on the first floor of the Mayflower, the second floor was a dance hall, and the third floor was a rather unusual apartment—there was a big living room, a kitchen, and three bedrooms. Two friends of mine had been living in that apartment, and they invited me to have the third bedroom. About four or five days after I moved in, my room was broken into, my clothes were stolen, and so was a box full of all my letters and anything of value. I had the lock changed. Three days later my room was busted into again, because it seemed that in the first visit the thieves forgot to take a round world bank about two-thirds full of pennies. Goddamn if they didn't break into the room just to get that box of pennies. Five years later, I got a call from the people who ran the dance floor below me: "We have had a box here for five years. We finally broke it open and found your name." They told me what was in it and to come down and get it. By that time I was out in Virginia in the real estate business.

I decided to take the advice I had got. I resigned, and it was tough. My two roommates agreed to pay rent for the three rooms and I could pay them later for my share, since I had decided to go to Virginia. Now came the break of my life. I had been working on weekends with a real estate woman who was a broker. She would get listings of properties in Virginia and I would go out on weekends and sit in the office and try to sell property. She had a listing of 20 acres in a place called Sleepy Hollow, which then was way the hell out in the country from Washington. It was eight miles by air from the White House to this property. The 20 acres on Sleepy Hollow Road were owned by a woman in upper Maryland state, where the Susquehanna River goes into the Chesapeake Bay. The price was $200 an acre. If I could get that land, I could remodel the barn on the property, sell it and get some capital to work, build No. 2, and so forth. It was a long shot, and the owner lived a long way away, but I was determined to try.

I had an old beat-up car—I think it was a Hupmobile. I drove up past Baltimore, way up to Havre de Grace, and I got to her property, which was up a long driveway—a big home overlooking the upper part of Chesapeake Bay. She had a lot of acreage, and in the woods she was putting some cabins in for the Girl Scouts. When I got there it was about noon. She was about 80 years old. I talked to her and told her what I wanted and I said, "Now, there's only one bad thing about my proposition—I have no money."

She said that she had taken the property off the market on the advice of her attorney, so I left. As I was driving back down the driveway, a team of horses with a flatbed wagon came toward me. On top of the wagon was a cabin. A hotel that had cabins and was converting into a motel had given the cabins to the lady for her Girl Scout camp, and the cabin on this big wagon was one of them. When I came down the driveway the farmers pulled over a little bit to let me by, and the cabin slid partway off the wagon. I stopped to help. I told them if they had a rope I would turn my car around, back up, and tow the cabin back onto the wagon. I stayed there until a little after dark helping them transfer that cabin to the foundation that had been made for it in the woods. We did a good job getting the cabin back in the trees in the right place. We propped it up and got some blocks under it.

As I was about to leave, a maid came out of the house and said, "Mrs. So-and-so thinks you should take a bath and eat dinner here, and spend the night and go home tomorrow." So I slept very well. I left in the morning after a nice breakfast, and as I was leaving, she gave me a big can of cookies. I put them in the front seat and bid her good-bye, and she thanked me for helping with the cabin. Instead of stopping for lunch, as I passed Baltimore I decided I would eat the cookies. When I got to the bottom of the can, there was an envelope that was addressed to Mr. Pickens, an attorney in Fairfax County. A note on it read: Mr. Poppelman, please give this to my attorney.

I called my boss and told him I wouldn't be in, that I had to go to Fairfax the next morning. I drove out to Pickens's office—he was a big burly guy, red-faced and bald, and smoking a big cigar. He looked at the letter and said, "Son, what the hell you been doing, screwing that old lady?" So I explained what had happened, and he said, "She has directed me to prepare a deed to 20 acres to you on your terms, with no interest for the first year." She was the one who put me in business. Later, after I built two houses, I went back to show her photographs, but she had died. I never had a chance to thank her.

That was just the beginning. The attorney said, "What are you going to do with the land?" I told him about the barn that was there—I was going to convert it to a house with my own labor and sell it. And I explained that I had worked with my father in California on construction jobs and that I knew something about construction. He said, "We'd better prepare a deed of dedication, preparing a plat for showing the lots. I'll work up an agreement there; you can pay me for the lots as you go along." So he lifted the phone and said, "Joe? I've got a survey job for you. Send the bill to me. I want you to go down to [so-and-so property], get a description, lay it out on half-acre lots on the street the way you think it should be subdivided, and get on it as soon as you can." So without me spending a damn nickel, a surveying crew laid out the lots.

All of a sudden I woke up to the fact that I had a subdivision recorded. The attorney wanted to know what I wanted to name the subdivision. I said, "I'll let you know in a day or so." Then I went to the library and got a book of all the cities in the United States and let the book fly open, took a pin, jabbed it, and it landed on Ravenwood.

To get money to remodel the barn, I was going to get what was called an FHA modernization loan. I made a sketch of the barn as if it were a house, and I went to the Federal Housing Administration and asked for a modernization loan of $1,500, which was the most they'd give me. "I want to upgrade my house," I told them. At that time the upper part of the barn was full of hay. The basement was concrete, and the lower part was for the cattle.

I paid the former owner, my angel, on a release basis as I used the lots. And I think the attorney had a slight amount that the surveyor charged for it, but it was negligible. He set the thing up on the basis of $200 an acre, which was very cheap. With the $1,500, I fixed up the barn so there was a place for me to sleep, and I ate in a little cheap restaurant up in Falls Church, Virginia, about two miles away.

A black man named Freddie Foote, who was the last of Robert E. Lee's slaves, lived near the commercial area. He had about 30 acres there that were left to him. We became friends. He had a team of horses. He charged me 35 cents an hour for his labor, and if I wanted to use the team of horses, it would be 75 cents an hour. He and I, with the team, hauled some rocks from a creek nearby to build a stone chimney. He was a good worker. Just he and I took the barn doors off and built a great big stone chimney. Hay was still up in the hayloft. The farmer who was leasing the land (he wasn't really leasing; it was just a gift from my angel) gradually pulled the cows out of there.

We had just started framing the inside and put a new roof on it, then I needed more money. A bank in Roslyn, Virginia, turned me down because I had no collateral. I got a tip from the loan officer at that bank, though—"Go up and see Ashton Jones at Rucker Insurance Company. Before you go, go to [a certain] Baptist church and sit in the front row. He's a real Baptist, and maybe he'll recognize you from that." So for two Sundays I went to the Baptist church and sat in the front row, knowing that the president of the insurance company was sitting a few rows back. I just wanted him to see me. Finally, I went to his office and told him that I needed a construction loan to finish a house on Sleepy Hollow Road.

At the time I went to Ashton Jones to see about getting a loan to finish the house, I had been working on an old house down the road that had a big tank about six feet across that I had a man haul up to my house. I put it in the barn for my water supply just before we built the chimney. The rainwater ran off the roof into the big tank. It was five feet high, six feet across, rusty and riveted together; a moonshiner had been using it. We needed the water for the mortar to build the chimney and the stone walls. I had put interior partitions in, a new roof on, some siding on the outside, and a stone wall. I just needed some money to finish the house.

When I told Mr. Jones what I wanted, he said, "Can you tell me how to get to your house?" So I sketched him a map. He came out one day, and I escorted him through the upstairs and told him what I'd done. We walked down a long terrace to look at the lower floor, which was concrete, where the cattle had been. I'd cleaned it up pretty well. We were standing directly under the water tank. It was resting over a subflooring that, since the wood was green, had shrunk a little bit and left half-inch cracks on the flooring that was diagonally across it. While we were talking below, the tank split and all the water came flushing down on top of us. Mr. Jones was practically saturated. I panicked and ran out the door and I looked up at the sky and I said, "Jesus Christ, I prayed to you, and look what you've done to me!" Mr. Jones came out sopping wet, in his beautiful coat and his hat. I took his coat off and shook the water out of it and said, "I'm sorry, Mr. Jones."

He said, "The foundation is certainly built well." It was concrete reinforced—whoever had built the barn built it real well. I walked up the hill with him back to his car and apologized again. "Why don't you have your coat cleaned?" I said. "I'll pay the bill." Then I noticed his car, which was old with yellow wheels. I said, "Mr. Jones, you deserve a better car than this. Why don't you get yourself a new car?" I figured I didn't have anything to lose, and he seemed to be having trouble starting it.

I started to walk away and he tooted his horn. "Come back," he said. "Why don't you come down to my office tomorrow morning? Let's see what we can work out." He gave me enough money to finish the house. I put it on the market in 1939: "Gentleman's Estate, Two Acres." People in about 300 cars came out to see it, and I sold it for $7,400 and made $4,000. (The barn later sold for $169,000. In 1995 or around then, it sold for $434,000. Can you believe that?) After that, Ashton Jones was my banker for years; he became a good friend.

When I went back into the service, my black friend Freddie Foote, who helped me in the beginning, came to me and said, "According to the will of General Lee, my property will go back to the state after the last heir dies. I have a lawyer who told me that I could deed it to somebody, and if you're going into the service, maybe when you come back you'd like to have my property. I'll give it to you; you just pay the taxes."

I said, "Go see my attorney," and I sent him to a man named Farr. Mr. Farr found some legal way of selling it for $750,000 to a developer who developed it and sold the whole bundle to the Queen of England. She still owns it. It shows you what a will can do.

I had developed about half of Ravenwood before the war came. The cheapest house went for about $32,000 and the most expensive one commanded $50,000. (Those are all selling for about half a million now.) Then luxury homes were outlawed; you couldn't get materials for them.

I took on a young fellow as a superintendent. Jon Roan was from Summit, New Jersey. He had some friends in New Jersey who owned a tract of land in the town of Falls Church, and he and I organized a corporation called Roan and Poppelman, Inc. To finance the project, we each put $50 in the bank for the corporation. We prepared a plat that we used for the deed of dedication, which went along with restrictions. The plat looked so impressive right in the center of Falls Church that our banker let us borrow enough money to pay for the land and to install sewer, water, electricity, curbs, and gutters.

We made a subdivision out of it, which was sponsored by the

U.S. government as a private defense housing project aiding families during World War II. I switched my activities over to the second subdivision, which we named Virginia Forest. (See Chapter 13 for details of our Virginia Forest development.)

I had two more breaks in my life. For Virginia Forest, we had to go to the War Production Board in Washington to get permission to buy materials. The only thing you could use materials for then was the war. A man by the name of Mr. Orr was the head of the War Production Board. In order to get materials to build Virginia Forest, we had to get approval from Mr. Orr. I dressed up in my Sunday suit one day, went down to the government office, and had to clear through about three secretaries to get to see Mr. Orr. I told him my proposition, what I was doing, and he approved it. I couldn't believe it; it seemed so easy.

At the same time, a former lawyer of mine, a brother of my current lawyer, had died and left a widow. She was heir to an office building in Fairfax and was in the process of remodeling it so she could get some decent rent from it and then the war came. The War Production Board shut her down, but she needed materials to finish the house. When she talked to me about it, I said, "Gee, I had a good break. I know the boss. He gave me materials for my subdivision. If you want to, I'll take you down there." She agreed. So we went through the same routine, and I introduced her to Mr. Orr and said, "My friend here, Mrs. Farr, widow of my former attorney, has got an office building about half-remodeled. She needs material to finish it." You know what happened? They fell in love and got married. So then I was really in. All my friends who needed materials came to me, and I'd call Mr. Orr and say, "I'm going to send [so-and-so] down. Take care of him, will you?" I was really in in Washington.

Dwight Eisenhower's nephew worked in my unit of the Resettlement Administration, and we became friends. His father lived in Falls Church, and when I left the government to start building houses I was remodeling a house next door. One Saturday I was there working when the Eisenhower I knew in the government came over to the fence with his father, who was head of the information bureau, and Dwight Eisenhower, who was then a lieutenant colonel. We were introduced and talked a while across the fence. That was the first time I met Ike; I met him again after the war, and he said he remembered me. (I also met four other presidents—Coolidge, back in 1928 during the championship football game between the Marine Corps and the Naval Academy; Harry Truman, over the phone one day— an important contractor was in my office and had called him, and I spoke with him briefly; John Kennedy, who was then in the Navy, at a photo studio before the war; and Richard Nixon, at a horse race in Maryland.)

One day in 1939, I got a call from George Winnick, an assistant in the government. He said, "Ray, how'd you like to go to a party Wednesday?"

I said, "What kind of party is it?"

He said, "Well, the girl I run around with is a good-looking gal, and we have some invitations to go to the Russian Embassy party; it's a big deal."

I said, "How the hell did you arrange that?"

He said, "This girl I want you to have a date with has a sister who is secretary to Arthur Godfrey, the famous radio announcer." (Godfrey lived in Virginia and Washington. He had a house on Leesburg Pike. Later, after I became a realtor, I sold his house for him, and he moved up to a big mansion in Leesburg.) Arthur Godfrey had turned his tickets over to his secretary, and she gave them to her sister, who was to be my date. So it was George Winnock and his girl, and myself, and the sister, Sue Goodwin, my blind date. We went to the Russian Embassy, and what a hell of a party it was. I think it was about the only time I was really drunk in my life. Sue looked like the queen to me. I wound up in her mother's home in Washington in the guest room and we had a Sunday dinner. We started going together. She had a job with the District of Columbia Compensation Board, interviewing people who had lost their jobs or didn't have a job and wanted some compensation.

Sue and I were married in Fairfax County in 1940; it was a very quiet affair. The clerk of the court, a friend of mine, owned the famous home in Fairfax where George Washington slept. I asked him if we could get married there, and he agreed, so that was where our wedding was. For our honeymoon we took a boat ride from Washington to Virginia Beach and stayed there a week.

My second house was a stone house that originally sold for around $28,000. The fellow who moved into it became a very good friend of mine. He's now retired and living at the Congressional Club in Washington, D.C. My condition for selling that house was that he would rent the guest room to me while I looked for someplace else for Sue and me to live. I found a small frame house up Sleepy Hollow Road to rent for something like $25 a month. Next we lived in a house I'd built in the back of the subdivision. We lived there for about four or five months, but I needed money so I sold it and made $10,000 on it. Then I built a big colonial house up the street, moved into that, and sold it for around $20,000. By this time I was running ads in both Washington papers. Every Sunday I'd have a big ad with "Raymond J. Poppelman" under it. I was getting calls from all my buddies in the government, asking, "What kind of price can you give me on that house that was advertised?"

I'd say, "That's the price." I was quite prominent as a builder. If only war hadn't broken out, I'd have been in good shape. But it did and I had to stop building my luxury homes. For $10,000 at that time you could get a medium-sized house on a nice lot in Arlington County with sewer and water. I was pricing my houses outrageously according to some brokers. I'd call a broker and say, "Do you want a listing on my house?"

"How much is it?"

"Thirty-two thousand."

"Oh, hell." They'd bang the receiver down. The same house today couldn't be bought for $400,000.

CHAPTER 13

The Development of Virginia Forest

The Virginia Forest property was on probably the highest land within 25 miles of Washington, D.C. It was beautifully wooded. It was actually a shame to use such beautiful land for a defense housing project, but we decided to incorporate art with the architecture to make the houses attractive. Walter Huenemoerder, the architect we hired, had done a beautiful project in Chicago. He was a natural artist, and he designed a model home for us to promote our sales. Jon Roan operated a bulldozer that we owned, and I took charge of clearing the streets, using a 50-foot right-of-way. We would saw the trees down, stack the logs on the side of the road, and remove the stumps with dynamite.

We had a lot of difficulty with the city of Falls Church because of noise from the bulldozer and saws and dynamite—the dynamite sometimes even broke windows. In one instance we had some stumps stacked to burn the following day. Our crew hid a box of dynamite in the stump pile, and the following day a different crew started the stump fire and got a fire going, and when the dynamite exploded, it was almost a catastrophe. Windows broke all over town. After that, the chickens of a nearby farmer stopped laying eggs. As settlement, I told the man who had the chicken farm, "We'll give you all the wood that's lying around the streets in the subdivision. You can set up a sawmill and make some money with cord wood." He fell for the idea and removed all the logs, doing us a favor, and he did very well selling all the wood for fireplaces.

When I went to the city hall to get information on the major sewer line, I was given wrong information. I eventually learned that the major sewer line was in a different place than I had been told, and I couldn't get into the main line. I woke up one night and said to myself (I call my inner self "Canny" for "uncanny"), "Canny, we're in a hell of a fix. We face bankruptcy. We've got 200 houses and no sewer. We've got to do something about it." A couple of nights later, I had the most vivid dream. I dreamed of a digging machine coming across a five-acre property adjoining our subdivision. That morning I went to my junior partner and said, "I had a dream last night that was so vivid I remember exactly how the machine looks and everything."

He said, "What was it?"

I told him about the sewer main problem and said, "I saw a machine coming across the Glasson property next to us."

So he said, "Well, let's get a surveyor and check." Sure enough, the main line was on the other side of that property. The surveyor suggested we get an easement across the property, but we didn't know where the owner lived. We would have to find Glasson or go bankrupt. We went to the tax office and found out that Glasson lived in Kentucky. I went to the bank, got out some money, and told my partner, "Just hold up everything till I get back from Kentucky—I'm going to find that Glasson guy if it kills me."

I made arrangements to go on a train—they didn't have airplanes going there then—and I had to get to the depot by 6:30 to catch the train going to Kentucky. I went in the bedroom and started dressing. Sue came running in and said, "There's a man at the front door who wants to talk to you."

I said, "Tell him I can't talk to him; I've got to get down to the depot. I've only got 45 minutes to get there." So I rushed like hell to get dressed, put on my coat, walked out, and there was the guy sitting in the living room. He had taken a taxi from Washington—a distance of 20 miles—to see me. I said, "You wanted to talk to me?" and he said, "Yeah." I said, "Well, I'll tell you what. You took a taxi from Washington out to see me? I'm going to Washington now. You can ride back with me and talk to me then." We got into my car and headed out, and I said, "What is it you wanted to talk to me about? I'm not interested in investing in anything. Who are you?"

He said, "I live in Kentucky and I wanted to talk to you about something. I found out that I have some land next to you and I want to sell it to you because we need a new car." And goddamn, the Glasson I was going to go see was sitting next to me! I didn't want to lose him, so I went to the hotel he was saying at in Washington.

I said, "Today I'm going to take you out to my attorney's office and we'll get the deed and everything settled up."

He said, "You don't have to do that. My father used to deal with a bank in town and we can go there. I've talked to the banker; that's how I found out about you." So we went to his bank and they made up the deeds and we closed it out. When I went back home, I had the deed. I went to a sewer contractor who was a friend of mine and said, "I've got to have a job done quick." Within a week, we had the sewer line in.

We finished the street work and got the property ready for promotion and had the model house well under construction, and Jon thought I should take a vacation, knowing how busy we would be when we went into the sales program and the building operations. Sue and I decided to go to Florida for a few days, but it rained hard every day. Rather than lose our vacation totally, we went to Havana, Cuba, which was only 90 miles away by airline.

Before I left for Cuba, I spoke to Charles D. Hamel, whose niece Doris I had been married to, and told him that I was going to Cuba. He said he had a client who was the richest man in Cuba; he owned six big sugar plantations. He suggested that when Sue and I got to Havana, we check in at the American Club and let him know we were there; he would contact his client, Mr. Gomez Mena. When we arrived in Cuba, rooms were not available at the American Club, so we were directed to another hotel for that night. The following morning, a big limousine with a chauffeur came to our hotel. The chauffeur instructed us to check out, and he drove us to a hotel owned by Mr. Mena. It was on a beach, and we had a suite there. We stayed one day, and then the limousine came to take us to Mena's ranch in southern Cuba.

We drove all day long through Cuba, through all the sugar plantations and the small towns that Gomez Mena owned, and finally arrived at the big estate, which was surrounded by a high iron fence with pickets sticking up to keep people from crawling over. One thing that impressed us was that there were no screens in the whole house. We thought that was strange—an expensive house such as it was—but we saw no flies.

The following day was an exceptional experience. We were sitting in the living room, which had tile floors. Friends of Mr. Mena, who sat in a circle smoking cigars, were introduced to us. Everybody would spit on the floor. And with the doors all open, chickens would walk into this luxuriant place, wander through the living room and out through the dining room to the kitchen, and go outside.

Nobody seemed to be concerned about them. Sue and I couldn't understand it, but we had a wonderful lunch and went to sit outside on the patio.

About 2:00 in the afternoon, three or four Cuban workers came running, yelling and shouting about a catastrophe: Mr. Mena's white riding horse had attempted to jump the fence surrounding the estate and had impaled himself on top of the pickets. It took about eight or nine Cubans to lift the horse off the fence. Its entrails were dragging on the ground. They laid him out, stuffed the entrails back into the horse, and with twine and a big needle sewed up the horse's stomach. The following day a veterinarian came and did a better job. The horse survived.

We stayed at the big mansion for two days, and Mr. Mena showed us around the town. Each big sugar-refining plantation had schools, stores, a hospital, and everything the people needed, all owned by the company. Mena owned six big plantation towns. On the third day, he decided that he would drive us back to Havana. In Havana, as we drove down the main street going to the San Susi gambling hotel and casino, Mr. Mena mentioned, "I own all the businesses from here down four more blocks." As we passed the bank he said, "This is our family bank. We have so much money in our family that nobody has a single account; we just all draw from the same account. And no matter how hard we could spend our money, we could never use it all up." I eventually asked, "Mr. Mena, do you ever invest your money?"

He said, "Oh, yes, sometimes."

I said, "I am thinking of building some apartments in Washington, D.C., after the war. Could we do some business?"

He said, "Oh, sure. Whenever you're ready, come back and talk to me."

In front of my field office at Virginia
Forest in Falls Church, Virginia, 1942.
The car at left is a V-8 Packard, a
prize car to have during World War II.

So I left Havana feeling very good about the fact that I had found
a Cuban financier who would take care of my future financing,
should I need it. But actually, we never met again, because years
later Castro came in, and that was the end of that.

When I returned to Falls Church, it was about May 1, 1942. The
dogwood trees were out, and Virginia Forest looked beautiful. We
ran a half-page ad in all the newspapers announcing Virginia Forest. We had about 200 lots in our subdivision and four model houses.
The homes were quite small by today's standards, about 1,000 square
feet. They were built of cinder block with one coat of stucco on the
outside. The inside was furred out with hardboard and lathe. The

most popular model went for about $6,000. It was a house on a small
lot with sewer and water improvements; it had two bedrooms, a
living room, and a vaulted ceiling. The first mortgage was $4,000,
we took back a second trust, and we required $1,000 cash. Those
same houses, some years later, were selling for close to $200,000.
Actually, at the time we were selling for $6,000, we could have sold
them on the open market with a little promotion for close to $20,000.
People really got a bargain. But by law we couldn't do anything
else. We decided that making $1,000 per house wasn't too bad—
with 200 lots, we'd see $200,000, which in those days was a fortune.
By nightfall, we had sold practically 50 percent of the subdivision
with the help of only four people—the architect, my partner, one of
the supervisors, and myself—none of whom were professional real
estate people. As a consequence, we had no real estate commissions
to pay. (With a $6,000 budget we couldn't afford much anyway.)

As World War II developed, my time in Falls Church grew short.
I had received my draft notice, and the draft board had given me 60
days to finish up my building. We went into rather desperate and
fast production to get the houses finished. To make a long story short,
our project, because it was so successful, created quite a sensation in
the Washington building business. We had no competition. People
were coming to us; we didn't have to go to them. And the White
House seemed to be interested in small houses. As a result, Eleanor
Roosevelt brought the queen of England to our subdivision. I happened to be absent that day, but our architect gave them a tour. Later
we received an award from an engineering society in England for
creating a prize subdivision in the moderate price range for the average family. Our customers were mostly service people and employees working for the war effort. Washington was like a beehive,
a boomtown. So sales were not a problem; the problem was getting

the houses finished on time. We had a clause in our contract that any complaints would be settled by canceling the contract, so we had the upper hand and things went well.

There were always problems. Once, the plumbing supplies were stolen. The lumber that was being delivered was sometimes highjacked. Builders who were desperate would see trucks loaded with lumber and would stop the driver and say, "Who is this delivery for?" The driver would tell them and they'd say, "Oh, that's us. Follow us." A lot of highjacking went on in the building business.

Near the completion of the project, there was a big snowstorm. We had about 20 houses ready to get a roofing draw, which is a draw on the bank's loan when the roofing was on (we'd get a draw when the foundations were in, and another one when the partitions were up, and so on). The snowstorm shut us down—all the houses were covered with about 20 inches of snow; it was terrible. We had to get the snow off the roofs and the shingles on to get the roofing draw, so we were gridlocked for a while moneywise.

On this occasion, our payroll was $4,000. We used to pay off at Saturday noon. Our credit was pretty much exhausted at that time because we had so many houses under construction with limited capital. The situation couldn't have been more negative. It looked like we were in deep trouble when a woman in an old beat-up Ford drove up. She wanted to know if we still had a house left. We said yes, we had a couple, but they were not completed; it might be six weeks before she could actually move in. When we explained the terms, she said, "I don't want to put $1,000 down. I want to put $4,000 down." That was a blessing out of the blue; we couldn't believe our luck. So we said, absolutely, we could work it out that she could pay $4,000 up front. And her $4,000 bailed us out.

Then the weather changed rapidly, the roofs melted off, and

within two weeks we were solvent again. That blessing, I think, was of divine origin. Why else would we get the exact amount of money we needed in the last hour?

In spring 1943 I was no spring chicken as far as the military goes. But men were eligible to go into the army up to 38 years old, and I was 37. I was just under the wire. I accepted a commission with the Marine Corps so that I wouldn't have to join the army. When I left for the corps, I had 40 houses to finish. Jon Roan took over and finished them. Later he had to go into the coast guard service. When Roan left, my wife, Sue, took over Virginia Forest. Ravenwood was in a static condition; it was just sitting there. We had lots there but could not build during the war.

When I came home in late 1945, I found that our attorney, Henry Clay, who had been closing out sales while Jon and I were in the service, had accumulated about $120,000 in our corporation. Henry Clay came from a prominent family. We trusted him, but we made a mistake: We gave him power of attorney instead of having two attorneys. Clay had another client who was a builder and was going to build some apartments under the federal housing financing program. One of the requirements was that a builder had to show so much cash and assets to get an FHA project approved. Henry Clay took our money, which was lying idle, and loaned it to the other client's corporation. His other client died. His wife, who was set up as secretary-treasurer, knew nothing about the business. Clay, desperate to cover up, had used some insurance funds illegally. He was supposed to take permanent loan money from people who bought houses and pay off the construction loans, but he was delaying that. He was finally prosecuted and disbarred, and the assets that he had were taken over by insurance companies. So when I came home, I got the sad news about him being broke, and he told me the story.

There was nothing I could do. He was working as a bookkeeper. I thought I had money to operate on, but I was broke, too. When I got home, the only damn thing I had was my dog tags—my personal bank account was practically empty. But that was probably a good education for me.

I did get one break. The income tax was never paid on that money by Henry, and of course, when I came home, I was also faced with every goddamn kind of thing—bills and the Internal Revenue Service. Two men came out to see me because I hadn't paid taxes on that $120,000. They were with me about a week, and they came to my office one day and the boss said, "Do you have $16?"

I said, "Yes."

"Write out a check for $16." That would close the case. Then he said to me, "For what you've been through in the war, I'm ashamed to take even this $16." I never had trouble with Internal Revenue again.

When my partner, Jon Roan, who had been in the North Seas aboard ship as a radio operator, got out of the coast guard, he joined me. Together, we reactivated Virginia Forest. We had about 25 lots left in Virginia Forest; I decided to build those out. Since the war was over, we could sell for whatever price we could get. I decided to sell those last lots in the $12,000 range. I ran a display ad in the paper and was very disappointed. Few people came out to see the houses, and I didn't sell any of them. I had one GI who wanted to buy one of my houses, but he wanted a big discount. I ran an ad the second week that was also disappointing.

A few days after that, I was in the Mayflower Hotel in Washington. As I was walking through the lobby, somebody yelled at me, "Hey, Ray! When in the hell did you get back?" It turned out to be a Jewish fellow who was known as a "fixer." You had a problem, you'd go to so-and-so, who was a fixer and would have an answer for you or could get money for you somehow. Anyway, Mr. Fixer (we'll call him that, I don't remember his name) and I talked, and I told him I was having a problem selling my houses in Virginia Forest. He said, "Do you have time to take me out to look at them?" I said sure. So we went out to Virginia Forest and looked at the houses, and he said, "Do you know what your problem is?"

I said, "No."

"You're selling them too goddamn cheap."

I said, "What do you mean?"

He said, "Hell, these houses should be going for $20,000. I'll tell you what you do. You used to have a raven that appeared in your ads, didn't you? Professor Raven?"

I said, "Yeah."

He said, "I'm going to make you up a new ad. You put your raven in there again, and he's giving a notice: 'In September, the carpenters' unions are going on strike, labor's going to go up. Now is the time to buy your house.' Put your old price in with an X over it and raise your price $1,000. Sell one house."

I said, "Jesus Christ, I'd be glad to sell one house. I'll sell all I can."

"No," he said, "sell one house."

So I ran the ad and about ten people came out. The GI came out again and wanted to buy one of the houses at last week's price. I said, "No, we're holding." We had raised the price $1,000 from $12,750 to $13,750, and we sold one house. The bank had wanted me to quit building. I called the bank and said, "I sold one house." They thought it was great—I thought they were going to declare a holiday.

Anyway, I called my Jewish friend and told him what happened. He said, "OK. Run the ad again and mark out the $13,000 and sell it for $14,000. And change the story of the raven—the raven's got something else that's going to make houses go up; something about inflation."

The following week, we had about 50 people come out and we sold two houses, just like that. To make a long story short, we kept moving up the houses $1,000 a week with different admonitions by Professor Raven. Each week, the same soldier would come out and want to buy at the last week's price. We went on up until we got the houses up above $20,000. When we got them to $20,000, we had at least 100 people come out to look at the houses. The psychology was fantastic.

We went down the street to the last six houses in the subdivision and sold all but one for around $26,000. The same house that we had a hell of a time selling at $12,750 was going fast at $25,000. On the last house, a pilot from the air force came in and plunked an envelope on the table. He said, "I'm just back from Europe. I have in this envelope $25,000 cash. Can you build me some kind of a damn house for $25,000?"

That $25,000 looked like big cash. That was my operating cash to move into Ravenwood. And we had a shack full of concrete and scrap lumber and other scrap materials, so I decided to use that last house to clean up our old material. There was no contract; it was based on trust. The pilot trusted me to build him a house for $25,000. He said, "I'll be back in about four months. Just have some kind of a house for me and my wife to move into." So the pressure was on me. I used surplus paneling, which I normally wouldn't use; it was an extra. I paneled the living room. I changed the roof to a Cape Cod–type house with dormers so that he could expand the house by two more bedrooms. I ran rough plumbing up for the second bathroom on the second floor. I ran a beautiful wrought-iron railing from the living room up the steps. I pretended it was my house to help think of ideas, and I told some of the suppliers, "I'm building a house for a GI hero; I need a low price." I even took the extra sheathing we had and put a fence around the property. When the pilot came home and saw what he had, he couldn't believe it. The only complaint I got was about three months later, when his wife called to tell me the rear screen door was sticking a little bit. I had to shave off the door some and put some paint on it.

After the war, I ran into situations that made me sort of cuss my bad luck about being drafted. For instance, a young fellow named Bob Stafford used to drive trucks for me before the war. One day he had delivered some stone on a lot for a man. The man had run off, and Bob was stuck with about ten loads of beautiful stone. The man had been buying the lot on time from a realtor in Falls Church whom I knew. So I told Bob, "I think you could build a house on that lot and sell it for whatever you wanted to. You go buy that lot from Mr. [So-and-so]. You already have your stone. You build a house on speculation—you, yourself."

He said, "Hell, I don't know how to build a house."

I told him what he had to do and gave him the names of some subcontractors. When I came back from the war, not only had he built that house but he had a great big subdivision—one of the biggest in Fairfax County. He was a natural builder. He didn't go in the service for some reason, and he made a lot of money in a very short time. But his wife, they found out, had cancer, and he sold out and retired to Florida.

There were a couple of comical stories about Virginia Forest. When I came back from the service, I built two Cape Cod houses on a corner. They had upstairs bedrooms with dormer windows. One of the houses had a stone facing and a stone chimney. My partner, Roan, told me that we were getting complaints from the people who owned the stone house about the chimney smoking in their bedroom. He went over and checked it out. He built a fire, went upstairs, and couldn't smell any smoke. He said, "Ray, you'd better go over there and talk to that woman. She's still complaining about smoke in the bedroom."

So I went over one morning. She was a beautiful blonde dressed in a negligee. I asked her if I could make a fire in the fireplace so I could see about detecting the smoke, which I did. I had the fire going, and I said, "I don't see any smoke here."

She said, "Oh, no, it's upstairs in the bedroom."

And I thought, "Well, that's strange." So I went upstairs. The chimney ran up the side of the house, and the master bedroom backed up to where the chimney would be. We went upstairs and I said, "I don't smell any smoke."

"Oh, you have to lie on the bed to smell it."

I thought, "Uh-oh." Well, what a come-on this was. I got on the bed with her and leaned over to kiss her, and goddamn if I didn't smell smoke!

When the chimney was built, the crew used tile liner and built the stone around it. When they got up to the baseboard area behind the bed, some mason was careless and left mortar out for the tile, so the smoke was going through the chimney, into the walls of the bedroom, and along the baseboard. You could even see a little smoke coming out. I pulled the bed away from the wall, and damned if I couldn't see the smoke. We had to tear the whole chimney down.

When we resumed building Ravenwood—Roan joined me and

got half the profits on the buildings—we could sell for what we wanted. I had a chance to buy some land adjoining mine, which I later dedicated as Ravenwood, Section 3. That land ran to the back of the original 20 acres I had bought all the way up to the major highway known as Leesburg Pike. That was a big deal. I went to my banker and told him I wanted to buy a piece of land on Section 3. He accommodated me by giving me a rather generous loan so I could buy the property. I had it subdivided except for the top of a hill, which was a break in the property. The land from the top of the hill ran down to the Leesburg Pike. I reserved the land from the top of the hill down for future commercial property upon the advice of a real estate man, and it was good advice.

I was quite successful in Section 2 of Ravenwood. There were no two houses alike. When we finished building a house we'd burn the plans so nobody could duplicate them. So every house was different. I built a house on the back end of the property out of stone. I had contact with some stonemasons in Virginia up near Leesburg. They worked very cheaply—they worked for less than I could get bricklayers for. The landscaping was being put in, and it was very muddy around the house. One morning a car drove up and a well-dressed man got out and introduced himself as an adviser to the president. He wanted to know about the house. I lay down a few planks so he wouldn't have to walk in the mud and got him into the house. He looked it over and said, "I like it. How much is it?"

I said, "We're getting about $35,000 for it."

He said, "Well, gee, it's nice." And he gave me his card, wrote out a check as a deposit, and said to call the office of his attorney on a certain day. "You can call me, if it is an emergency, at the White House," he said. He wanted some shelves put in the closets upstairs for his shoes and other minor things. He didn't like the light color

This is the house in Section 2 of
Ravenwood that I built and sold to
Atherton Lee, an adviser to the president.

we had on the varnished handrail going upstairs and wanted us to make it dark. So I sent a bill for the changes to him at his attorney's office. I got a letter back, signed by the attorney: "Mr. So-and-so [I think his name was Atherton Lee] thinks you have overcharged him for the work. He could have done it cheaper himself."

I couldn't believe it. I was charging him less than $25 for the varnish on the handrail and probably less than $50 for building the shoe racks. Then I got a call one day; he wanted something else changed. I changed that, and he complained about me charging too much again. The third time, he wanted me to enclose the porch so he could grow orchids. We did that, but I told the foreman, "This time, we'll double the bill on the son of a bitch and let him complain. Then we'll just compromise." I charged him $800.

I got a call from the attorney: "Mr. Poppelman, when you're in town, would you stop by the office? I've had a complaint from Mr. Lee." I went down to the office. The complaint was that I undercharged him. "That job would have cost him at least $1,200, so here's a check for $1,250."

Now, that wasn't the end of it. He fell in love with a secretary at the White House, divorced his wife, and wanted to sell the house. I told him that he should get a broker. "No," he said, "I want you to have the commission." So I sold the house to a couple for about $40,000, a good price. The couple didn't have enough money to close the deal, so there was a $2,500 second trust involved. I called Mr. Lee at his attorney's office in Washington. I told him that I had a buyer for the house, but I would have to include a $2,500 second trust deal. Otherwise, it was a pretty good deal. The couple could get a first trust and they had a certain amount of cash, which was pretty substantial. Mr. Lee would have to take a second trust, and he would have to come out to the settlement office to sign the deed, which he agreed to do.

We were all at the settlement office—Mr. Lee, his attorney, the buyers, and me. I was the broker; I got a 6 percent commission. The settlement officer was reading off the terms, when Mr. Lee said, "What is this second note business?"

The attorney explained to him, "That's a condition of the contract, and you agreed to it when you signed the contract. The buyers are putting on a mortgage; you'll get that money. You'll get their cash, and you'll have to carry the $2,500 second trust."

Mr. Lee said, "Hell, I don't want a second trust. What can we do about it?"

The attorney said, sort of facetiously, "Well, you could reduce the price, Mr. Lee."

"Yeah, that's it! Reduce the damn price. I don't want to bother with second trusts."

The couple just about fainted—they couldn't believe they were going to get a house for $2,500 cheaper.

No wonder our country is screwed up. And so the sale went on. I got 6 percent less of the $2,500. And the buyers got a break; they had no second trust. Everybody was happy. That was unusual, but this world is full of surprises.

PART 4

Service During World War II
(1942–1945)

CHAPTER 14

Being Drafted, Obtaining a Commission in the Marines, Training in California and Hawaii, and Landing on Iwo Jima

In 1942, while engaged in building those 200 private defense housing houses in Virginia Forest, I got my greetings from the president—a draft notice. At that time, Fairfax County was basically an agricultural county, and agricultural employees were exempt from the draft. Most of the quota was filled from adjoining Arlington County. I was in that area. Although I made pleas to the draft board, it insisted that my partner, Jon Roan, could finish up the houses.

But I didn't want to go into the army. I felt that since I had training and connections in the Marine Corps, I would go back to that outfit. Most of the men I had known as young officers in China were by then high-ranking officers. One was General Fegan, who had become head of the Camp Pendleton Marine Base in Oceanside, California. He had been the football manager in 1928 when I was playing football. I knew him well and I figured he could help me, so I made an effort to get to San Diego to see him.

My trip was successful, except I would be required to go to Washington headquarters and pass an examination, which would be mostly oral. The Marine Corps was top heavy with regular line officers, and the only people who were getting commissions at that time were specialists. The only category I fit into was motor transport because I'd had experience driving cars in China and had a third-interest in a racing car in California. I was told that I would be interviewed by a Major Osmondson, who had been once a colonel but had been busted for drinking. He was supposed to be a tough SOB. If I could get by him, I'd probably get my commission. So I made an appointment. I'll never forget the day of my appointment. After he saw my name, and asked me a few questions about my early years, I learned that Osmondson had been a friend of my father's and as a boy had worked on the farm in Marvin for two years.

I got my commission, but when my creditors learned that I was going into the service, they panicked and they immediately wanted all their bills paid up. At that time I had approximately $40,000 outstanding in bills, which would eventually be paid off when the settlement of the homes was completed. But everybody figured that I might never come back and they might never get paid. So I went to a bank that I had never gone to before and approached a banker there. He listened to my story and said, "Here's what we'll do. We'll go down to my vault and get some cash that I'll put in my bottom drawer. You carry a certain amount of cash with you and go around visiting your creditors. Tell them that they can have a payment now if they give you a substantial discount," or I could tell them that under the Soldiers' and Sailors' Act I would be protected and they would have to wait until after the war for their money. I was able to pay off all my debt with only $18,000. The money was never put in my account; it was cash in the bank officer's bottom drawer. He never even had me sign a note. So I left Virginia Forest in good shape as far as bills were concerned.

Afraid that I might not survive, I decided to have an updated portrait photograph taken of myself as a civilian. I arranged an appointment with Harris and Ewing, the best photographic studio in Washington, D.C. By coincidence, John F. Kennedy, who was then an officer in the navy, had an appointment at the same studio following my appointment, except he arrived earlier than scheduled. The photographer introduced us to each other and explained my situation to Kennedy—how I was about to leave for duty in the marines.

While the photographer was coaxing me to smile, Kennedy interrupted us, suggesting that a man going to war should express concern and not smile. "Poppelman should appear serious!" he said. The photographer agreed to shoot a somber pose. (I later learned that a marine in a foxhole under heavy fire doesn't smile much. Kennedy was right—no smiles before or during combat!)

I left for California, but was bumped off the plane on a priority. In Denver, Colorado, I had to sleep on a rubbing table in a Turkish bath. An attendant piled up six or seven towels; it was the only place I could find to sleep. But I finally did get to California. With the endorsement of General Fegan, I became a second lieutenant. I had the alternative of taking a commission as a captain, but I was advised that a second lieutenant would be safer for me—I wouldn't have to know as much. A second lieutenant could make mistakes and not be reprimanded as much as a higher-ranking officer.

So I joined the 5th Division being organized in Camp Pendleton as a second lieutenant. I was the third officer to arrive in camp, and on one weekend when the temporary commander was gone and his assistant was gone, as a second lieutenant I was in charge of the marine camp at Camp Pendleton.

A few weeks later I was sent to the army chemical warfare school in Grass Valley, California. I joined up with about 40 paratroopers from the Marine Corps. The Marine Corps had disbanded its paratroop group because jumping into jungle territory in the South Pacific was too dangerous. I then entered the Marine Corps officers' school at Camp Lejeune, California, in August 1943.

I was at officers' school through October of that year. It was rather tough for me. However, I had an advantage: I had been a drill instructor in the Marine Corps back in 1928, and in the fieldwork I was at the top of my class. As a matter of fact, on graduation day the big shots from Washington, D.C., came to see an example of our drilling. I was appointed to direct our group in drilling, and we made a beautiful display. I had taught our men some special maneuvers, and we got a big hand from the crowd. Everything we did was perfect, and I got high marks. In the classroom work I had some difficulty with the technical parts. But my average brought me up so I graduated with a 90.3—I had one of the top scores. At the rifle range I was top in our class. I had become an expert in all three weapons that we were practicing with—the M-1 rifle, the carbine .30-caliber rifle, and the .45 pistol. We had bivouac exercises: We chose teams—one team would be the enemy and the other would be the American team—and we did a lot of work in the field. Some of the officers who were specialists were quite old for what they were doing. They were photographic experts and engineers. I was not an engineer, but I did pass most of the examinations in good shape.

In addition to our classes, we had to learn all about the chemical warfare gases used in World War I, such as phosgene and mustard gas. We were also trained with flamethrowers, which were kerosene and another explosive that would stick if it got onto your body. It would embed itself in your clothes and your skin. I didn't like to use it because, first of all, I didn't believe in using chemical warfare on humans. I thought the Geneva Conference overlooked one thing when they were making up rules about chemical warfare. We could use white phosphor shells and flamethrowers on the Japanese, but we could not use cyanide gas, which would put them asleep painlessly. Had we used cyanide gas I think we could've taken the island of Iwo Jima just by putting all the Japs to sleep without any pain.

From Camp Pendleton, in late 1944, after hard training, we were transferred to the island of Hawaii, to Camp Tarawa in the northern part. When our ship arrived, the lieutenants got the dirty work of taking charge of unloading the ships. During that process, two of us lieutenants came down with what they thought was polio. We were immediately transferred into the army hospital just outside Hilo, Hawaii. One of the officers was sent back to Washington, D.C.

General Rocky, who was commander of the Fifth Division, claimed he needed me in our division and used influence to have me put into a special hospital where civilians would not be contaminated. They put me on a beach up on the north end of the island, not too far from Camp Kamuela. There they had doctors and male nurses and I was checked hourly. They couldn't determine exactly what I had—I had some of the symptoms of polio but was functioning OK. So for two or three weeks I was on a private beach in a tent with medical help. Nobody was allowed to visit me. I was finally declared clean, and I returned to my engineering group in Hawaii.

At Camp Pendleton, I had been assigned as operation officer of a motor transport battalion. Our camp was located in a low area. When it rained, we were sort of flooded out. Our parking area for trucks was under water; some of the water even got into our shops. We requisitioned the engineers to come down and do some grading and put in drainage ditches and fix it so the water would not flood our camp, but the engineers were busy training far up on the mountains and couldn't get to us. So I asked permission from the battalion commander of the motor transport to do it myself. He went to General Rocky and got permission for me to borrow equipment from the engineers, and under my direction, we graded out the premises of the motor transport area. I put in drain ditches, which functioned well and properly.

When the commander of the engineer battalion, Colonel Shuey, found out about the incident, he went to General Rocky and said, "Poppelman has no business being in the motor transport; he's too valuable. I want him in with the engineers." So I was assigned as motor transport officer of the engineer battalion. They had a lot of equipment—trucks and bulldozers and everything you'd need on a construction job. It was a big assignment, and a tough one, much tougher than being in motor transport because I had so many other things to worry about.

One day, while we were training in Hawaii, supposedly getting ready to go to China, a jeep drove up. During my days as a civilian contractor in Virginia Forest a marine sergeant named Morris had come in wanting to buy one of our houses. He had no money, and so I loaned him $1,000, which he turned over to our corporation so he could have a house. But the house was not ready and he had to have a place to live. He moved in before we had the house glazed and camped out there. Later he was transferred into Marine Corps officers' school in Quantico, Virginia. There he became a lieutenant. I didn't see him again until he drove up in a jeep in Hawaii and said, "You won't remember me, but not only did you build me a house, you loaned me money to buy it. If I can do anything to help you, you let me know. I have been appointed aide to General Rocky."

That was good news for me because I knew General Rocky from the old Marine Corps, but being of low rank, I had little access to him. I was not allowed in his officers' club, which was for colonels and generals only. And to go through ranks—through my company commander, battalion commander, and regimental commander—to get a request to the general would take a lot of time, and my request would possibly have been intercepted and denied. I wanted to get word to General Rocky about the enlisted men's complaints—about the food and liberty and furloughs home in case there was a death in the family. So I made an agreement with Lieutenant Morris that we would meet about twice a week in the junior officers' club, where I would tell him directly what the enlisted men were griping about. The men trusted me because I had been a sergeant in the old Marine Corps and I always accommodated them when they wanted to talk to me.

Our system really worked, and it built up the morale of our division. Lieutenant Morris and I would meet, I'd tell him what the word was, he would tell the general directly, and the general would take action. We improved our food and liberty, and we improved our morale. We were located on Parker Ranch, which was one of the largest ranches in the world. Rocky had complete control over the ranch. I sold General Rocky on the idea that we should use some of the ranch's cattle so our men could have steaks. That was accomplished. So that was a very important connection.

We were training hard, but our equipment was breaking down because of the volcanic ash on the ranch. As we approached the deadline to leave the island, we needed a lot of parts for our trucks and equipment for both motor transport and the engineers. Since I was familiar with motor transport work, General Rocky sent me over to Pearl Harbor on Oahu to expedite replacement parts. There I met a very unusual person, someone I think would have been a great commandant of the Marine Corps. He was a warrant officer, which is sort of half–enlisted man and half-officer. He doesn't have the qualifications to become an officer but his knowledge from experience is very valuable. When I arrived at the big depot at Pearl Harbor, the warrant officer was assigned to take care of the 20 pages of parts we needed. He read over the part list and said, "Let me take you for a ride."

We drove down what was practically a city of parts. Great big boxes were stacked up maybe 20 feet in the air in street formations. You could drive from one street to the other and find the part you needed. The warrant officer said to me, "Are you a genuine motor transport officer?"

I said, "Yeah, I have a certificate. I went through the motor transport school."

He said, "Well, hell, you've got it made. Let me show you something else." We went down to a big field where, as far as you could see, there were rusting trucks. They were just sitting there, unused. He said, "I can get you the trucks quicker than I could ever get the parts. I think you guys are going to be shoving out in not too long. By the time I get the all parts it'll be too late."

I said, "Well, I'd like to go back and talk to my general."

He said, "Hell, you don't need a general; he'll screw it up. Let me take charge."

So I said, "What do I have to do?"

He said, "Just sign your name."

I said, "Jesus Christ, I could get in trouble for this. If I have to pay for all these damn trucks, I'll be broke for the rest of my life."

He said, "You won't have to pay for them. Besides, where you're going, you're not coming back anyway."

I said, "Do you know where we're going?"

He said, "Yeah. Japan."

I thought, "No, the word around our camp is we're going to China."

There was a problem about shipping the trucks back to Hilo, which was the port for the big island of Hawaii, but he said, "I'll take care of that; I'll get the damn ship for you. All you've got to do is sign your name."

I thought, "What the hell do I have to lose?" I'd be killed anyway. What could they do to me? So I arrived back at Hilo with 1,200 vehicles, including jeeps.

The general came to me and said, "Who the hell do you know in Washington?"

I said, "Not a damn person. I know somebody that's even better than anybody in Washington—a warrant officer that knows what the hell's going on. We've got a shipload of material. All I need are drivers and a railroad to get them all back to our camp." So as a second lieutenant I gained a lot of respect. Everybody figured I knew somebody in Washington who was pretty important.

The irony was that we only needed a small portion of what we had when we got to Iwo Jima. Of course, we never made it to China—that information was just to throw everybody off. We did not want the Japanese to know that we were going to make a surprise attack on Iwo Jima, so we took a lot of our old trucks, pretending we were putting extra gas tanks and spare tires on them and getting them fixed up for China. The officers who knew what was going on knew damn well we weren't going to China. We were going to a little

Japanese island with eight square miles of land. The Marine Corps would lose nearly 6,000 men and nearly 18,000 would be wounded. For 20 percent of them, it would have been better if they had been killed instead of wounded. We didn't know all that then, but that was in the cards.

I used to lie awake at night wondering if something did happen to me, how would my poor wife handle all the property we had. It wasn't like you were picked up off the street and suddenly told, "Hey, you're going to die. You're going to war." The training was so gradual that you had a certain resistance against any of these thoughts. You knew you were going to lose some men; you knew there would be some casualties, but somehow or other you never realized that it could really happen to you. It always happened to the other guys.

I remember one time when I first took over the job at the motor transport in Hawaii. The discipline was rather poor, nobody was too serious about anything, and I got all the men together with Sergeant Basilone, a veteran of Guadalcanal who had earned the Congressional Medal of Honor. He gave a talk about how actual combat was not a picnic. He said, "You boys have buddies in the crowd. Some of you are going to get killed and some of you are not. You're in a serious business. The harder you can train now, the easier it's going to be in combat." The boys began to sober up after that. For myself, I was not so worried about losing my life as what a hell of a mess it would be back home. That's what bothered me. And out of all the marines on Iwo Jima who died, many were my friends. In fact, I knew practically all of them because they'd been in chemical warfare and engineering classes with me.

One of the assignments I had on Hawaii was interesting. Our maneuvers were disturbed by Japanese radios coming from other islands. We knew there were Japanese stations on the big island of Hawaii where we were, but we didn't know where the hell they were. I was assigned to take charge of a detail posing as civilians to explore some of the remote valleys on the north side of the island. I had two lieutenants with me who had formerly been paratroopers. One of them was a fellow by the name of Drinker, who was a sweet-heart of Doris Duke, the tobacco heiress. We posed as civilians and rented horses to get through the valleys because the mountains were running to the sea in 300-foot cliffs.

We had been in the northern part of the island almost a week when, on a Sunday, we came to a little grass church with a big tall priest—they're known as *kahuna* priests in Hawaii. They have the reputation of being able to walk over lava flows. We peeked into this little church and there was this big six-and-a-half-foot-tall *kahuna*. There were about ten benches in the church, and the people sitting in there were native Hawaiians. The front row was vacant, and the *kahuna* priest said, "Come in. We've been expecting you." We won-dered, how in the hell could he expect us? He gave a little talk and then asked the congregation to say a prayer. And when we left, he said, "You boys have nothing to worry about. I will see to it that you come home safely." To jump ahead a little bit, practically all the other paratroopers were wiped out at Iwo Jima. But the two paratroopers I was with and I came home unscathed; we didn't even get wounded.

We had been out for two more days when we came upon a farm-house. We noticed an aerial running from the house to the barn. We walked up to the house and knocked on the door, claiming we wanted a glass of water. When the woman opened the door, we could look on through to the dining room. On the dining room table was a modern Japanese machine gun—on the island of Hawaii. We pre-tended we didn't see the machine gun and we asked for water. She brought us a Coca-Cola, and we left. I wrote up a report for our general, which was turned over to the FBI. I never learned what happened, but I'm sure that somewhere in that house they had radios. But what they were doing with a machine gun, I never did learn.

We now come to the question, "Why Iwo Jima?" When the word got around where we were going, everybody wanted to know, "What in the hell are we going to Iwo Jima for?" It was only five miles long and two-and-a-half miles at its widest part, and 750 miles from Japan. Why Iwo Jima? The answer was that we needed a place for our damaged B-29 bombers returning from Saipan. Iwo Jima would be a good semi-port to land on. Also, the island was bristling with Japanese planes that were making bombing raids on Saipan. Their fighter planes were a nuisance to our planes, flying from Saipan 1,500 miles from Japan, so we had to take long routes to get around Iwo. It was also necessary to take Iwo Jima because Japan had been fortifying it for over 40 years. One of their greatest generals was in charge of the island—General Kuribayshi. He was educated at several universities, including one in the United States.

The island was shaped like a pork chop. At the tip end—the southeastern end—there was an extinct volcano that was about as high as a five-story building. At the top were remnants of a crater. The planners at the fleet marine headquarters in Pearl Harbor and in Washington figured we would take it in three days and move on to Okinawa. But after three months of bombing, the only thing we did to the island was knock off some superficial buildings. All the real installations—the big block houses and cave entrances with fortifications and the tunneling under the island—were still intact. That was a surprise for our fleet of 700 ships and many planes. We had two or three aircraft carriers and a battleship for each of our three divisions.

But I'm a little ahead of the story. The trip from Hawaii was long because the air force was stalling for more time. Our big fleet zig-zagged all over the damn ocean on the way to Eniwetok. It was a miracle the ships didn't crash into each other. We were blacked out at night so submarines couldn't spot us. And with all that, the navigators were perfect in everything they did. We were running out of supplies, so they cut us down to two meals a day.

We finally landed at Eniwetok, which our forces had recently taken. Eniwetok was like a pearl necklace resting in the middle of the ocean, forming a harbor. Each pearl was a little atoll with what had been palm trees. All the palm trees had been destroyed by fire power. But the island was bristling with supplies. There must have been 100 bulldozers on the beach that were completely rusted out. Inside the harbor were several hulls of Japanese ships built of concrete. Instead of steel, the outside plating was six inches of reinforced concrete. (The Japanese were running out of steel and they substituted concrete to make their ships.) The harbor was quiet, and it had good protection from the seas. We had aircraft carriers standing by—they were too big for the harbor. After we had recovered from the sea (and we were really tired of it, what with tight quarters and hard training, calisthenics, reviewing relief maps that we had of Iwo Jima, and being groomed on what each outfit was going to do), it was a relief to have two or three days in a new environment right in the middle of the ocean.

After our stopover there, we proceeded on to Saipan, which was our big bomber base. B-29 bombers were flying on regular schedules from Saipan to Japan, 1,500 miles away, and a lot of them didn't come back because they were shot down by fighter planes in Japan. In Saipan we laid over about four or five days to rest and take on more supplies and get the fleet organized.

In the ward room one night where the officers were going over some maps and photographs, a sailor popped his head in the door and said, "You fellows need anything?"

I said, "What have you got?"

He said, "Everything. We've got it all here."

None of us had had any candy in a long time, so I said, "How about Hershey bars?"

The sailor said, "Yeah, we got those. How many you want?"

I said, "Oh, I don't know. Ten thousand."

About 3:00 in the morning, the officer of the deck came to my bunk and woke me up. He said, "Poppelman, there's some sailors out here got an order for you."

I said, "What's that?"

"Ten thousand Hershey bars." And they had them! We stacked them up between my bunk and another tier of bunks. I asked Colonel Shuey, in charge of our ship, what I should do with all those Hershey bars, and he said, "Don't give them out yet. Before we make a landing, we'll ration them out." So 10,000 Hershey bars were rationed out to the marines on our ship. As they went over the side on D-Day, they would grab a handful and jam them in their blouse. With an ammunition belt around the jacket, the blouse made sort of a big pocket where they could put K-rations and Hershey bars. And the chocolate bars were the one thing that we could keep in our stomachs to hold the butterflies down.

On our journey to Saipan, the junior officers took turns being what they call the officer of the deck. The officer of the deck would make announcements over the intercom and patrol the ship. We had guards in our ammunition holds and each officer, during his tour of duty at night, made two or three rounds of the ship, just continually walking. If he saw something fouled up he could make a report.

On one of my tours, I went way forward in the bow of the deck and came across thousands of white grave markers all beautifully made and painted—most were crosses and some had Jewish stars on them. I thought, "Jesus Christ, what is all this? We're going to a little tiny island and they need thousands of crosses? What's going on?" I kept it to myself—I didn't want to panic anybody. But I never dreamed that we would not only use all those crosses, we'd run short of them.

On Saipan, a lot of planning went on. When we had been at sea, a destroyer might come up beside our ship. If the destroyer wanted to transfer photographs they'd shoot a line to our deck and we'd pull over a bag of photographs. Once we were at Saipan the photos were delivered to the officers. One day my colonel, who later became a general, called me into his private quarters and said, "Ray, I want you to look at some photographs." When I looked at them I couldn't believe the accuracy of the photographs. Our P-51 fighter planes were equipped with cameras. They would fly in real low and would even get guys sitting on toilets outside. They'd have their mouths open because they were so surprised an airplane was so low coming in at them.

We had very accurate photographs of Iwo Jima. Marines were diving along the shore looking for obstructions, and they gave reports about which beach to land on. The Japanese thought we were coming in on the west beach, and we had our water boys expose themselves deliberately so the Japs would think we were going to land on the west beach when we were actually coming in on the east beach. The east beach was not contaminated with obstructions. Our photographs showed a lot of the installations, even through the water. I'd never seen combat photos that were so accurate. The colonel said to me, "The aerial bombers have scarred the whole surface. They've taken off the vegetation and a few buildings, but the installations that we have to take out are still there. The navy has to save the day with their big 16-inch guns from the battleships. The air force has only taken the superficial stuff off the island. They have not taken out the pillboxes." So we were running very scared going into Iwo. We thought that after three months of bombing with fleets of B-29s, there'd be nothing left of the island.

We left Saipan headed for Iwo Jima and were approaching our D-Day. We were completely equipped. Colonel Shuey summoned me and said, "Ray, we have a lot of specialists in our group that are officers. They outrank you, but they've never had any combat experience; they're technical people. I'm going to do some shifting here. I want you to take in our No. 1 landing craft. You're only a second lieutenant, but I'm giving you authority now and I'm going to convey a message to all my officers that you will be my aide. You'll be with me."

On the morning we were to land, we had our last good meal—steak and eggs, or anything else we wanted. After the landing, we'd live on K-rations. The men didn't like the K-rations. They'd usually tear them open, take out the cigarettes, and throw the rest away. But that stopped when we realized we weren't going to take the island in three days; we were merely getting started. But the Hershey bars were the only thing that I could hold down.

On the D-Day, as we approached Iwo Jima, about all we could see in the early morning were clouds of powder dust; you couldn't see Iwo for the smoke. Our navy poured everything they had from the battleships, cruisers, destroyers—anything that would shoot. They wanted to pulverize the beach so it would be safe for us. This pounding of the beach with aircraft and battleships continued as we approached what they call the line of demarcation, where we'd load up our landing craft. I would be in charge of 40 men in what was called a Higgins boat, which was made of wood and would not adhere to floating land mines. All our men crawled down on the landing nets, which lay over the sides of our ship. Everybody got aboard the Higgins safely. We had a supply of burlap sandbags and a plastic bomb—stuff that you could wrap around a pipe that would blow it apart.

I'd say about 200 yards from shore the Japs were firing at us. The bombardment that we gave them put the Japs in shock, but after about the fifth wave of marines went in, they began to recuperate and started firing at us from Mount Suribachi (the extinct volcano) in the south and from cliffs in the north. So we were subject to shellfire. When we hit the beach, we ran off the front of the boat, which would be the bow. It fell open forward, so we'd have a good run off the boat down the ramp and onto the beach. The beach had two steep terraces; there was very little actual hard ground to walk on. When we landed, we stepped into about a foot of water, which had a terrific undertow. Then we noticed a tank that was mired down just in front of us. We crawled in behind the tank until the navy came to our rescue by bringing escort boats—small destroyers—practically right up to the beach, putting a barrage in front of us so that we could get up the beach and inland a little ways.

My assignment was to go ashore, resurrect some rails from a small railroad track that ran from Mount Suribachi up toward the north and make a command post, using a B-29 crater that seemed to be well protected. I was very lucky—everything went smoothly. We filled the sandbags to make our walls and cut the railroad track up into rafters—or floor joists, you might call them. Those would extend across our sandbag walls, and then we would lay tarpaulins on top of the rails, and on top of that we'd stack sandbags. Even with all the artillery and mortar machine gun fire and every other damn thing that was coming after us, we didn't lose one man building that command post. Later, when we abandoned the command post to move farther north, the corpsmen used it for an aid station, and surgeons patched up wounded marines to get them to the beach, waiting for their transport onto a hospital ship. I felt good that not only did I not get killed but none of the men got killed and we got the job done.

Chapter 15

The Battle for Iwo Jima

One of the first problems we had on Iwo Jima was getting our tanks landed and moving forward. The beaches were not the ideal place to bring a tank in—they were heavily mined. After we got our command post built so our general and colonels would have a place to operate from, all the engineers among us had to go back to the beach and attend to the land mines. We would crawl along the beach holding steel rods about 18 inches long with a curve on the end (like a button hook), and we would tap the ground for mines. When we would hear a click, we would tie a red ribbon, which we carried under our belts (we had a whole belt full of ribbons), to the rod and leave it there to indicate a mine. It's really an eerie business when you hear that click because you know damn well if you hit the wrong place you'll be blown to smithereens. We marked the mines, and at daylight another crew from our demolition battalion took over. The men in the crew would crawl around to the red ribbons, dig out the mines, and do what they called "delousing"—they'd take the fuses out. Later we used those to blow up Jap caves. But our problem the first morning was to make paths for the tanks to get up the terraces. We needed the tanks to go ahead of us with flame-throwers so that the infantry could follow them. So even after a tough day we worked practically all night to get the paths cleaned.

At 4:00 in the morning, just about daylight, the Japanese started their big bombardment. Every morning at 4:00, as though it was written in a book, they'd start up their guns. You could set your watch by the time the Japs started their barrage. My first night, a mortar shell, which is sort of a torpedo shot out of a tube that makes a high arc like a rainbow and whistles when it comes down, landed near me. Two marines in a foxhole near mine were blown out of their hole. They had to go somewhere, so they came over scrambling and dived in our foxhole on top of us.

The Japanese made one mistake that was a big help to us: They had set their fuses for landing on normal ground, but we were in soft volcanic ash mixed with sand. Their mortar shells would bury themselves before they'd explode, and then they would splinter with the parts flying in all directions. But they had enough power to lift a lot of sand. The two marines piled in on top of me and the sergeant I shared my foxhole with, Sergeant Richey from Norfolk, Virginia (we had two in each foxhole so you could be back-to-back and could cover all the territory). I was on the bottom with a marine on top of me; we were just lying there quietly. I was tasting blood; it was coming down my neck and into my mouth. I yelled at my sergeant, "Rich, you'd better get me to a station—get a corpsman—I think I'm hit; I've got blood all over me."

When things eased up a bit, the marine on top pulled his buddy off and we found out that I was not wounded at all; it was blood from the boy above me. We asked him, "Are you hurt?" He had a big gash in his shoulder. He said no. He was in shock; he couldn't even feel pain. That was just part of what happened during the night. Everything was blowing up around us. The beach was cluttered with boats that were damaged and blown up. The seas built up to about 12-foot waves; we couldn't get our wounded off the beach and we

This photo shows a Japanese artillery
installation that our ships, with their 16-inch
guns, blew up some time after we arrived on
Iwo Jima. When we landed, these 8-inch
caliber artillery guns were shooting at us.

couldn't get any marines in. We had 2,000 marines ashore fighting 23,000 Japs. Our main force was still to come and we couldn't get them ashore.

The next day was D-plus-1, which means the day after D-day. We had 71,245 officers and men who were supposed to go to the beach. On D-plus-1, we only had half of them ashore. The Japs were pouring it on us. The seas were rough and we were getting fire-power from all parts of the island.

The bombardment continued pretty well as steady fire until D-plus-2. All the time, our aircraft were bombarding the Japs as soon as they'd find a position or could see fire and knew where the caves were. They set up a new system—for the first time the marines on land were telling the gunners aboard ship where to fire. Each marine officer was given coordinate maps. Our unit would, say, have a destroyer with guns available to us, and we would call into the ship, sometimes with code talkers that the Japanese couldn't understand. If we saw a target and knew the navy couldn't see it, we'd call in to central command and they would get the ship that was best lined up for it, and they'd zero in with a test shot. When we saw where that shot landed, we'd call back to the ship and tell them the coordinates of the hit. The gunners needed two shots to get zeroed in; the third one would be right on target. So the navy with their guns (and the aircraft carriers with their airplanes) saved us. If we had to depend on hitting the beach and trying to take things ourselves, we couldn't have done it.

Sometimes companies and teams would have men in an area we didn't know about. That was one of our big problems: to know where our men were on the line. We didn't want to shoot our own men. Some of that happened during the first couple of days.

The third day, General Rocky came ashore. I was one of the first officers he talked to. He said, "I was going to pull you guys off the beach, but we couldn't do it." He said, "We were relieved in the morning to know that any of you were alive." We were losing officers so fast—the junior officers, especially second lieutenants and first lieutenants and captains. The second lieutenant is the only officer who leads his men; the others stay back and have sergeants lead. My colonel said to me, "Ray, we cannot send you into combat; you're a specialist. We could be court-martialed. You'd have to volunteer."

I said, "What do you want me to volunteer for?"

He said, "Take over a machine gun company" (a platoon). He

General Keller E. Rocky, the head of the 5th
Division at Iwo Jima. In 1928 he had been
athletic officer for the Marine Corps football
team that I played on, and despite his high
rank and my low one, we were friends.

said, "That'll be part of your job at night now. Instead of sleeping,
you're going to have to be on point on the west beach with a platoon
of machine-gunners. You have .30-caliber on one terrace, and .50-
caliber on the higher terrace."

The machine gun business was new to me. I'd had some training in it, but I'd never had charge of a machine gun company. I had
a runner—we didn't have a telephone at that point—on the beach.
Visualize two big terraces, one lower than the other. We had the .30-
caliber for Japanese sneaking out of Mount Suribachi and coming

up the beach to get to our water supply. And in case the submarines were unloading people, we had the .50-caliber out to sea, in back of us. About the second night I was on duty, we had cleared off the beach with a bulldozer. We put canopies over the bulldozers so the drivers would be protected. With one of those armored bulldozers, we cleaned out all the brush along the beach so we had a big wide beach. The Seabees, who are navy engineers, started coming ashore and cleaning up the debris along the beach, and they were a great help. At night, we would throw flares up, so when the Japs came up the beach we could see them. This particular night I was a little weary. I had sent my runner back to Colonel Shuey with a message, and I was in my foxhole alone. Being in charge of the group, the last thing I could do would be sleep, so I fought the sleepiness.

I saw a black object that looked like it was crawling up the beach. I'd squint my eyes and look and look, and I'd think, "Hell, he moved. I didn't see him move." Finally he got bigger. Then he turned from the beach and started up our terrace. I thought at first it might be my runner, Spicer—I thought maybe he got lost and was coming up the back way towards me. So I yelled out the password at him. No word came back. Then I began to smell a Jap. They hadn't had baths for months so they had a strong odor; you could smell them in the ocean breeze. I knew he was a Jap. He kept coming closer and closer and I thought, "Geez, I can't shoot him. I'll get these marines all shooting, and if one starts, they all get trigger-happy. We'll have a barrage going all around the place."

So I figured I'd let him come to me and I pulled out my bayonet. When he got close enough, I'd stab him in the back. It'd be just the two of us—one-on-one. I thought, "Maybe my eyes are still fooling me." But he just kept getting larger and larger and finally, as he came up the terrace to me, I got ready to pounce on him when he made a turn and went around my foxhole. I don't know why he did that. And he did not have a helmet on. (We found out later he had a hand grenade in each hand.) He just worked his way up past me; he was about three feet from me. I felt that if I could possibly reach him I would stab him, but it looked like he was going to pass me. So I thought, "Well, I'll let him pass me." When he got by me I yelled at the boys in back of me. "Hey, there's a Jap coming up on your terrace. Don't shoot him with the machine guns. Lay back. Let him come into your foxhole and shoot him with your .30-caliber rifles." And that's what they did. The Jap kept coming right on up and he made a dive into their foxhole, and as he did they laid back and turned loose with their automatic .30-caliber carbine rifles.

We let him roll down the bank and left him there until daylight. Then we got a rope around his feet and dragged him into a shell hole. We called the intelligence officers. They always wanted a Jap to get information. When we saw him in reality he was not a great big imaginary monster—he was just a young kid. We had to cut his muscles to get the hand grenades out. Then we took his leggings off because under the leggings the Japanese kept personal things from their families. We found a letter that the intelligence officers who could read Japanese interpreted. The letter was from his mother. It told him to fight on, that the Japanese had invaded California, the president of the United States was begging for mercy, and the war would be over in a few weeks. Then there was a paragraph about his family and "Love from your mother."

He was an innocent boy dragged into war. He's fighting us for God knows what; he probably doesn't know himself. And he was given false information from his mother, who believed it too. That's what the Japanese people were being told—that they were winning the war. As I looked at the little fellow I thought, "All that worry

This photo shows a typical "blockhouse,"
a Japanese cave reinforced with steel
and concrete. We had to be careful
because artillery guns and machine guns
were in them. The ships couldn't see
them (the ocean was off to the left and
right), so we had to neutralize them with
flamethrowers or get airplanes to dive in.

and I would actually stab a little boy like that." His stomach had
about as much fat as my shirt. He had a few rows of little sacks like
our old Bull Durham sacks with dried rice in them; he had no water.
We found out the Japanese were completely out of water on Mount
Suribachi.

On about D-Day-plus-3, at a cave near Mount Suribachi, an interpreter from the 28th Regiment with a bullhorn yelled that we

This photo shows a typical terrain. We
had little protection and would crawl from
rock to rock. One marine is using a
flamethrower on a Japanese bunker.

wanted to talk, and a colonel in the Japanese army came out in response. The officer (who had been educated in the United States)
talked to Colonel Liversedge (I served with him in China), head of
our 28th Regiment. He said he had talked to his men about surrendering. The colonel offered to take the wounded soldiers out of the
hospital the Japanese had in the cave and put them on board ship
and take them to a hospital on Guam. The officer went back inside
to talk to his men. Then he came back out and told the colonel that
they voted to remain in the cave and die because they knew their
ancestors would resent their surrender. If they died for the emperor
they'd be heroes, so they preferred to stay and die.

This photo shows the headquarters of the Japanese commanding general's fortified blockhouse being blown up. We didn't know the general escaped to the north end of the island.

The two officers shook hands. The Japanese officer went back to his men, and we piled up land mines that we'd taken off the beach at the entrance and blew the whole damn cave up. The rubble sealed them there. Those were only some of the Japs who were sealed in caves. Today Iwo Jima is like our Arlington Cemetery—it's a national cemetery, with the bodies of 20,000 Japanese all sealed up in caves.

We were fighting soldiers that were brave. They knew they were going to die, and so they tried to do all the damage they could before they died. We intercepted some wonderful speeches that General Kuribayshi made, encouraging his men to fight on. He radioed the speeches back to Japan, and we intercepted them. We gave the Japanese plenty of chances to surrender; they just would *not* surrender.

The 28th Regiment of our 5th Division was assigned to attack Mount Suribachi. The 4th Division was to go up the east coast. The remnants of our group would go up the west beach. The 3rd Division would stay aboard ship as reserves. They finally came in on the fifth day.

In my records, for D-plus-3 I wrote: "Rain." It was rather cold on Iwo, and cold rain in a foxhole is about the most miserable damn experience you can have. Medical supplies and more K-rations dropped in by parachute. Some of us would cut up the parachutes, which were waterproof, and use them to cover our foxholes—but they had colors on them, and the colors were good targets for the Japanese. So we would cut away the colors or be sure they weren't showing; we used the white part only. A cold rain is about the most miserable thing you can experience.

D-plus-4, February 23rd, was the great day that everybody today celebrates. It's the day we put up the flag. The flag was erected to save face for the planners in Washington and Pearl Harbor, the fleet marine force, who had said we would secure the island in three days and move on to Okinawa. The brass figured that they could claim that we had secured the island if we had the U.S. flag up.

The navy launched a big bombardment in the early morning so it would be easier to get a patrol up to the top of Mount Suribachi. But it didn't work too well. As our patrol pulled up a little canyon, the Japs would roll hand grenades down and we lost a few men that way—I think a total of 23. When the patrol got to the top, the men raised a small flag. The crater had a little valley in it, so when you were looking up from the bottom, you couldn't see the flag. The flag was too small and the staff was too short, and it was placed too far inland to see from the shore.

Lieutenant Schryer, in charge of the detail, called for help from a

ship, and the men tore out a big long plumbing pipe from one of the
damaged ships. That pipe was sent up with another detail. Shooting was going on all around the damn mountain. I was halfway up
with a detail that was supposed to blow a cave to keep some Japs
sealed in there. I guess there were probably 1,000 Japanese in the
cave, and we were crawling on the outside with a flag, so we had to
protect our men. I was about halfway up when I got a telephone
message from a code talker, an Indian, who said, "They want you
down at the beach."

Being a motor transport officer, I had to round up some vehicles
to bring the high command in off the flagship. It was Secretary of
the Navy Forrestal and Colin Smith, in charge of all the marines—
the big shots. They wanted to come ashore and have a second flag
put up so they could have their pictures taken and see the flag. They
couldn't see it from the ship. So we hauled them up to a place that
was quite level. Several marines had been killed that morning right
where they were all standing.

When the second flag went up, Joe Rosenthal, who came late,
took the famous picture. He had his camera there when the second
group put up the second flag—a bigger one—on a longer staff out
toward the edge of the crater so you could see it from below. One of
my buddies, James Griffith, now living in Florida, was in back of
Rosenthal. The cameraman was shooting away, and James was facing away from the photographer to protect him. In doing so, he got
shot in the hand and was wounded. Ordinarily, for security reasons
photographers had to send all their film to the island of Guam to
have it developed. Admiral Nimitz didn't want any bad photos to
get back to the States; he didn't want the people in America to know
how tough the battle was. The routine was that the correspondents
would send their material through the flagship, it would be flown

to Guam, and censors would send it back. We had a developing trailer in our engineering outfit, and Captain Vogler, a friend of mine who was in charge of all the photographs the marines took, developed them in that trailer. Some of the correspondents would go to Vogler and say, "Would you do me a favor—would you run off my film for me?"

So Dave Vogler had some film from Rosenthal, whose picture became famous. He said to me, "Hey, Pop, I have some good shots here of the flag-raising. Why don't you pick one out?" He had all of Rosenthal's pictures. My print was the first one of the official flag-raising. Later, when Rosenthal was up in San Francisco working for a newspaper office, he autographed it for me.

The following day, February 24th, there were what appeared to be white phosphor shells coming from the Japanese. They were illegal according to the Geneva Convention. Whenever a peculiar smoke came up, the marines would yell for a chemical warfare officer (there were about five of us on the island), so that we could test the smoke. I had a testing kit, and whenever I got a warning, I would have to get smoke as fresh as I could—jump into the hole and test the smoke—then give a report. According to the White House, no gas could be used except by order of a chemical warfare officer who had training and knew what the stuff was. An admiral couldn't call the White House and say, "We're going to use gas" if he hadn't been trained in chemical warfare. I was warned to stand by our command post in case the president of the United States called to verify the fact that the Japs had used gas. In a couple of cases, the Japanese had used little vials of cyanide gas on our tanks. They'd climb up on our tanks, and if they could find an opening, an aperture, they'd throw it in, trying to kill the crew. Cyanide is terrible—you can't smell it, there's no evidence it's around, you can't see it, and about

My personal print of Joe Rosenthal's
famous photo of the raising of the flag on
Mount Suribachi, Iwo Jima, February 23,
1945, autographed by the photographer.

ten whiffs of that stuff and you're dead. Even so, it didn't justify having us go all out with a gas war against the Japs. We tried to get all the boys to wear gas masks, which they didn't want to do. They figured we'd never use gas anyway and to crawl around with a damn gas mask on was a damn nuisance. I had to practically start my own war to get everybody to wear gas masks.

The 3rd Division landed on D-plus-5. They came ashore to give support because we were having a rough time with the Japs. The engineers were about to cross the neck of the island, the pork chop, to protect the west beach. Colonel Shuey sent me on a reconnoitering expedition with one man to determine what the sniper situation was. The snipers were a problem for us. They would crawl through tunnels from one point to another. The places they would come out were known as "spider traps." They would lift a lid up, shoot, get back down, and move. I was supposed to go over to the west beach and see if anyone would fire at me.

I went out reconnoitering with my man—his name was Spicer— and we went up as far as the first airport, which is what they now call Motoyama No. 1. There was a cave there and it was getting fairly dark. At night, the Japanese did about what we'd do—they'd send out patrols in no man's land. We were out there and saw some Japs coming. I told Spicer, "You get the hell back to Colonel Shuey and tell him not to move into this area. There are Japs and I haven't covered it all yet." I crawled into a cave, not knowing what the hell I was getting into; it had six dead Japs in it. I was afraid to leave the cave because the Jap patrol would pick me up. So I stayed in the cave but I got my head and shoulders out far enough to get away from the smell. They were just lying in there, dead, partially covered. The Japs had a practice that was important to them: Always pull your dead back so the enemy doesn't know what your losses are. So practically all the caves that were vacated were full of dead Japs.

I was in just such a cave and one of our ships started shooting in our area—I think it was ahead of the 3rd Division coming up. They were shearing down rock, which was covering up my entrance. I didn't dare go further inside, and I was afraid to go out. So as fast as the rock would fall down over my entrance, I'd drag it back inside and throw it over the Japs. As daylight came (this would be D-Day-plus-6), the Jap patrol moved back and I escaped. I later found out that the marines didn't come to rescue me because my runner got wounded on the way back and was dragged over to the beach, and the message didn't get to Colonel Shuey. They didn't know where I was.

I started going up the bank to the edge of the airport. About halfway up, Jesus Christ, a B-29—all shot up—flew over me. The tail was shot off; the belly was shot out. It came right over me, and I thought it was going to hit me. But it went over me, and its wheels were down. It landed on the runway, went down and made a U-turn, and raced back because at the other end were Japs. The crew jumped out and pushed that big plane off the runway. Then the 3rd Division came ashore and got them safe, and a while later we sent a bulldozer up there to push the big plane over the edge toward the west coast. It was quite an experience.

It was now February 26th. My notes from that day read: "The engineers cover the west beach; we finally move over to the west beach." In seven days, I hadn't washed my face or even shaken the sand from my socks. And I had hardly slept. I was trying to run a machine gun platoon at night and also furnish vehicles for our motor transport department, engineers, and a million other things. And I was an aide to Colonel Shuey—once you're hanging around a place,

This photo taken on Iwo Jima shows the sandbag "offices" that we built inside craters created by our B-29 bombers. This was my headquarters for motor transport and the engineers and chemical warfare. The arrow points to me. Mount Suribachi is to the right of the picture. This photo was probably taken four or five days after we landed.

even though you're trying to sleep, if a general or colonel needs somebody, right then they would summon you

The Japanese were desperate for water, so they made a charge up our beach. We had a distillation plant going there, pumping salt water inland to a big unit that would make fresh water out of salt water. The only drinking water Japs had was water condensed off the ceiling of their caves; it really had a sulphur taste. So, on D-plus-9, they made a banzai charge up the beach (this is in all the books). Some may have escaped, but we killed over 300 of them; it was just

We all got a cold shower and fresh water
to drink after a distillation plant was set up
near the beach. On the terrace above
were tanks and weapons to cover U.S.
forces coming in from the beach, which is
to the left of the photo, and to protect us
against Japanese attacks at night.

like shooting ducks walking through a pasture. It was complete murder. I thought to myself, "What the hell is the war all about? Jesus
Christ, a guy can't even get a drink of water. If he tries, he gets killed."
I got very sympathetic towards the Japs, because I realized those
guys didn't volunteer to go on that island and hurt us, and here
we're out to kill them.

On the same day, D-plus-9, we finally took Hill 382, "the meat
grinder" (the hills were marked according to their elevation). That

was a tough one to conquer. The Japs had arsenal material in a cave, whose walls were ten feet thick with reinforced concrete, and they were holding up the 4th Regiment and the 3rd from going to the north end of the island. My notes from that day read: "Am very tired. I changed pants." I had come ashore weighing a trim 195 pounds after a lot of training. (When I went in the Marine Corps originally I was 220 pounds.) After nine days of fighting, I was down to 172 pounds, and I couldn't keep my pants up. So I detailed two fellows to get me pants. They went down to where there were piles of dead marines who were brought back from the front. (We didn't have ground to bury them in.) They stripped off the pants from a dead marine and put mine back on the body—that was the only way I could get a smaller size of pants.

One of the worst nights I ever had was on D-plus-10. At 2:00 in the morning my colonel called me over the lines at my foxhole. My mate was a Sergeant Richey. He could sleep through anything. The colonel said, "Ray, all hell has broke loose down at our ammunition dump. Get some of your drivers down there with the covered bull-dozers and cover over the ammo dump."

So I stuck my head out of my foxhole and, Jesus Christ, it was like the Fourth of July down there at our ammunition depot, which was in from the beach about 100 yards. We had built revetments like a waffle, and in each cell we put different ammunition. I was concerned about our chemical warfare shells with cyanide. If they blew up and the wind blew over our area, we'd all be killed. I got three bulldozers with armored hoods over them and drivers, and we went down and started bulldozing the dirt over the depot. The 27th Regiment, I believe, sent some boys over to carry ammunition out of some of the cells to get it away from the fire. We lost 25 percent of the ammunition we had on the island that one night. (The last time

An overview of our 5th Engineer Battalion camp on Iwo Jima. There's so much camouflage over the ground that you can't see the bulldozers, trucks, guns of all types, ammunition dumps, and all the other equipment that was stored there. This was the west beach. We arrived on the east beach, so our division moved to the west beach and went up that side to Mount Suribachi.

I was in Florida I went to see a fellow who had written a wonderful book on Iwo Jima. He was a friend of mine. We talked, and I said, "You know, in your book you tell about the Japs blowing up the ammunition dump on Iwo. You mention in there a certain marine who was in charge, and you never could get his name. You know who that was? That was me.")

The Japanese were firing down at the dump from Mount

A view from our engineering camp on Iwo Jima,
looking southeast toward Mount Suribachi.

Suribachi. In their caves, the Japanese had big guns on railroad tracks. They'd roll those things out to the entrance, fire, and then roll them way back into the caves. Even though we'd shear the mountain down with our bombing, they'd still have their guns back in there, so they could zero down on top of us. They got a line on our ammo dump and just kept firing those big heavy guns until they made a strike. They had to do quite a bit of firing to hit the right cell to get it to fire up. It sure made a racket and lit up the sky. I was walking around there, and debris was hitting my face; it was a mess. Everybody got decorated but me. Afterward my colonel came to me and said, "Ray, you didn't volunteer; I sent you. I could be court-martialed."

I said, "Oh, forget it, Colonel."

He said, "I can't decorate you; you had no business being in there. You were a specialist and you were not a combat man for your commission. I don't know what to do."

I said, "Well, just forget about the whole damn thing. I'm glad I'm alive. You can do one thing, though: There's one bulldozer operator who did not get a medal." (I think it was because they ran out of medals. Each company was given a certain number of medals.) I said, "One of our drivers was killed. Send it to his parents." So they sent a medal home with a letter about how brave the bulldozer operator had been and all that—it's consolation for a family whereas the medal didn't really mean too damn much to me personally. I was just praying I'd get out of that damn hell hole with my dog tags. That'd be enough medal for me.

The next day was D-plus-11. My notes read, "Colonel Chandler of the 28th Regiment, killed." Earlier that same day, Captain Klotz of our outfit, in charge of our demolition squad, was shot in the back by a sniper. (Whenever an officer would get shot, usually it would be between the eyes. The snipers would wait till they got a perfect shot.) But Klotz got hit in the spinal cord and was in a hospital in Philadelphia for about 20 years. After Klotz got taken out, there were just two officers left there—me and a lieutenant by the name of Ernie Chennault, a brother to the famous Flying Tigers General Claire Chennault. We both volunteered to take over the demolition squad, and we flipped a coin to see who would go. Chennault got it. Two hours later, he got hit in the field by a mortar shell; it ripped his arm from his elbow up to his shoulder. He had to be taken off the island; that's how bad it was. So I was the only officer left there until some officers from the 3rd Division came in.

(Many years later I was at a reunion in Scottsdale, Arizona, and Colonel Shuey was there. He was sitting at a table and I said, "General [he'd been made a general], what the hell ever happened to Ernie Chennault? I know he went to a hospital, but whatever happened after he got out?" Turns out Ernie was standing right behind me.)

My notes from D-plus-11 read: "March 2nd. Discipline is waning. The navy refuses to allow the army to come in to support us." That was the one thing that bugged the hell out of me. The army had 80,000 troops floating around in transports five miles offshore. Sometimes when the wind was right we would lie in our foxholes and hear their music. The navy didn't want the army to take any credit for winning the battle. They were only allowed to relieve us when we left. I objected to that because we had guys all crapped out, and here were fresh guys five miles away, playing music.

On D-plus-12, March 3rd, I got a notice that I had been promoted to first lieutenant. On that same day the first hospital airplane landed on Iwo Jima at Motoyama Airport No. 1. The plane was called *Peg o' My Heart*, and the only woman to land on Iwo Jima was the nurse who jumped out of that plane to help the marines aboard. I went up to her, introduced myself, and told her I could get some men up there to help her; she should not be lifting. She said, no, she wanted to help.

My notes from that day read: "On D-plus-12, bucket of water." One of the boys came up to me and said, "Lieutenant, I've got a present for you. I just came from the beach and I brought you a bucket of water." That would be like somebody today saying, "Ray, I've brought you a new Mercedes-Benz." A bucket of water all to myself to take a bath; it was unbelievable.

The Japanese were continuing their firing from Mount Suribachi south to the beach and from the north down; we were in a crossfire, and we had no place to take the wounded. We had to get them to the beach so we could board them on boats to take them to the hospital ship. A lot of the marines were getting wounded a second time as they lay in the open, waiting for the transport boats, so the Seabees coming ashore and some of our outfits started to bury the wounded in sand up to their necks on the beach so that they were less exposed to the Japs.

During the last days of the campaign, we were fighting up at the north end of the island. I was there with a platoon of marines and we killed a Japanese officer. Since I was in charge of the detail, the officer's flag was turned over to me. The flag had signatures all over it—it was a farewell gift signed by friends at a party. All the Japanese soldiers carried them on their left legs under wrapping, along with letters and maybe a Japanese bible.

When I came home from the war, I gave the flag to my brother Clyde, who was a lieutenant in the Marine Corps during World War II and served aboard the USS *Salerno Bay*, an aircraft carrier operating in the South Pacific theater. He had it framed and on a wall for a long time. Then a friend of mine wrote a book on Iwo Jima, and on the last page he had written that the Japanese had created a museum in Yokohama: the Iwo Jima Museum. They were appealing to Americans to have all Japanese personal items returned so they could be put in the museum. So I got the flag and sent it to the Iwo Jima Museum with the name of the person and copies of the letters—and I received a flood of letters, not only from Japan but from the U.S. State Department. They wanted me to go to Japan and present the flag to the widow. I was sick at the time and couldn't go, so an American consul in Japan was appointed to represent me. The dead officer had been an employee of Japan's largest steel company, and the company declared a holiday on the day that the flag was going to be presented to the widow. My gift sort of set a precedent. It was pub-

This photo shows a detail of marines in the north end of the island near a little town called Nishi. During fighting, they got hold of a Japanese flag from a dead soldier and gave it to me because I was commanding the unit. Years later I returned it to the soldier's wife in Japan.

licized in the Marine Corps, and after that, many of the marines sent back the personal bibles they had.

We took no prisoners on Iwo—the marines had vowed not to because of an incident that had taken place earlier (in August 1942) during the battle for Guadalcanal. The marines had landed on the island of Guadalcanal and were in a battle along the beach area when the Japanese dropped a message by airplane stating that if we would send a full colonel with marines up to the beach to negotiate, they

Queenie, as the Marines called him, had been a
Japanese mascot dog on Iwo Jima until we
found him. Dried rice was all he had ever eaten,
and he wouldn't touch the food we tried to give
him. We sometimes took the little sacks of rice
tied to the ammunition belts of dead Japanese
and brought them back to Queenie. He was
eventually weaned off rice and onto American
food. He was later transported to Hawaii and
became somewhat famous among the Marines.

would surrender. At the beach was a colonel, Frank B. Goettge, who
had been an all-American football player. (He was one of the coaches
when I was on the team; I knew him well.) Frank Goettge went up
the beach with a detail of 20 men and was ambushed. Two marines
made it into the ocean far enough to swim back to camp and tell
about it. Frank Goettge's body was dropped from an airplane by

parachute—in a basket—cut into two-inch pieces. The marines were so incensed that they decided from then on to take no prisoners. Even when I was in officer school, they told that story and said, "When you get into combat, take no prisoners." On Iwo Jima, every marine who passed a Japanese corpse put a bullet in it to be damn sure.

I'll tell you how crazy it was. Japanese were taking the uniforms off dead marines, putting them on, and disguising themselves. We captured one standing at the north end of the island, wearing a marine uniform. One of our colonels drove up with a jeep, and on his way back he saw that lone figure standing there. He gave him a ride—brought him back to camp. The Japanese fellow jumped out, signaling that he wanted a shovel to dig a foxhole. They realized he was a Japanese and turned him over to our intelligence group, which was begging for prisoners to interrogate.

A young fellow from the University of Maryland—I forget his name—jumped into my foxhole one day and said, "What the hell are you digging—a well?" My foxhole was very deep. He hung around for about 20 minutes, just shooting the bull. He'd heard about me and my football days at the university (he attended after I had graduated). We talked a few minutes, and goddamn, I later found out that 45 minutes after we spoke, he was killed. That's how bad it was.

Iwo Jima was a rough battle. They say it was the fiercest battle the marines ever fought. I think we lost 2,000 in the first 36 hours. I'd say the 5th Division's 28th Regiment on Mount Suribachi took the heaviest loss. They lost so many officers, they had even non-commissioned officers running companies at one time.

The worst part of Iwo Jima for me was about the last ten days. When we'd gone through 26 days of battle I got to thinking, "Will I

A funeral service on Iwo Jima, probably in
March 1945. Nearly 6,000 marines were
buried—with great engineering difficulty—on
Iwo Jima, but the bodies were all removed
back to the United States after the war.

ever make the next day?" Fear comes in various levels: As you get
on the ship to go to sea, and as you get closer to your target, and
after you see the beaches—it comes in gradual levels, so that when
you get into the real combat, you sort of feel like you've been in
combat before. You've heard so much about it, you've seen so many
films, that you automatically know what to do. When men in your
outfit were killed you'd figure, "Well, gee, that's too bad." And you'd
grieve about it. But you always had the feeling "I might get through
it." Even so, we'd swap letters with another officer. We'd go to a

buddy and say, "When I get killed, send this to my wife." Not if, but *when*. You'd give one to him, and he'd give one to you.

I was in a foxhole. I was 38 years old and had a 39th birthday coming up in three days. The way things were going, I knew I would never get off the island; it was just a matter of what day you were going to get it. The lucky ones, we always thought, were the ones who got wounded in the beginning and were taken off the island. And maybe they were. Anyway, for some reason, I just hoped to hell I could get to my 39th birthday. So I prayed to the Lord that I be allowed to live to see my 39th birthday. We had so damn many casualties and wounded—nearly 7,000 men killed and more than 19,000 wounded in all the forces. I figured my chances for surviving were getting worse. In fact, my colonel told me, "Ray, you've been so lucky, you'd better stay out of that front line area. Stay back here with me for a while." Anyway, I prayed that I'd get three more days. And he gave me those three days 56 years ago.

The United States gave Iwo Jima back to Japan. The island has been landscaped and restored. The only way you can get onto it now is with a special permit from the Japanese government because it is a national cemetery. The Japanese allow U.S. Marines to go back there once a year. I never want to go back.

CHAPTER 16

Last Days at Iwo Jima, and Returning Home

March 7, 1945, was D-plus-16. My notes read: "Our 5th Division overtakes Nishi Village, or what is left of it." Admiral Chester Nimitz was urging the marine generals to make a great push. We had taken nearly the whole island. There were about 2,000 or 3,000 Japanese at the north end of the island, facing Japan, down in a valley. That last valley was full of caves, and it took all of our three divisions several days to get them under control. We bombarded the hell out of the valley and went in, blew up caves, and sealed the Japs in there. Long after armistice was declared, almost 2,000 Japanese came out of their caves, not realizing the war was over.

At the time we blew up the caves, I was given an assignment, along with our demolition officer, to take a tank with a bulldozer blade and, using a large water tank, haul 300 gallons of aviation gasoline behind the tank. With a fire hose from one of our damaged ships, we pumped all 300 gallons of gasoline into the Japanese general's headquarters. Then we exploded it with a white phosphor shell. It practically shook the island, and we thought no human being could ever survive within that cave. But the Japanese general did—he escaped through tunnels to a new headquarters on the Containment Point area. We found out he was alive when we intercepted a broadcast from him to Japan.

Death was all around me on Iwo Jima. A good friend of mine, Lieutenant Leonard Isaacs, was wounded the third day on Iwo. Someone told me he was down at the beach with a fragment of an ammunition shell lodged between his collarbone and his head, so I grabbed a jeep (since I was a motor transport officer, I had a jeep available) and drove to the beach to find him. He could barely talk— just a whisper—and was highly sedated. He laid there that night, and the next morning the rough seas had subsided, so he was taken aboard the hospital ship. He had surgery and was put aboard a ship going to the hospital at Guam. On the way to Guam he died and was buried at sea.

When the boys went after pants for me, the pile of dead marines must have been six feet high and half a block long. The vehicles would come back from the front with dead marines. As they came up alongside the pile of marines, they just threw them out like sacks of potatoes. In a few days the bodies would be in different shapes because of rigor mortis. It was really a terrible sight. Once the Seabees came ashore they dug big long trenches with bulldozers. They'd lay the marines out—they had a plan so they would know where each one was buried. They'd take one dog tag off the body and leave one. Later they dug all the bodies up and brought them back to America.

The wounded and dead were transported in several ways. A "duck," which looked like a tank with an open top, was the only vehicle that could get up the beach terraces. The ducks would take ammunition and guns to different units that were ideally situated to fire, and they'd also bring back the wounded and dead. Jeeps were also used, which meant that those like me who had a jeep seldom ever rode alone. I was either taking some marine some place or

I was bringing back somebody who was wounded or dead. You never knew what the hell you would come back with.

Our corpsmen were heroes. They were absolutely fabulous, even thought they had no weapons. The Japanese soldiers would try to lure them closer by yelling "Corpsman!" so they could shoot them. The corpsmen were right up front, picking up boys that were wounded and helping them. An awful lot of corpsmen were killed and wounded. They were the bravest. And the Jap soldiers had no mercy. Two corpsmen would be carrying a stretcher with a marine on it, and the Japs would shoot at them. We wouldn't do that.

About my last day on the island, I was assigned with a detail to go around to the caves looking for stragglers who were shell-shocked. We were trying to get everybody aboard ship so we could move out. I got a telephone call from one of our officers, Lieutenant Kenney from Chicago. He said, "Ray, all hell's broken loose up here near Airport No. 2. The army put a battalion of black boys up on the ridge to keep the Japanese sealed up in their caves, but the Japs have made a banzai charge, and they've come down. They're hopped up with dope (they all had opium pills that they'd carry in little sacks on their belts, and before they'd charge, they'd get high on opium) and they've killed about 45 pilots who were living in tents up near Airport No. 2. If you've got any ammunition or shells or anything at all, get on up to the airport. Our Pioneer Battalion is the only one intact. They're up there fighting and they need all the help they can get." I rounded up all the boys I had and headed toward the airport. We had turned in our machine guns—we only had rifles and carbines. It was early morning, just beginning to get light. I dug into available foxholes with my boys, just before about 250 Japanese soldiers came toward us, yelling and raising hell. They had beheaded somewhere between 45 and 90 pilots and were continuing toward

Airport No. 2. The few marines we had left killed almost all of them. A Japanese officer charged at me, and I lay back and unloaded my .30-caliber carbine rifle. He was killed.

A black boy who had previously jumped into my foxhole with me was yelling for his life. He said, "Oh, there's a million of them coming up! A million of them coming! Save me! Save me!" We lost quite a few marines in that battle. The Japanese soldiers were masters of the sword, and they took to beheading our men. They were tremendous fighters. How they stood the punishment on Iwo I'll never know.

Finally General Rocky told the army general who relieved us, "Either you protect my marines or I'm bringing them back off the ship and shoving the whole goddamn army in the ocean!" That's the way he felt about it. The army had no training compared to the marines. Once they came ashore, the first damn thing they put up was movie screens and ice cream machines. They put up tents instead of digging into foxholes. They thought the fighting was all over. We told them that several thousand Japanese were still in the valley, and their job was to keep them sealed up in the caves so we could get off the island, but they failed in their mission, which was one reason the marines resented the army. When an army truck driver used our ramp to come up the west beach, our marines went down to him and said, "What have you got aboard?"

He said, "Pineapples." The whole damn truck was full of pineapples! We took half of it as a toll for the use of our road.

Some young army major who couldn't have been 20 years old— not dry behind the ears—wanted me to tell him what it was like up front. I told him, "Hell, you'd better sit down in this foxhole here. We've got Japs out here listening to us." He got scared to death. And I told him, "Don't call me 'lieutenant.' Don't use my rank. And tell your men not to say their ranks. The snipers are lying around here and they'll take care of you. Some of them can understand English. The only people they shoot are officers, and that's between the eyes." He took off like a scared rabbit.

Another incident with the army occurred the first night the army came ashore. Two Japanese boys who had been hiding in a cave—unarmed, and hungry—sneaked out and sat on sacks alongside some army boys, watching the damn movie. After the army boys left, the Japs went over to where some candy wrappers had been thrown away and were licking them. An army fellow spotted the Japs and started yelling, "Marines! Where are the marines? Get the marines!" Instead of taking care of the two Japanese fellows, they were yelling for the marines to do the job.

The way the army relieved us was poorly organized. They thought that our leaving meant the island was secured, but it was not. I think it would have been better if we had brought the army ashore earlier, possibly by five or six days, and put them up front fighting the Japanese.

I had been working pretty hard. We took all our engineering equipment, some of it practically new, and put it on the LST (tank landing ship), which would go offshore about a mile and dump everything overboard. None of it came home—it was cheaper to jettison it than to ship it back. The army had brand new equipment, which they were bringing ashore. Turns out the new stuff was never used. The waste was unbelievable. And I thought of all those bulldozers going over the side—if I had just one of them at home. Life isn't fair.

But we finally boarded ship—the last ship out of there. The last marine to leave the island was General Rocky. The second-to-last officer to leave was my old friend Colonel Liversedge, who was a lieutenant in China when I was there, and later became a general. He was the head of the 28th Regiment that captured Mount Suribachi. (We were very close, but because of his high rank and my low one, we didn't talk too much in company with other high-ranking officers. I went up to his officers' club in Hawaii one time with the colonels and generals. He told me to take off my second lieutenant bars, which I did. That way, nobody knew who I was. Some of the admirals coming in probably thought I was a marine general.) And I had the honor of being the third-to-last marine to leave that damned island.

It was sunset when we left, and we could see Iwo sinking into the sea. Then I broke down. Being with the dead fighting on Iwo was one thing, but when you leave them behind. . . . You trained with them for two years, and suddenly you're coming home and they're lying back there. Every man that came back had lost at least several buddies. We had a guilt complex—we were coming home while so many others were left behind. It was not easy.

Aboard ship was a big wardroom full of intelligence officers deciphering and translating Japanese material we'd captured in caves. We had a ton of stuff. In the paymaster's cave, we found and brought out a lot of Japanese money, with which the marines were gambling. And lo and behold, the merchants in Hawaii would buy up that money—they'd give 10 percent of the face value of the yen. The Japanese on Hawaii thought the Japanese still might win the war, so they were willing to buy the foreign money.

There were many regulations aboard ship. General Rocky appointed me as permanent officer of the deck, and I made announcements over the intercom. For security reasons I had to sleep up on the deck in a bunk. The captain of the ship slept opposite me. He would tell me the orders and I'd announce them over the intercom.

All the way home my sleep was interrupted because I had to make patrols on the ship; it was terrible. On rainy, stormy nights in the middle of the ocean, as far as you could see were just shadows of the ships—no lights. Waves would break over the bow and water would run down the deck. I would be out there all alone on patrol on that goddamn ship. A wave could have washed me overboard and nobody would have known it. I'd go up on the bridge, and if there was an alert about a submarine, I had to announce to the men and tell them to be sure to wear grease on their faces and not to come aboard in their T-shirts in case there was an explosion. Security was high all the way to Hawaii.

When we arrived at Hilo, the sugar trains were waiting to carry us to our camp. As we passed through the village we saw some Japanese flags flying. The Japanese natives would turn their heads in shame; they wouldn't look at us.

Out of our whole division, about 25 marines were selected to go, sort of secretly, to Washington. I was at Camp Kamuela in a tent with my company commander, Suchek, who did not go to war. At midnight, a jeep pulled up with an officer who said, "Poppelman, get your gear together. You're going to catch a plane to Pearl Harbor, and you're going back to Washington."

When I arrived at the Hilo airport, who should be sitting next to me on the plane but Colonel Liversedge, my old friend. His hair had been black when we went ashore, but it was perfectly white when I got on the plane. And I said to him, "General [he'd been promoted to general], you're going to have to get your hair dyed." He laughed. When we arrived at Pearl Harbor a delegation of high-ranking officers was there to greet General Rocky and General Liversedge. There was also a big Chrysler station wagon decorated with flags. When we got off the plane, the officers came up to

Liversedge and told him the car was for his service while he was in port. It came with a female driver and a female doorman. Liversedge turned to me and said, "Ray, I have no damn use for this car. You take it and use it; it's yours."

I went over to the girls and said, "What am I going to do with this car?"

They said, "Anything you want. We'll be with you until you leave."

I said, "Well, what do you recommend?"

One of the girls said, "Doris Duke has a big place out on Diamond Head that is for high-ranking officers. They have good food and drink, and there'll be some entertainment. Would you like to go out there?"

I said, "I don't want to go alone."

She said, "With this car you can take anybody."

So I went up to BOQ, which is where the officers' quarters were, and yelled, "Does anybody want to go on liberty?" A lieutenant colonel and another fellow got in the car with me and we went out to Diamond Head. We were treated like royalty. There was every damn kind of food and drink you'd want and women all over the place. The next night we went to another officers' quarter that was popular. The town was jam-packed with people.

The next stage of my return home was a flight to San Francisco. When we were out about three hours over the ocean, a big pipeline in the seaplane broke. Oil was splattered all over where I was sitting. The pilots flew the plane back to Honolulu. Once I finally got to San Francisco, I flew on to Washington, D.C., and went to the assigned meeting place. There I was escorted into a room and told, "Nobody else can come in here, except one officer." Who should be the officer assigned to be with me but a fellow I'd known in officers' school—Chris Battles. (He later was inducted into the professional football hall of fame in Canton, Ohio.) He hadn't been in combat but had been kept at headquarters. He stayed in the room with me to make sure no one else entered and to keep me from communicating with other people. The brass wanted 25 different opinions as to why it took us 36 days to capture Iwo Jima when we were scheduled to do it in three days. I took two days writing out my opinions. Finally I was called into the commandant's office—he was A. A. Vandergriff, who had been a major in China when I was there. He was the head of our 3rd Battalion. He said, "Ray, we meet again. I've read your critique. I want you to do a favor for me."

I said, "What's the favor?"

"You've got three paragraphs in your critique I want you to re-move. It'll hurt the Marine Corps, and Congress won't like it." (The U.S. Congress was going to be reading all these reports.) The parts he wanted me to take out were these: I complained about the 80,000 army boys floating around outside of Iwo Jima when our boys were crapped out. I complained about the way the medals were distrib-uted—officers in Honolulu (guys who didn't even go to Iwo Jima) were getting medals for the planning that had been all screwed up. And I complained about chemical warfare—that we were using flamethrowers. I had written about seeing Japanese run out of caves, their clothes burning, and they were yelling and crying. I thought we could have used sleeping gas or cyanide and there'd be no pain. I wrote, "There's no greater pain than being burned alive." I told Vandergriff that I saw so much that I had to put it in my report.

He said, "Well, there's nothing we can do about it now, but I'll see what we can do about it in the future. We may forget these flamethrowers." He agreed with me that using them on humans was a terrible thing. So I agreed to delete the three paragraphs he wanted me to. Then he said, "Now, Ray, what can I do for you?"

I said, "You can get me out of this damn outfit. I don't ever want to go to Japan. I'm through with it."

He said, "You don't have to worry about going to Japan." He knew about the atomic bomb and how we were planning to use it on the Japanese. He said, "If you have any buddies that you're going to correspond with, you can tell them we're going to be home for Christmas." He didn't say why. So we shook hands and he said, "If you're not feeling well, you let our doctors check you over."

A couple of weeks later I was at my home in Falls Church, and an officer that I had gone to school with came by. He said, "The commandant sent me out to see you. He thinks that you deserve to put the Iwo Jima monument together." Felix de Weldon was doing the sculpture. He had made a model and then the bronze statue of the men putting the flag up, which was going to be a memorial by the Pentagon in Washington, along the river. At the time, it was in Philadelphia in different sections. The general who was the hero of Guadalcanal was head of the monument committee—Colonel Merritt A. Edson was his name. I told the officer who came out to see me, "I don't have the kind of money it takes to put that monument together. I'm just a small guy, I just got back, and I haven't even got organized yet."

He said, "Vandergriff thinks that since you were a contractor, and in the engineers, you should have the honor."

I said, "I appreciate it, but I can't do it."

A few days later I got a call from the officer, who said, "I talked to the general and he said they want to make you a consultant. Would you be a consultant?"

I said, "Yeah, I could do that." So I met General Edson, and Gene Tunney was on the committee and a couple of admirals and another general or two. They asked me what my thinking was and I said, "My thinking is that we should not put the monument by the Pentagon, along the river. It's going to cost $100,000 for pilings." The bronze statue weighed 45 tons.

They said, "Where do you recommend we put it?"

I said, "I have a friend, Mr. Flather, an insurance man. He's a vice president of the Riggs National Bank and owns land near Arlington National Cemetery. He had given an option to Arlington County to build a hospital there, but the zoning board turned it down. I think that land's still available. If we can get our congressmen busy, we could grab that land."

So General Edson went to the commandant, Vandergriff. They went to friends on Capitol Hill and told them, "We want some land." Meanwhile, I went to see Mr. Flather, the man who used to loan me money, and told him, "It would be a great honor if you could hold that land for the Marine Corps for the monument they're going to put up." He agreed to it. Congress passed a bill to purchase the land and we got it. Felix de Weldon, the sculptor up in Philadelphia, who argued against the whole idea, practically became my enemy. He wanted the monument to be near the Pentagon.

There had been some concern among some of the officers at Hilo about the mental state of the returning men. The navy sent a bunch of psychiatrists to our camp to interview anybody who seemed crazy. A lot of fellows were breaking down and doing crazy things. One of my boys was picked up by the MPs [military police] on Hilo with a big trailer truck we used to haul tanks with. In the middle of the trailer was nothing but a pair of shoes. He was in Hilo looking for a shoemaker to repair his shoes. In addition, he took the trailer truck down the coast road, where he was not supposed to go—it was very dangerous. You had to be a damn good driver to get a big thing like that down there without going over the cliff. I made an appointment with the navy psychiatrists to bring him in. When we came to the appointment, we had to sit on a long bench and wait. Finally a yeoman—not a nurse, but a guy who sort of serves as a nurse—came over and said, "Lieutenant?" I said "Yes," and he said, "So-and-so will see you now."

I went in to the office and a navy officer was sitting behind a desk. He talked to me gently and then finally said, "I've got a test here I want you to try." It was what they call the Rorschach Test. When he put the ink blots in front of me, I said, "Hold everything, Sir. It's not me. I'm the commanding officer. It's one of my boys. He's out there. He's the one." I told him what my runner had done. So he said, "Yeah, I understand all about that. You tell me what you see here." I had to get him to call my commanding officer to get me out of there.

A lot of the guys from Iwo were a little balmy. They'd get certain notions in their heads and it was hard to get it out of them. They'd get sullen and not eat. They were cracking up pretty badly, I thought. You just don't fight Japs for 36 days and not have something wrong with you. When I told Colonel Shuey—he was going to be recommended for general—about my taking Spicer over to the psychiatrist, he said, "Well, I'm not so sure you shouldn't have stayed there and gotten that test. How do you feel?"

I said, "Hell, I'm OK!"

Spicer was sent to a hospital back in the States somewhere. It was common to transfer the men into a different environment. The men's letters back home were being read to find out who was crazy. If a guy was writing a crazy letter home, he'd be sent to a psychiatrist. The Quonset hut that was put up for the psychiatrists—Jesus Christ, it was full. Guys were there all day long.

I did have some emotional problems when I first came home. For instance, I had a few friends around Washington who had been in the war—one fellow was a major who got killed. His wife lived in Arlington, and I went to see her. I was OK until I started talking to her. Sue, my wife, thought it would relieve my distress if we want to California for a vacation and to visit my family. While we were there, a Kiwanis Club or some other organization in San Fernando talked me into making a speech. I broke down; I cried and I couldn't talk. It still bothers me.

Being in the war actually helped me in my business. The bank practically gave me a blank check for what I wanted; the mortgage companies were a big help; the carpenters' union was also a big help. They were all sympathetic to me. I got a lot of breaks that I wouldn't have gotten if I hadn't been viewed somewhat as a hero. I didn't have a lot of decorations and medals, but I certainly had enough experience to deserve them. And Iwo Jima, then, was getting an awful lot of publicity. I'd get invited to parties and such, but I had to refuse to go to them because everyone would ask me questions, and memories of all these damn experiences would flood back; I couldn't take it.

I think what saved me mentally was the fact that I had a goal at home. I wanted to get Virginia Forest cleaned up, and I wanted to get back to building at Ravenwood. As for surviving in battle, I figured it must be destiny. For instance, I was on a patrol with five guys. A sniper turned loose, the others all got hit, but I didn't. I developed a phobia of snipers. Whenever I'd be somewhere and it would suddenly be quiet, I'd be scared and would get the feeling "There's a sniper that's got a bead on me." And then on that last goddamn day when the Japs made that banzai charge, I thought, "Lord, why do you do this to me?" I figured this was it. But I lived to be the third-to-last marine off the island, after Rocky and Liversedge.

I was in Falls Church reactivating my civilian life when I got a phone call from the father of my buddy Leonard Isaacs, who had died on the hospital ship going to Guam. Leonard was the kind of a guy who could make you feel good after just a few minutes with him, no matter how bad you felt when you got there. He was always laughing and had something good to say. When we were in training at Camp Pendelton, Isaacs was a motor transport officer, so we socialized together. He rented a big house up at San Clemente and would entertain a lot. We were practically brothers. When he was killed on Iwo, it shook me up badly.

Mr. Isaacs was a wealthy lumberman in New Orleans. He said, "Ray, I need you. Can you fly down here so I can talk to you?"

I said, "What's it about?"

He said, "It's about Leonard. The only thing I can get from the Marine Corps is that he died at sea." They wouldn't give him any particulars; nobody seemed to know anything about it. He said, "Do you know anything?"

I said, "Yes, I know a little bit."

He said, "I'll pay your expenses if you can come down and tell me what you know." Leonard had been the only son in a rich family. I flew down and checked in at the Roosevelt Hotel, which was then the best hotel in New Orleans. The next morning I met Mr. Isaacs in the bar area. I had brought some maps and material with me that I thought he'd be interested in, and I had made notes. He was very quiet, and we sat down and he said, "I appreciate your coming. Don't hold anything back."

So I didn't. I showed him on the map of the island where his son

had been wounded and told him what I knew of how it had happened. He finally broke down and started crying. Goddamn waiter
came over in his fancy red coat and said, "Is there something wrong?"

For some reason I said, "Yeah, you forgot the peanuts."

But then I told him, "His son was lost in the war and I'm telling
the story." The bar was lined up with people and pretty noisy. The
waiter went over and told the bartender the story, and suddenly the
room was quiet. Anyway, Mr. Isaacs pulled himself together. I
showed him on a map about where in the ocean Leonard was buried, and I described the ocean—it was a deep blue—and said that
Leonard had been a great hero to his men. I built that part up to
make him feel better. He said, "You know, you were a good friend of
Leonard's wife." I said yeah. "Well, would you mind if we rode over
and saw her?"

I said, "I'll do anything you want. My time is yours here." So we
went over to see Leonard's wife. I had known her back in San Diego, and she'd been a beautiful girl. Since Leonard died, though,
she'd become a derelict—gone to liquor and drugs. Her two daughters had to be taken away from her to live with Leonard's mother.
She was completely shot.

Then we went back to my hotel. Mr. Isaacs said, "Ray, what are
you doing for yourself?"

I said, "Well, you know, I was a small builder in Washington.
I'm trying to reactivate my building business."

He said, "If Leonard had lived, he'd have been a very wealthy
man. How would you like to take his place?" I knew that was out of
the question.

We finally parted, and I thought to myself, "How many more
families in America have been shaken up? They talk about boys getting killed in battle, but how about the families back home?"

Leonard's father had told me he'd pay my expenses to come down there, and when he left he handed me an envelope with a ridiculously large check in it made out for about $10,000. I wasn't going to accept that, so I took the check and tore the signature off and wrote on the back of it, "My reward was advanced to me by your son's friendship," and I mailed it back to him.

The A-bombing of Hiroshima on August 6, 1945, came as a great relief to me because I had a whole division of friends waiting in Hawaii. I had fears that I would be called back if the fighting continued. We had heard stories about the Japanese training their women to fight us with broomsticks on the beach. And we knew that we would lose a million marines trying to invade Japan. So naturally when we found out that Japan was going to surrender, it was a great joy to everybody; it was unbelievable.

There had been rumors that we had a secret weapon, but no one around me knew what it was. Some of the high-ranking officers in the fleet marine force in Hawaii knew we had an atomic bomb, the president certainly knew it, and the staff in Washington probably knew it. But we common enlisted men and officers of the lower ranks had no suspicion of it. I did get wind of a rumor, though, through the chemical warfare men that we had something new that we were going to use on Japan. I thought it was just a new type of chemical warfare, probably a development of cyanide gas that would put all the people to sleep—not kill them, but put them all to sleep—and then we would invade while they were handicapped that way.

President Roosevelt had died, and Harry Truman had become our president. We didn't know much about him or if he had the courage to use the secret weapon on Japan. After Hiroshima, we all learned about the bomb, and I couldn't believe the damage we'd done. My division, as well as a lot of other Marine Corps divisions, went into Japan after the surrender. When we saw what the real destruction was, how we'd really flattened out Japan and how many civilians we'd killed, we had a collective guilt complex. We wondered, Was it necessary to drop the second bomb? There was a lot of controversy. A lot of people thought we should never have used the bomb. It was just too cruel; it didn't affect only Japan's military, it wiped out so many innocent civilians. We had mixed thoughts: If we had invaded Japan, we would all have been killed, so it was better to kill them. I would say if you took a vote of all the servicemen, probably 90 percent of them were damn glad we used the bomb.

Had Japan never attacked the United States at Pearl Harbor, I don't think we would have used the atomic bomb. But retaliation was the cry word. Also, the Japanese had been cruel to our prisoners, and we didn't like that. Now we had a weapon that would make Japan surrender, so why not use it? Why do it the hard way? It was bad enough to invade the islands—to go to the mainland of Japan would've been really devastating for our forces.

PART 5

Commercial Development and the Oil Business (1945–1964)

CHAPTER 17

Vacationing in Mexico, Building Homes after the War, Commercial Development, and Corruption in Washington and Virginia

In 1945, in addition to completing the critique for the Marine Corps on Iwo Jima and assisting with the construction of the Iwo Jima monument, now known as the Marine War Memorial, I had about three other projects that I had to take care of. But my family was pressuring me to visit because I had not seen them since 1943. So, in spite of the difficulty in getting new cars at that time (most of the automobile manufacturers had been stripped down to build tanks, trucks, and other vehicles for the war effort), I used the influence of Senator Chavez from New Mexico to obtain a Cadillac. I had done him a favor prior to the war, assisting in getting his son, Dennis, a commission in the Marine Corps. So the senator used his influence and I ended up with a 1945 Cadillac sedan. Sue and I drove it to California to enjoy the Christmas holidays with my relatives.

Before we left for California, I had our construction crew start on a new building in Ravenwood—it would be a combination office and home. It was a two-story house, all built of stone, with three bedrooms, a den, and a wing that faced Sleepy Hollow Road. The office could be reached from the house or from the street, and it accommodated about seven real estate salesmen. There we established what we called the Ravenwood Realty Company. We were quite successful. We were not only selling our own homes but were on the open brokerage market. (I had worked as a salesman for a real estate broker during the last two or three years that I was with the government. With my reputation, I merely had to apply to get a license as a broker.)

My partner, Roan, had been released from the service, and when we completed Virginia Forest he was with me in the final phase. Then while I went to California he looked after the various projects we had going. It was important to get our credit established with subcontractors and supply houses and to clean up loose ends. Several real estate offices that had made settlements on some of our homes while we were away were holding the money for us. The lawyer to whom we had given power of attorney had lost about $120,000 of our money while we were in the service, which would be like $5 million today. It was practically all our operating cash. So during the last part of 1945 and 1946, we were very, very busy tying up loose ends plus dealing with new business.

The subcontractors and supply houses were glad to see us come back and get back in business again. They had seen very profitable years during the war and had gained a momentum that they wanted to keep. I don't know whether it was their loyalty to us because we were servicemen or some other factor, but we had very little difficulty. Generally, costs were way up. We had hired good carpenters before the war at 75 cents an hour. When we came home the price was up around $3.50 an hour. We had to really educate ourselves to the new postwar era. The carpenters' union was very good to us and gave us some of its best carpenters. All around, everybody was very nice to us. We were some of the first servicemen released from the war. I had been discharged from the Marine Corps early, so when I came back to Falls Church I was one of the first servicemen they'd seen back there.

But to resume my story: In California, upon the advice of a friend of ours who was a Mexican attorney, Sue and I decided to take a break and go to Mexico City. The new Pan American Highway would be great for our new car. And most of the members of my family felt that before I got back into the harness of building new houses, which was a lot of pressure, I should have a break. I probably showed some stress and concern when I went home because it seemed like my hometown was a little different; things weren't the same. So I agreed, and we took off, not realizing what we were going to get into.

The first negative thing that happened was that we ran into a snowstorm with accumulations of about 20 inches as we were touring through Texas along the Mexican border. We pulled into a town called Del Rio. The hotels were all filled, and the only room we could get was a cheap cabin that was remodeled from a chicken house. About midnight, Sue woke me up claiming something was biting her. The lamp we had was ridiculous—it was just a cord hanging from the ceiling with a bulb on it and a chain. I pulled that on, and when I threw the sheets back, every square inch of the sheet was covered with bedbugs. So we checked out and went to the lobby of the hotel and complained and sat in chairs till daylight. Then we proceeded on to Mexico.

In Monterey, which was a very nice town, we looked for a hotel. On the way, we went the wrong way up a one-way street leading to a factory. We were about halfway up the street when the factory employees came pouring out in their cars, and we caused a gridlock of traffic. The attorney friend of mine in San Fernando had told me that if I ever got into trouble in Mexico, the first thing to do is reach in your pocket and get a fistful of pesos and hand them to the cop. That's the way you greet him. You don't say "How are you" or anything, just reach out and give him a handful of money. And that's what I did. As a consequence, he decided to be our guide, and he had all the cars that were going the right way get out of *our* way so we could go down the street to our hotel the wrong way on a one-way street.

He showed us all around the town and later showed us a drugstore where we could get medicine for our bedbugs. We got a product called Cuprex. On the bottle was a caution sign written in Spanish that said, "Do not leave on for more than 15 minutes. Wash off." After you leave Cuprex on for 15 minutes, it starts nipping at you like little bugs are biting you. But not knowing Spanish, when we had that feeling we thought that the solution was just to pour more of the Cuprex on. So we proceeded down to Mexico, using that medicine, which, as I'll explain later, practically ruined our trip. The scenery was beautiful, the fields were beautiful, the crops were beautiful, the highway was new. We stopped at a little tropical town called Tamazuncharle. We found cabins there that were quite nice and comfortable. We enjoyed our rest there. The little town was located at the base of some very steep mountains, which we had to drive over to get to Mexico City, and as we left the motel the owner gave me some pills. He said, "If your wife should be nervous about going over the mountains, give her one of these."

I said, "What are these?"

He said, "They are knockout pills. They'll put her to sleep."

Actually, I was one who should have used them. Going up those steep mountains, we were confronted by Mexican truck drivers racing down the mountain in the middle of the road. On our right going up was a steel fence, which was broken through about every mile where some truck had gone overboard and fallen about 500 feet down the canyon.

The ride to Mexico City was quite difficult for me because I don't like heights. But I managed to get through, and the scenery was fantastic. In Mexico City, we found the traffic so horrendous that we just parked the car. And where we parked was interesting. Most of the Mexicans, when they stored their cars, put them in a pawn shop. It was much cheaper to pawn your car than it was to pay the high price of parking. We were advised to use taxis. At the hotel, before we parked our car, we were besieged by what they call coyote salesmen. Cars were so difficult to get into Mexico that we had to sign a statement at the border in Laredo for the State Department agreeing not to sell our car. We had at least 20 salesmen hanging around us, begging to buy our car for as much as $10,000 (we paid $2,300 for it in Washington). We were advised by the manager of the hotel not to do it because the coyotes would turn our names in and get a reward anyway—they'd double-cross us.

We had a beautiful room in a very quaint hotel where a group of Mexican movie actors was filming on location. We got the same treatment they did, which was wonderful, except our waiters were wary of us because we were always scratching ourselves. The Cuprex was really unbearable. We had to scratch our eyebrows, our hair, under our clothes—every place we had Cuprex was just biting into us like little insects. Even at a boxing match we went to—I sat next to a Mexican who knew the fighters, and they gamble on the fighters. For the first three bouts, he picked winners for me. I was making money with him. But I was scratching myself and he said, "What's wrong with you?" I said, "I've got lice," and he left me, fast. Even in the restaurants it was embarrassing. The waiters would look at us, wondering why the hell we were scratching ourselves.

The best part of our trip, I think, was our visit to the pyramids out of town in the valley of Teotihuacan. It was a popular place for tourists. While we were walking around one pyramid, a young boy came up to me and wanted to sell me a small figurine. It was a face of a person who lived 4,000 years ago, made of baked clay. He sold it to me for 35 cents American money. I asked him if he had any more and he said, yes, over at his house they had some for sale. Sue and I went to this Mexican stone house. The father was away, and they had a whole big basketful of stuff that they'd taken out of the pyramids a couple of nights before. They'd dig under the corner of the pyramid and get stuff that was buried long before the lava flows came in. I bought a whole clothes basket full of stuff mixed with mud and clay from the boy for $5. When we took it back to the United States and crossed the Mexican border, the guards didn't even pay any attention to it. All they were worried about was some liquor we had in the car.

Because of our problem with the lice, which was getting worse, we decided to leave Mexico early. We would stay for a bullfight and then leave the following day. Traffic in Mexico City was governed by automobile horn. The first person to blow his horn at the inter-section had the right-of-way. So it was not only noisy but scary as hell. We took a cab to the bullfight and shared it with a young couple in our hotel. Cars were parked not only on the curb but in the center of the street, leaving just a very small aisle to get through. The char-acter we had for a driver came to a tight place and just crash-banged right on through, ruining all four of his fenders and scratching up the fenders of the cars to either side. Eight fenders got marred at once, and he didn't even look back; he just kept racing down the street to the bullfight ring.

Sue couldn't stand to see the toreador ram the sword down the back of a bull's neck—she practically fainted. So we left after three bulls were killed. The Mexicans go absolutely crazy at bullfights. I had a movie camera with me and I took pictures of the whole thing; it's very colorful. There were 150,000 people all cheering for the toreador against the wild bull. I'm glad to know that in America we don't allow that sort of killing. But the bullfighters in Mexico were greater heroes than our movie stars.

Our return trip from Mexico City to Laredo, Texas, was not as exciting as riding down. We were anxious to get back to the States. We had made a deal with a dealer in Laredo that we would consider selling the car to him for $4,000. Sue was worried about our upholstery being contaminated with lice. We had decided to keep using the Cuprex till we got to Laredo. If we still had the bugs biting us, we would consider selling our car. At the hotel in Laredo, the Mexican car dealer met us for breakfast on a Sunday morning. We had decided that we'd accept his offer. We didn't even have to have the title in case we'd had it financed somewhere. In turn, a little syndicate that included the president of the bank, who opened the bank so we could get the cash and make a deal, would take the car across the Rio Grande River, clean it up, and eventually ship it to Spain, where they'd get $20,000 for it. That was the deal. The bank workers were very polite. They said, "We will furnish a car for you to use while you stay in Laredo, and we'll have your clothes sent home." Sue decided that our clothes were full of lice and we should give them away. We told the bank people to disinfect them before they gave them to anyone.

After two days in Laredo, we went to Dallas, Texas, on a small plane and then caught a Capitol Airlines flight to Washington, D.C. As we approached Washington, a big storm had moved in and we could not land, so the plane proceeded on to New York City. New York was snowed in; we couldn't land there, either. Because fuel was getting low, the plane touched down in Buffalo, New York. We were lucky we didn't crash, for there was about a foot of snow on the ground. Fortunately a strong wind had swept most of the snow off the runway. The passengers were all taken to a nice hotel. I immediately went to a barber shop and told the barber I wanted to get a haircut. He said, "What the hell is smelling in your hair?"

"It's Cuprex; it's supposed to kill lice," I said. "You'd better give me a short haircut."

He said, "I've got a better idea. I'm going to turn you over to this other fellow, but don't tell him you've got lice." He wouldn't cut my hair. After I got my hair cut, I went to a drugstore to get more medicine. I found the Cuprex, but with the label written in English I learned what the caution sign said: "Do not leave on for more than 15 minutes."

The following day, we were transported by train to Washington, D.C. Sue and I were glad to get on the train for a change because we'd been on airplanes for half a day and all the previous night, and we were getting a little scared about it. We stayed in a hotel a few days. Then we rented a small house for a couple of months until our new house was completed in Ravenwood. We were again without a car—I couldn't believe the scarcity of cars and how hard they were to get. The best I could do, through a friend, was to buy a used DeSoto. I kept that for about a month. It had so damn many things wrong with it that I wanted a new car. I managed to get one through an old connection. Before the war, a young Jewish doctor—Siegel was his name—came to ask me if I could help him find a place to open an office. Fortunately, I knew of a place over a drugstore—the only drugstore in Falls Church, Virginia. He converted that space into a chiropractic office. Patients would deposit $3 in a cigar box in the waiting room and proceed to the living room for treatment, which would usually be more of a skin massage than anything else. He had a clicker in his hand that sounded like vertebras were popping. He became very prosperous. I had learned that he was a silent partner in a new Lincoln agency out in Bethesda, Maryland. I contacted him and through him I got hold of a new Lincoln. (I was happy with the Lincoln. When we were driving through Mexico, wherever we'd pull up to a hotel, everyone would come running out just to see our car. Cadillac was *the* car, and if you owned a Cadillac, you owned the world. In Washington after the war, the kind of car you had didn't seem to make much difference. Hell, if you could get any kind of a new car you had to be somebody, since cars were so damn scarce. But I liked the Lincoln. I drove it to California twice in later years without any problems. I did notice that my employees, when I had the Cadillac, would call me "Mr. Poppelman." When I had the Lincoln, they'd call me "Ray.")

Getting back into the harness as a builder was difficult at first. We set up a crash program to finish the houses in Ravenwood. By about 1947 we had built Section 1 of Ravenwood. We had 14 houses there; that was about half of what we had planned. Section 2 was about the same—we still had building to do there. Section 3, our new development, ran all the way to Leesburg Pike—and Leesburg Pike then was *the* commercial street. It was also a historical spot—Robert E. Lee had made the last stand there of the Southern army coming into Washington during the Civil War. Out of the 25 acres I'd bought in Section 3, I reserved ten acres for future commercial development. The top of the ridge there, which was the highest point within 25 miles of Washington, D.C., was the dividing line between my commercial property and my residential property.

In about 1950, a man by the name of David Tishman, a leading entrepreneur from New York City, walked into my office and wanted to talk to me in private. He said he had a problem, and he thought that perhaps since I knew most of the officials in Fairfax County, I could be of some help. He had placed a $6 million bid for some real estate property for a large housing project with Judge Brown of Fairfax County. The bids were to be opened on the following Monday, but he was very anxious to retract his bid, which he thought probably would be the highest one presented to the court, because the property had been misrepresented to him—it did not have a major sewer line nearby. His problem was that he might not get back the money he'd put in escrow; he might be forced to turn it over to the property owners.

By coincidence, I knew Judge Brown very well. He had handled a divorce case for me, his law partner had gone to school with me at the University of Maryland, and I had served on a couple of his juries. I did not indicate this to Mr. Tishman, but told him I would see what I could do.

I went to see Judge Brown, explained the situation, and said that I thought Tishman had a reason to complain, that there was merit to his wish to retract his bid. Judge Brown asked me if I had been paid a fee for coming to see him and I said, no, I did not want to put a cloud on his reputation, and a payment might reflect some sort of bribery or seem like I was using my friendship with him to get the favor done for Tishman. (Tishman probably would have paid me dearly had I asked him, but all I wanted in return was for him to take me to dinner.)

He listened to my arguments and told me to have Mr. Tishman

come out to see him—that the judge would have to prepare a legal document. When I called Tishman at his hotel, he was in ecstasy—he couldn't believe what I had accomplished. The following Monday, he went out early to the courthouse by taxicab, talked to Judge Brown, and Judge Brown released his bid so that the money he'd put in escrow would be returned to him.

Tishman then invited me to dinner at his hotel and told me that any time I needed any help for anything, I should call him because he sure appreciated my help. He said he had never had anybody treat him so well. So we parted. Through the years, he always sent me beautiful Christmas cards and added a thank you note and reminded me to be sure to see him if I ever came to New York City. Today, if you drive through Beverly Hills off Wilshire Boulevard on Miracle Mile, you see a tall office building—I think it's the biggest one in Beverly Hills—and the sign on top of the building says "Tishman."

In about 1953, when I was developing the last section of Ravenwood and just as I was progressing nicely, a bombshell hit the housing business. Inflation had hit the country. Building prices were going up and the government thought that if it required greater down payments on housing, it might retard the housing business. Also, building materials at that time were a bit scarce because so much had been used in the war effort. So Regulation X was imposed by the government. It was a deterrent to all the building businesses. It almost bankrupt a lot of construction companies. I was in trouble, too, because I had sold a lot of my houses that were under construction by contract, specifying the amount of payment that would be made. In some cases, I was specifying mortgage loans at 75 percent of the building cost and requiring as little as $10,000 down payments. (That was popular at that time—low down payments and big mortgages, which is what Regulation X was designed to counter.)

I was in a bind. I went to see all the mortgage brokers in Washington for suggestions about what I could do, but no one had any good advice until I ran into a small-town broker who said he had heard that there was a man in New York City by the name of Joe Markel who was a genius at arranging financial deals. He was sort of a magician with money. My thought was, What could I lose? I was not making anything and I was facing bankruptcy.

So I went alone to New York City to find Joe Markel. I went to the Stock Market to ask some of the brokers there if they had on record a man by the name of Markel. They said no, but suggested that I go to the Chemical National Bank Building, which was just down the street. Many entrepreneurs and mortgage brokers and financiers were in that building, and I might find his name posted on the directory.

And sure enough, I found the name "Joseph C. Markel." I went to his office on the 20th floor, and his secretary said that he would be there in about 15 minutes, and I could wait for him. While I waited, I explained my problem to a young attorney who was there. He thought that if anybody could help me, Mr. Markel could. When Mr. Markel came in, I was expecting to see a short, fat, bald-headed man, a typical Jewish financier. To my great surprise, in walked a tall, handsome man who could have passed for an older John Wayne. He asked what I wanted to see him about, and I told him that I had a problem with Regulation X. He said, "A lot of people are having that trouble. Have you had lunch yet?"

I said, "No, I'll just wait here for you."

"Oh," he said, "come on. I know a place where they've got good food."

We walked down the street a couple of blocks and went into a businessman's club mostly filled with Jewish people. I had never seen such a beautiful display of food. There were beautifully carved images of birds and ducks and geese made in ice atop a long table with a great spread of food. In addition, there were waiters who would bring your food to your table. Mr. Markel introduced me to a few people as "Mr. Poppelman from Washington, D.C." They assumed I was some sort of a big shot.

Then came the biggest surprise of all: Who should I see but the man I had aided in Falls Church—Mr. David Tishman! I didn't realize at the time that he was such a big operator in New York City. He'd built lots of skyscrapers and was quite a promoter. Well, he got up and embraced me. And this was quite a surprise to the man I was with. They were friends; they stepped aside and talked so I couldn't hear them, but I caught some of what they said anyway. Tishman told Markel, "Take care of Poppelman. Give him anything he wants. I will underwrite any project he has." It was almost too much for me. I just couldn't believe that suddenly I had two of New York's greatest financiers behind me. Of course, the dinner was very elegant, but I was too nervous to enjoy it.

When we went back to Markel's office, he said, "I will turn my attorneys over to you. But before you leave, give me a clue as to why your property should be exempt from Regulation X."

I said, "Well, for one thing, I served our Marine Corps in China in 1927 and I was in World War II as a line officer with the Fifth Division on Iwo Jima. I served my country well. I also played on the Marine Corps football team for two years. I had a good record as a marine. Another thing I think I should have credit for, and the government should respect, is that before 1945, I built 200 homes under the Private Defense Housing Plan—houses for workers who were coming to Washington to help in the war effort. They needed places to live, and housing was very tight. I built over 200 houses that were sold practically at my cost at $6,000 apiece to make it easy for the workers. (That was the law—no house could be sold to a war worker for over $6,000.) Under the pressure of the draft board that wanted to take me in the army, I had to finish up 200 houses when obtaining materials was tough; they had to be approved by the War Production Board. I accomplished that before I went into the service. I think the government should take that into consideration, especially when I'm facing bankruptcy."

Markel had a secretary taking notes, and he asked me a few questions. I told him there was also one thing that he might be interested in—that in 1931, the *New York Daily News* picked an all-Jewish All-American football team, and I was on the team. (Because my last name has *m-a-n* in it, they thought I was Jewish!) I also told him that the *Washington Post* had interviewed me and wrote a story stating that Ray Poppelman was the only German who ever made the all-Jewish football team.

He said, "You look like a football player." I told him that a man on the same team was a movie director in Hollywood whose name was Aaron Rosenberg. I had met him on a fishing boat one time. Aaron Rosenberg had told me, "Ray, what you should have done is kept your mouth shut" about not being Jewish. "You'd have been a movie director out here with me." The interesting part, though, was that while everybody thought I was a Jew, I was getting all kinds of offers for jobs. And when the *Washington Post* noted that I was not Jewish, all my invitations to make speeches at banquets and so forth, and offers for jobs, were retracted.

Anyway, Mr. Markel told me that he was going to have his attorneys in New York appeal to the proper government officials. Shortly after that I got a phone call requesting that I go to Richmond, Virginia, to see a man by the name of Snow—he was a bureaucrat, the head of the Regulation X program. I went to Richmond with my secretary. Mr. Snow was very polite. "Mr. Poppelman, we have reviewed your case. I just have a few more questions about your subdivision of Ravenwood. Did you have any of your loans under federal housing?"

I said, "A few, a few years ago. Not many."

He asked me a few questions. Then he said, "I see by your report that you were on Iwo Jima."

I said, "Yes, I went the whole program—36 days. We had 7,000 marines killed, and I knew most of them."

He turned to his secretary, who was taking notes, and said, "By God, I'm not going to let the government treat our veterans this way." He said, "I will take care of your exemption. You may not get the official papers for a few weeks, but from now on, you go back there and just go about your business the way you want to."

This was just another instance in my life where I did a good turn for somebody and then somehow it came back around and something good happened to me.

I saw Mr. Markel two or three times after that for dinner when he was on business in Washington. In addition to being a mortgage banker, he also owned one of the largest trucking firms in America. He sold the idea to the president and Congress that we had to be very careful about foreign countries taking over any of our trucking businesses because if a foreign country got control of the trucking industry in America, it could call a strike and cause a catastrophe. So many people in the cities depend on trucking for their food, and to shut down the trucking industry at one time would bankrupt America. Markel apparently had an "in" at the White House because he told his secretary, "If I have to, I'll take Poppelman's case to the president."

In New York, when I met Tishman at the Jewish club, he asked me, "Why the hell didn't you come and see me? I would have taken care of you. I have connections in Washington, too." But it hadn't dawned on me to go see him because he was not a mortgage broker; he was an entrepreneur. He built things, whereas Markel was supposed to be a mortgage broker. Tishman had told Markel that I had done him a big favor and not charged him anything. Markel also gave me mortgage money for permanent loans. He said, "You don't even have to ask me; just tell my secretary what you want." I had a blank check. And he would even take my second trust paper if I wanted him to take it.

I had a life of ups and downs, but I had a life of some great breaks. There had to be some divine power behind me to have things occur the way they did, to have Tishman walk into my office and then to meet Markel under those circumstances. I caught Markel when he was hungry and he wanted to go to lunch, so he took me with him, and there was Tishman.

One thing I learned about New York: It's a great city, and people shouldn't let those great big buildings scare them. Because when you get inside, they reduce down to rooms. And in that one room, you're still with a human being. It's like a piece of advice Tishman gave me after I knew him better—that to be a good businessman, you have to learn how to talk to bankers. "When you talk to a banker, remember, he's selling you money; he's not giving you money. You're buying money from him. Don't let him look down his nose at you. You're his customer when you ask him for a loan."

He said, "If you ever have a banking problem, let me do your talking. I can get that banker squared away."

During the height of the Cold War, everybody wanted houses with basements—for use as radiation shelters. So I and two other men dug out a basement under my last house in Ravenwood. Of all the houses I ever built, this was the most difficult one to sell. The market had dropped; we were going into sort of a depression. I advertised the house with realtors for three weeks in a row. I started at $32,000 and worked my way down to $28-something but couldn't sell it. The brokers weren't having any luck, so I decided to advertise the house myself and sell it on offers.

The first man who came in the door was an army general. My pickup truck was parked illegally in front of the house going downhill on the left side. The general drove up in his car and parked on the right side, the correct way. When he came in the front door, he pulled the knob off the door—gave it a jerk and the knob came loose. He walked in and said, "What the hell kind of a house is this? Goddamn hardware won't even hang together." He looked around and picked on the house a little bit. I knew I was in trouble then; I knew he was not going to buy anything. His wife sort of liked it. It was a small house, but the rooms were nice. There were two bedrooms with a den, all on one floor. Half the house underneath was cleared out for a basement; the general liked that. But they were not interested.

They went out the front door and I thanked them for coming in. I thought, "It's about lunchtime, so I'll go too." So I left with them. We went out to the street; he got in his car, and I got in the truck. I forgot about shifting and got the wrong gear, and I went forward and slammed into his car—bent the radiator and the fender. He was pretty decent about it. I gave him my insurance card and told him to fix it up, and if he wanted the house, I'd knock $1,000 off. He didn't want to see the house or me again; he'd had it.

Nobody else came; there was no response to my ads. I called the brokers and said, "What the hell should I do?"

They said, "Just hang on." I decided that if anybody offered me $26,000, I'd grab it. It was my last house; I wanted to get out. I had finished up the curb and gutter and sidewalks all by myself, and I had no crew there anymore. My partner had gone out on his own and took most of my key men with him, which was OK.

Now came a break; I used to get a lot of them. The following week, an admiral from the navy and his wife came to look at the house. They were from California. He was a general counsel for the Navy Department—the head of their legal department. He came in, looked around, and liked it. He went in the bathroom and yelled at his wife, "Come here. I want to show you something." I had used some extra tile left over that was all white to make the whole bathroom white, which made the room look bigger. At that time, colored tile was the rage, and you had to have a colored bathroom to sell the house. But the navy officer of high rank loved that bathroom. "Thank God somebody had the guts to build a white bathroom," he told me. "We have three more houses to look at. Then we will come back."

I said, "Well, don't come back here; come to my house. I live down the street," and I gave him the number of my house.

About 2:00 in the afternoon the doorbell rang and it was the admiral and his wife. I told them the price was up for offer. They said, "We hope you won't be offended at our offer, but we have looked at other houses and we think that a fair price on your house would be $34,500." He said, "Now, that'll be cash, and there's a few little things we'd like to have changed," which were minor. I was hoping I'd sell that house for $26,000, and here I had an offer for $34,500 cash, with no mortgage or anything!

Now the story gets interesting. About three years later he came to see me and said, "I have been transferred to Europe. We're going to have to sell our house. Would you sell our house for us?"

I declined but gave him the name of a real estate company. He wanted to know what they should ask for the house. I said, "I'd push it up close to $40,000. You deserve some profit out of it. There's inflation, and you're in the best part of the subdivision—you're up high." Guess who bought the house? The army general I'd run into! When the admiral told me the general's name, I didn't tell him about my episode. I thought to myself, "Geez, it's funny what goes on in this world."

Another interesting incident concerned the two-story colonial house I'd built for the vice-president of Westinghouse Corporation. His wife was somewhat of a nut. After we had the house almost completed, she went to Washington, D.C., and bought a very expensive rug for the living room that was six inches too long. It was a monster rug; she must've paid a fortune for it. She wanted it to look like wall-to-wall carpet, so instead of exchanging it for a smaller one, she had us tear down the whole end of the house, with the fireplace and all, and add six inches. We had to split the bricks to make it fit—it was a hell of a project. Her husband fussed about it, but there was not a damn thing he could do to change her mind. She must have had the money in the family because at first the husband did not object to all her idiosyncrasies.

Changes came so fast and furious under this woman that I told her husband we'd have to renegotiate the contract. We did, and one of the conditions was that the wife, who was really screwy in my opinion, would remain in Florida until the house was finished; she could have no more to say about the house. I would finish the house only with her husband; his orders would be my command.

We finished up the house and were ready for the painters to come in. We had built a large storage cabinet in the center of the house for the owner's hobby—collecting rare and antique wines and liquors from Europe. Instead of taking the liquor out and putting it under lock and key while the house was painted, the owner left it in the closet, assuming that the painters wouldn't touch it. Now, most of the painters I worked with had something of an alcoholism problem. When they went to paint the house, they really made a dent in that liquor. That was only one thing that I had to make compensation for.

When the wife came home, we had a problem with the doors. She had ordered some extra-thick padding to go under the rugs and carpet. She also had changed the doors. Instead of the authentic panel doors for a colonial house, she fell in love with straight doors without panels that you use in a modern house. And those were usually quite flimsy. She wanted me to trim the doors down because the padding she was putting under all her carpet raised the rug so that the doors wouldn't open and close. I told her I refused to do it; she'd have to get another contractor. And I wasn't going to talk to her husband about it. One day while the carpenters were all having lunch out of their lunch buckets under a tree, she drove up and said, "Which one of you carpenters would like to make some extra money after work?" (I didn't know about this.) A carpenter's helper, who was really not a carpenter, volunteered to do it. The other carpenters just laid back; they knew about her. After work the helper went with this lady and they sawed off the bottoms of the doors. But because the wood was flimsy, the doors splintered and were ruined. The owner had to get another builder—I refused to touch it—to come in and replace all the doors. She was a nuisance right to the bitter end.

She held a housewarming party when the house was completed. All their friends came to see their new house. She did one thing that upset the whole neighborhood: She told her guests that all the people who lived in the subdivision were her servants and that she and her husband owned all the property! I don't know whatever happened to the family. They lived in that house about two years, sold it, and moved, which we were quite glad about. She was just an absolute nuisance. But the husband was an important guy and he had money, and he was putting up with her for some reason or another.

Another story concerns an heir of the Union Pacific Railroad, whose husband was a colonel in the air force in Europe. She bought a house in our subdivision. And of all the houses, I'll be damned if we didn't forget one thing, which was a complete oversight: We left out a closet in a bedroom. Well, that was easily taken care of. When we got to the painting stage, we called up a company known as Bunny Painting Company (on the side of the truck was a picture of a rabbit). The owner was a roly-poly guy weighing almost 300 pounds. Much to our surprise, when we got close to finishing up the painting, the woman decided to change the paint color or there was something else wrong, and she wanted Bunny to do the work. "Don't send anybody down but Bunny." Bunny was the owner; he had several painters. Much to everybody's surprise, this woman and Bunny had an affair. One day Bunny came to my office in a new Cadillac. He said, "Ray, Mrs. [So-and-so] bought me this new Cadillac. She's also going to buy me a farm out in Kansas. She also wants to do some work in the basement." And he said, "By the way, if you ever need any payroll money, just let me know. This woman's giving me all the money I need and more."

Next thing I knew, the colonel arrived from overseas. He said, "I want to talk to you privately. What are these stories I hear about my wife and a guy by the name of Bunny?"

I told him the truth. I said, "I think your wife needs some psychiatric help. I can't believe what's going on." She had really fallen in love with that fat fellow. So they gave up the contract and I resold the house. I hadn't seen Bunny for months when he came in one day, and I said, "Where the hell you been, Bunny?"

He said, "Out to my farm in Kansas." He finally went back to his wife (he was married) and he got out of the painting business and I never saw him again.

The next story concerns the third house I built in Ravenwood, which would take us back to probably 1940. The house, which was on a corner, had a vacant lot behind it. One day a big limousine drove up and a little old lady got out of the car, came in, and said, "Oh, if I had this house I would change this and change that." And she wanted to know about the lot next door. I said it was available. Well, she wanted me to get a bid from a swimming pool company to build a swimming pool there. And she went over the whole house with some wonderful ideas. She said, "I will be back tomorrow to talk to you again." She didn't ask the price of the house or anything, and she had a chauffeur waiting for her. So she got in the car and left. The next day she came back with a list of stuff—all good suggestions—about what I should change.

I jumped the gun and got my gang in there and we started making changes. I assumed she was going to buy it, the way she talked. One day I said, "Well, Mrs. [So-and-so], before we go any further, I've got to get a contract."

She said, "Oh, we'll have to talk to my lawyer about that."

So I agreed to go to town with her. I got into her limousine and the chauffeur drove us into Washington. We went to her lawyer's office, which was quite swanky. I explained to the lawyer, "Mrs. [So-and-so] is interested in a house I have, and she has a lot of changes. Maybe you could make up a contract for us."

He said, "Mr. Poppelman, I'd like to talk to you in private." We went into the next room. "She is Mrs. [So-and-so]. She is in a mental hospital, but she has an arrangement in her estate for her chauffeur to take her riding. She has bought at least 50 houses around Washington. Her hobby is going in and making suggestions on how to change houses. She's in a dream world. Whatever damages you have, make up a bill for me." And she had suggested some wonderful changes. In fact, they were so good that I used them in the rest of the houses I was building, and I eventually sold some to the general consul of the company that controls federal communications.

The house she had made changes to was bought by a young fellow named Cattone who was an attorney. The day he bought the house we had a mob of people out to look at it in response to an ad, and he was running around saying, "I'm going to buy this house."

I said, "Don't bother me." I thought he was a nuisance.

Finally his wife came up to me and said, "Why won't you sell us the house?"

I said, "He's your husband?" He was just dressed in casual clothes; looked like he'd been working in the garden or something. (He was the kind of fellow that, to look at him, you wouldn't appreciate his intelligence. He was a smart lawyer.) They bought the house.

We weren't on city water then, so we had a well dug—at about 50 feet you had all the water you wanted. We also had some kind of a bottled gas that you'd run into a stove, which was put in the back of the house. Whoever put the tank in on that house didn't have it connected right, and some of the gas dripped down and got into the well so that when you drank the well water you could taste it. I called the well-driller out and told him to go down to the bottom of that well and see what the trouble was. (I didn't know the gas was leaking at that time.) He got into the well and lit a match, and the well exploded—flames exploded six feet out of the well.

He got burned, and the fuel company's insurance later settled with him for $3,000, which I didn't know anything about; he could've gotten more. After we got him out of the well, we put a cover on it and I called the fuel company about it. But in the meantime, you could take the lid off the well, light a match, and WHOOM! the gas would go up. A guy from the Interior Department came out to examine it, and he decided that it was a certain kind of fuel—that we had struck oil. Word went around Falls Church about striking oil on Ravenwood. The owner, Cattone, moved out of the house and had to live somewhere else for a while because there was no water. The company that furnished the bottled gas settled with Cattone, too. But for a long time, the word went around Falls Church, Virginia, about how "they struck oil in Ravenwood." Later, of course, Falls Church extended its water lines down to Ravenwood. Then the county eventually grew up around it. We were way out in the country in those days.

The property facing Leesburg Pike, which would also be facing Washington, D.C., was a problem. I had three acres on one side with a nice main street going through my property, and five acres on the other. The county zoning map showed that property as commercial, but I could not develop it until I paid off the board of supervisors. It was a corrupt county at that time. I had decided to build an apartment house, and I had the plans drawn up. When I went before the board to get the apartments, they turned me down. Through Jim McIlvane, my friend who was established in the county and knew how to pay off the board of supervisors, I found out that the fee was generally $25,000 per vote (there were seven board members) if you wanted the property zoned. One of the supervisors came to me and said, "I'll get your zoning on one side of the road if you'll deed off the property on the right side of the road to me."

I think I had paid $50,000 on the first time around. Two guys claimed they could get it for me, but they couldn't. I went to see my friend McIlvane, who had been an inspector in Washington on some big projects, sewer lines, and so forth. He got inside information that the White House was going to run a tunnel from the White House up to the mountains, to Camp David, which is the camp where presidents spend weekends. McIlvane went to a couple of sewer contractors named Nance and Vividelli. (They did sewer work on my project later; I knew both of them.) Nance had gone to school with the millionaire H. L. Hunt of Texas. They were friends, and once a year they'd meet somewhere and have old-time get-togethers. McIlvane told Nance, "If you guys can get yourself bonded—you're going to have to have a $10 million bond—I can tip you off about what the bids are going to be. You can underbid the other contractors." Nance went to H. L. Hunt, and Hunt agreed to guarantee their bonds. To make a long story short, Nance and Vividelli got the major contract to put that tunnel in and they subcontracted a lot of the work out. I went down to see them at work one day. They had taken Dupont Circle, the most prominent memorial circle in town, and put a big hole in the ground for an elevator so their trucks could go up and down. They trucked out all the dirt, mostly at night, and the tunnel was put in. McIlvane got enough money kicked back to finance a private bank. He opened up a building and loan association in Fairfax County and also bought land. Nance and Vividelli made millions and retired to Florida. McIlvane bought a house from me—a nice stone house, beautifully built, in Ravenwood. Anyway, when he found out I was having trouble with my zoning, he said, "Ray, Ann Wilkins is chairman. She and I are doing a lot of business together. I think I can get your zoning for you."

I said, "If you can get the zoning, we'll go in together. I'll put up the land, you get the financing, and we'll put in a shopping center."

About that time—it must have been about 1960—I was palling around with a fellow by the name of Bob Plimpton. He and I were trustees in a dowsing organization in Vermont. We met in New York City to have lunch with his cousin George Plimpton, who is now a writer. Knowing about our interest in dowsing, especially water witching, George said, "Did you hear about the woman who predicted that a certain stock would jump 12 points on a certain day?" We said no. He said, "This woman is at [So-and-so's] restaurant. You can get readings from her if you tip the maitre d' pretty well. She predicted a stock would go up 12 points on a certain day, and it did. From that time on, people have flocked into this restaurant to talk to her. Why don't you guys go up and talk to her?"

So we decided we would. The restaurant was up on 63rd Street. We went in there and Bob went first. We gave the maitre d' $10, and the psychic charged $3. Bob went out and he said, "Jesus Christ, that woman told me all about my past. She's fantastic!"

I went in, and she had some cards she laid out on the table. I said, "You don't have to worry about all that fanfare."

She said, "Mr. Poppelman, I get the impression that you're involved in an oil well." And I was. We were drilling a small well down in Kentucky through some friends of mine. She said, "You're going to get a dry hole. You should've moved 2,000 feet southeast."

I thought, "Where the hell's she getting that information? She must have talked to Bob."

The next thing, she said, "Are you involved in a real estate deal?"

And I said, "Yes."

She said, "Whatever you're involved in is going to be a failure." At that time McIlvane had put up an application for the apartment house for me. I had advanced $50,000 for payoffs. It turned out that some women in the area stormed the hearings at the board of super-visors' meeting, and they got scared and backed off and it was de-nied. I think there were other supervisors who wanted to get paid off, too.

I figured, "Well, that damn Bob, he's the one who tipped this woman off about me." Because Bob knew I was interested in all this stuff. Next thing, she said, "You're going to take a trip very soon."

I said, "How soon? Within a year?"

"No, sooner than that; in a few months."

I figured all fortunetellers say you're going to take a trip. Some-time you *are* going to take a trip. Anyway, she also said a couple of other things that really surprised me because I knew Bob didn't know that information.

The fortuneteller said, "You know, Mr. Poppelman, when I look at you I see a big department store. The zoning you're trying for is failing, but I think you'd be successful with a department store."

When I told Bob Plimpton about it, he told me, "Hell, that woman told me about things that she could've never known." I went back to Washington and found out that our zoning for the apartment house had failed. Jim McIlvane stopped at my house for breakfast and said, "Ray, the goddamn zoning last night went to hell. You're not going to get it."

I said, "Well, Mac, tell you what. I went to a fortuneteller in New York City and she said when she looked at me she saw a depart-ment store, and she said we were not going to fail."

As he went out the door, he took a bunch of envelopes from his pocket. He said, "Ray, sketch me what a department store would look like over on your property."

I said, "Why?"

He said, "I'm going to New York. I heard from somebody that Lord & Taylor [the department chain] was looking for a place."

He went to New York that day and talked to the Lord & Taylor people and up and got a commitment—if we could get the zoning, they would lease it from us. Then McIlvane said to me, "Ray, this is going to take a little time. Why don't you take a vacation somewhere?"

I said, "Well, I'd like to go to Europe." The reason I wanted to go to Europe was because that psychic woman told me I was going to take a trip. In the meantime, I had received a letter from the British Society of Dowsers—they wanted me to come to England and make a speech because I was a trustee of the American Society of Dowsers.

He said, "Hell, go on to Europe, and I'll take care of things here. I'll give you a $10,000 fee for an option."

In the meantime, Sue's aunt had died and she inherited $5,000. So we had $15,000 to go to Europe. We went to England and leased a car for a few days and went to Tunbridge Wells, where I made a talk to a roomful of British people interested in the phenomenon of the dowsing rod. Their organization had been going on for over 20 years. I gave a good talk about what was going on with the farmers in America and how they would find water wells with divining rods. The rest of the trip was quite successful, too.

McIlvane got his boys together and they had our hearing with the board of supervisors at 4:00 in the morning, and that's when they forced my zoning through. We got the zoning for a department store and McIlvane got a 99-year lease with Lord & Taylor. All of a sudden, within 30 days we had a big building going up. McIlvane put up $20 million to build the building that became the department store. In addition to that, he later leased the other corner for a big office building, which is still there. I'm still getting income from

The Lord & Taylor
Department Store in
Falls Church, Virginia,
now owned by Sears.

that and I still have title to the big building. Lord & Taylor was forced out in later years after the character of the area changed, so Sears now has the big store. It's quite interesting how it all worked out and how the prediction of this fortuneteller turned out. (Altogether, McIlvane paid five of the supervisors $25,000 apiece. We got our controlling vote.)

When I was initially turned down for the apartment house, I went to an attorney who was running for the board of supervisors. I told him the story and he said, "If you let me use your office area for a big sign, I'll represent you and see what I can do." I also went around to women's groups and told them the story. I campaigned like hell against Ann Wilkins, chairman of the board. I also went to the Internal Revenue Service and the FBI and found out they already had investigations against the board. When I went to the FBI, they said, "Mr. Poppelman, we have a big file on these people. You don't have to do anything; just lay back."

Ann Wilkins's husband was the one who wanted to make a deal with me—if I'd give him half my land he'd get the other half zoned. Turns out he went to the federal penitentiary, as did two others. They had been making deals with everybody who came to the county.

One member of the board of supervisors even called me up and said, "Poppelman, if you can have a white Thunderbird in my driveway by Sunday morning for my wife and leave a sack of small bills, not over $5, in the car for me totaling (I think it was) $15,000, you'll have my vote and you'll get your zoning." That's the way the bastards talked; I couldn't believe it.

The American people have no idea what's going on among their elected officers. When I worked in the government, there was a woman who was in charge of a section near mine. Her husband was a necktie salesman in a haberdashery. After I left the government and went into business in Virginia, she found out I was getting pretty important. She called me and said, "Ray, do you think you can get a job for my husband in Fairfax County?"

I said, "Well, I don't know. What kind of work does he want?"

She said, "Anything. He's got to get out of that haberdashery job."

So I got him on the zoning commission through friends of mine. And you know what? That son of a bitch wanted $25,000 from me when I needed his vote. After all that I had done! I said, "I don't have that kind of money."

He said, "Well, I'll take a couple of your lots down at Ravenwood."

When McIlvane told me what was really going on, he said, "Ray, you've got to play ball." He did all right on that deal, too. McIlvane today is a big millionaire, but his eyesight's bad. His two sons just finished the deal on a big Coca-Cola bottling plant in Hagerstown, Maryland. Jim had buddies in the White House and could get anything done. Jim's always said to me, "Ray, wherever you go, take old 'Bill' with you. Money talks."

CHAPTER 18

Sailing Days, Living in Florida, and Drilling for Oil in Kentucky and Texas

When I was completing Ravenwood, Section 3, I hired Howard Chappell, a historian and a great marine architect, to design a boat for me especially for use on Chesapeake Bay. The boat was 34 feet long with a hull that was ideal for the shallow waters of the tributaries and rivers of the bay. I'd finish work on Fridays and drive down to Galesville, Maryland, get on the boat, spend two days on the water, and come back. During the next few years, Sue and I took two trips down the Inland Coastal Waterway to Florida. We had fantastic experiences on these trips. We'd usually run the engine about half speed, put a jib up front to catch the breeze, and where the canals were wide, sometimes I'd put up full sail.

When we began sailing, Sue and I were novices, but we decided to go by ourselves to Florida. The first day out there was a big storm in Chesapeake Bay. We pulled into the Solomon Islands in lower Chesapeake Bay and were laid up there for about three days until the big blow was over. During that time, we met people from other boats who were also going south. One of them was an old sea captain who used to sail fertilizer ships out of Australia. He'd been on the water since he was four years old. He and his wife were in a

ketch-style sailboat. One of the editors of *Rudder* magazine was in a
40-foot schooner-type sailboat. There was also a young fellow who
had worked in a shipyard in Maine. He had married a widow who
had three or four children. With the widow's money, he bought a
big schooner about 55 or 60 feet long. Another young fellow had
lost his wife and was so grieved that he quit his job in Washington
and bought a small sailboat, about 26 feet; he was alone.

So we had a rather mixed bag of "sailors" in a fleet going down
the Intracoastal Waterway. We would all anchor and tie up at the
same place each night, and in the morning our commodore, the old
sea captain, and his wife would read the tide books and decide when
we'd leave, where we'd go, and when we'd stop. In the South Carolina area, we got separated in a storm. But through our ship-to-shore
radios and some shrimp boat captains, we got back together again,
except for the one fellow in the small sailboat. We never found him,
and we assumed he had been lost at sea.

We went on to Florida and spent the winter on our boat and
came back in the spring. Five years later, I was in Fort Lauderdale,
walking down the dock, when somebody yelled, "Ray! Ray!" I looked
up at a great big 60-foot yacht, and there was the fellow from Washington in a beautiful sports coat with brass buttons and a seaman's
cap! He had reached Florida, and he married a very rich woman
and stayed there. She bought him the big yacht, and they were living in a very fine home. He took Sue and me to his home and showed
us around. Here was a boy who had been really dejected, had quit
his job, and he wound up marrying a millionaire.

On my second trip to Florida a few years later, I went down
with a friend. Two-thirds of the way down, at Christmastime, we
docked so that my friend could go home. Sue, who joined me for the
rest of the trip to Florida, had a friend in Washington named Gracie

Sue in front of our boat the *Amber Sue*,
Fort Lauderdale, Florida, circa 1950–1952.
The borrowed Cadillac is at left.

Siglock. Gracie had a brother in the Coral Gables area of Miami who owned a big restaurant. When we introduced ourselves he said, "You folks don't have a car, do you?"

I said, "No."

"Well, I have an extra Cadillac you can use while you're down here."

So we spent the winter in Florida using his Cadillac, and we had a great time. On the way back the next spring, it must have been about 1952, we met two brothers in Savannah, Georgia, who were nationally known sailors. They had been tugboat captains. Most of their lives had been spent taking tankers up and down the seacoast, and they knew the Gulf Stream well. Adjacent to the shipyard that we stayed in was an Airedale dog that had gotten loose some months earlier and killed their dog. In return, one of the brothers went to England to buy the fiercest bulldog he could find. He brought the dog back to Savannah, threw it over the fence where the Airedale was, and that was the end of the Airedale. He named his dog Jiggs. The dog wore a seaman's cap and would walk around carrying a Sherlock Holmes–style pipe. He was a character who would come up to you, and when you'd pet him, he would lay the pipe down. Then when you left, he would pick the pipe up and take off. He was a very popular dog.

One of the brothers had a hobby of fixing up old boats and selling them cheaply. He had banker friend who tipped him off to the fact that some oil tankers were going to be put up for auction. Through the banker, he and his brother got title to those boats and resold them, with bank financing, and they became rich. One brother spent a lot of time with his racing sailboat, but the other brother didn't care about anything but fixing up old boats and drinking.

He had a reputation for getting drunk and tearing up places (he was an alcoholic). Then he would pay for the damage or settle the lawsuits that resulted. He got so bad that he decided to commit suicide. He jumped off a very high rainbow-shaped bridge in Savannah. Everybody who tad tried to commit suicide by jumping off it had always died, but he didn't die. As a result of that, he became very religious and very generous with his money. It is interesting how people can change.

When I completed the houses and had the Lord & Taylor building well under control, we moved to Florida for two years. We took the boat and had a wonderful time going through the Intracoastal Waterway. But I was bored to death in Florida. The only thing I had to occupy myself with was my sailboat and fishing. I retired too early.

While we lived in Florida, I became friends with a fellow, Fred Taylor, who had an airplane. He was looking for some way to charge off the gasoline he used—it was a pretty good-sized plane and was expensive to operate. When I was still completing Ravenwood, an oil promoter came to see me about buying an interest in an oil well in Kentucky. I invested, and the well hit oil. (Wells were very cheap to drill—I think the contractors were drilling for about $3 a foot. With a $1,000 investment you could buy an eighth interest in a shallow well in Kentucky. Most of the drilling was in Wayne County and Cumberland County, Kentucky, fairly near the Tennessee line.) When I told my friend with the airplane about the Kentucky oil well, he said, "That'd be great for me. We'll go up there, drill some oil wells, and use my plane to go back and forth, and I'll charge off the expense." Fred knew all the yachtsmen who had money, and we easily raised the money to drill more shallow wells. In total I drilled 40 wells in Kentucky, five of which were good producers. I also got what oil men call "shows," where oil was present but not in an amount sufficient to produce it. (In a wildcat drilling situation in Kentucky, the odds of hitting a producer are about one in 30. The formations are badly broken up; it's hard for a geologist to find a good location. So you just take your chances in an area where wells have been or where others are coming in.)

Starting in about 1950 there was an oil boom in Green County, Kentucky. I drilled a dry hole and got saltwater. Some fellow who knew the oil business went in that same territory and hit a discovery well by pumping the saltwater for 12 days to bring the salt down to a level where oil would come down. (In an oil formation gas is usually on top, then oil, then saltwater below. If you hit the oil, you've got a good producer. If you hit too high up on the structure, you get gas, which you can't use. If you come in too low, you've got saltwa-

Sue Poppelman in front of a drilling rig in
Monticello, Kentucky, 1955. Sue occasion-
ally accompanied me when I would drill.
This one didn't produce.

ter, which condemns the well.) The Green County field was about
29 miles long and 8 miles wide. In that perimeter, you could get a
good producer and could get rich. Some wells, at 500 feet, would
bring in 500 barrels a day.

   After I drilled saltwater, I decided to get the hell out of there. I

The Fred Smith lease, five miles south of Euell, Morgan's Farm, in Clinton County, Kentucky, May 1960.

had met a fellow from Indianapolis named C. C. Summers who had had bad luck and didn't even have the leases to promote. I told him, "I've got some land in Green County. If you want to pay the rentals you can just take my leases over." So I deeded off my interest, 100 percent, to C. C. Summers.

I decided to go to Texas and do something with the 80 acres my father had traded me for my interest in French Village in Newhall. I could drill two wells (in Texas, you could only put in one well every 40 acres). Standard Oil had wells all around my land. (The corporation was called Standolin, but it was owned by Standard Oil.) I talked to some men at Standard Oil to see if they were interested in drilling on my land. They said, "Our geologists think you're on the wrong side of a fault because about two miles from where you are they got a dry hole. However, we'll make a deal with you. There are two Babcock brothers who own quite a bit of acreage in an area we call a 'window.' Standard Oil owns all the land around there, but we need the Babcocks' two leases. If you can get the Babcock brothers to lease to us, we'll drill your 80 acres; we'll take a chance on that." The Standard Oil guys knew the Babcocks had oil on their farms—they were on the good side of the fault. They considered my property problematical; it'd be a wildcat. But they said, "If you can get the Babcocks' leases for us, we'll drill your property first."

I leased a car in Houston, Texas, and went down to Liberty County to the property they were talking about—the little town of Dayton, where my father's land was. I had a scintillation counter—an instrument that costs about $5,000 for a portable one, which you can carry in an airplane or car. It shows the gamma radiation coming up from the ground. Gamma rays hitting on oil reserves will give a different reading than a dry hole. So you can get an indication of the perimeter of an oil deposit pretty well with a scintillation counter if you're careful and know what you're doing.

With my scintillation counter, I went to see the first Babcock brother one afternoon. The story was that they were feuding and they would shoot each other on sight, for some reason or other. The first farmer I went to was sleeping on a cot on the back porch with a shotgun. I knocked on his screen door. He said, "What do you want?"

I said, "I'm an oilman."

He said, "An oilman? What do you want? Everybody's been after my lease. No, I'm not going to lease."

I said, "I'll tell you what. I heard that you're mad at your brother."

"Yes, I'm mad at that son of a bitch."

I said, "I have a good idea how you can get back at him."

He said, "What's that?"

"I think it would kill him if you got a gusher and he got a dry hole."

"How do you know I'd get a gusher?"

I said, "I've got an instrument that tells whether you have oil or not. If you want to get in my car, we'll drive around and I'll show you something." He agreed, and we drove around his property. I was able to control the hands and the meter of the counter. One of the hands would go up and I'd say, "If the hand's this way, you've got good oil. Now let's go down to your brother's place." When we got there I shook the instrument and said, "See how the hand's lying down? That means no oil here. You give me your lease, I guarantee you'll get oil. And he's going to be sick as a dog when he finds out he's got a dry hole and you've got a big well."

So he signed the lease at a notary public at the bank. And he was very happy he was going to get a well and his brother would get a dry hole. Then I went to his brother. I gave him and his wife the same pitch: "You're mad at your brother? He's got a dry hole and you've got oil." After about two weeks of running between the bank and the preachers and everybody else, declaring what a good guy I was, I got both leases from the two feuding Babcock brothers. I turned them over to the guys at Standard Oil. They couldn't believe what I'd done.

Standard Oil then drilled on one of my 40 acres and hit oil. They drilled on the next 40 acres and also got oil. They moved to the Babcocks' leases, and wherever they drilled, they got gushers. They didn't even have to put in pumping jacks—they just automatically flowed. Both Babcock brothers became millionaires. One day when I was driving Sue to California (Sue's mother was with us), I stopped

A good producer in Dayton, Texas (about
40 miles east of Houston), 1961. It checked
in at 3,000 barrels a day, but we pumped
20 barrels a day out of it for 20 years.

in at Standard Oil in Texas. I said to one guy, "Listen, I made the
Babcock brothers rich. Do you think if I talk to them they'd give me
some money as a bonus?"

He said, "If you talk to either one of them, you're going to be a
dead man. They don't appreciate the fact you made them rich.
They're both mad at you because the other one didn't have dry
holes." So I stayed away.

My own wells produced about 3,000 barrels a day. But the law in Texas limited you to 30 to 40 barrels a day after you got your cost back for drilling. The old railroad law was passed years earlier when everybody had gushers and they couldn't haul the oil, so they had to ration it. They did that by allowing only so many barrels out of each 40 acres. I divided the royalties from my wells among my brothers and sisters. We pumped for about 20 years. Those oil wells helped me get started in the building business in a bigger way.

Chapter 19

Learning the Oil Promotion Business from Jack Manning, and How to Use a Doodlebug

While I was in Texas, the gentleman in Green County, Kentucky, who had a saltwater well and pumped it until he found oil created one of the biggest oil flurries in the United States. Everybody rushed to Kentucky to get in on the deal, but I didn't know what was going on because I was working on the Texas land. But C.C. Summers, the man I gave my leases to, followed suit and drilled the same kind of well on the 4,000 acres I gave him. When I went back to see him, he said, "Ray, you've got to get into this play. Those leases you gave me are bringing me about $30,000 a week." He had oil tanks all over the damn place.

I said, "I'm not going to break the oil code." One oilman never begs off another. I said, "I congratulate you on getting the oil. If I'd stuck around here, I'd probably be in the same shoes you are. I'd have done what the discovery well man did. But, I had good luck in Texas, so we both came out."

He replied, "I'll be glad to deed back half of my land to you. You gave it to me and made me rich."

I said, "No. That's not the way oilmen play the game. It's all yours." So we parted friends.

It's strange how life is, though. At first I regretted not taking the other half. Then I got a proposition from some investors from Florida who had bought a lease but had a crooked promoter they didn't get along with. They got rid of him and asked me if I'd take over their block of leases and manage it for them. My wife objected to the idea that I would be in Kentucky so much, and a geologist I knew told me, "Ray, this whole thing is an anomaly; it doesn't fit the pattern. These wells are not going to hold up. Don't get into it." His name was Bird. (His father was an oilman; he was in partnership with an independent businessman who manufactured bricks, and they were known as Hanley and Bird. They were the men who got Quaker State going in the old days in Pennsylvania.) Bird figured that eventually the Green County wells would all go to saltwater. Two years later, that's exactly what happened. I'd have lost my shirt if I'd gone in there and gotten heavily involved.

I had other experiences in oil. Some friends of mine—doctors—in Washington had a block of leases in Kentucky and had a chance to sell out to Reynolds Aluminum Company. I met them in a hotel and told them, "Listen, I have information. You guys sell out. You've been offered $2 million by Reynolds Aluminum. Take the $2 million, split it up, and get the hell out of there. That whole field is going to go dry." They didn't believe me. Years later they told me, "We should've listened to you. That's what happened."

One restaurant in Green County was like the New York Stock Exchange. Oilmen were offering leases for sale while people were eating. John Wayne was there one time when I was there. He decided to invest. If you got in early and then got out, you made money. If you got in late and hung on, you lost money. When I was drilling early on, you couldn't see an oil tank for miles around. I went back later, and the whole goddamn countryside was full of oil rigs and oil wells. I once saw $600,000 counted out over the hood of an automobile. That's the way the oil business was. Once you got an oil affair going, a lot of money could be made.

Cumberland County was one of the early counties in oil production. In 1829, the first oil well in America was discovered there. The pioneers were drilling for saltwater to get the salt. (In fact, the medium of exchange at one time was salt. If you had a barrel of salt, you had a lot of money.) I was intrigued with the history of Kentucky oil because I had been on some farms that had wells that had been pumping for 50 years, in the so-called Beaver Sand. If you could get into the Beaver Sand formation, it was a long-lived proposition. And Kentucky had no limit on the number of barrels you could pump. If you had a 500-barrel well, you could sell all of the oil without restrictions. That made it attractive—cheap drilling and a chance to get rich if you were lucky.

The first well I got into in Kentucky, where I had an eighth interest, was on a lease of about 1,600 acres. A doodlebugger was there, using a simple device, like a divining rod or a ball on the end of a piece of string, to find underground oil or other deposits. Doodlebuggers were all over the oil fields. George Morris, the doodlebugger who located our well, had a little ball about the size of a small hen egg with string on it. He would stand holding the string, and if the ball would swing in a certain circle, oil was there. If it went the other way or didn't do anything, there was no oil. I was anxious to talk to him. It turned out that he used to lease for Shell Oil Company up in Illinois. Wherever he'd say the oil was, Shell Oil would lease. If he said, "There's no oil here," they wouldn't lease. So I decided that a person could own the world if he owned George Morris and Morris was right. Morris lived in Monticello. I said, "George, I want to do some experimenting with you."

He said, "What's that?"

"I want to go to the geologist's office in Lexington, Kentucky, and find out who's taking out licenses to drill. And I want you to tell me whether they're going to get oil or not." So I got a list of all the men around Kentucky who were drilling. We'd drive up to their leases and George would get out and suspend his doodlebug. If the doodlebug went wild, it was going to be a good well. I found that on dry holes, he was almost 100 percent right. On predictions of oil, he was about 87 percent right. I thought, "Jesus Christ, if I could get 80 percent of production on everything I drilled, I'd get rich."

I decided I'd do one thing better. I would go to the state geologist and find out what you had to do to be educated as an oilman. The state geologist was very accommodating. He said, "First, go to the University of Kentucky and get [a certain book] and read that. Then come back and talk to me." So I got it and went to a motel, spent about ten days reading the book and going around looking at places. Then I went back to the geologist. He said, "OK, here's what you do. If you want to be an oilman, go to find a lease man and spend some time with him seeing about leasing." Well, I already had him: George.

The next thing I was supposed to do was go live with a geologist in the hills—rough it—fight the snakes and help while he studied formations. That's how I met John Bird. I found out he was a good geologist and I said, "I want to travel with you and learn about geology." He told me about some more books to read and let me go out to the field with him. Next, I was supposed to work with a driller on the platform—get some old clothes and work with him. So I did. The final course I should take was to travel with a crooked oil promoter.

I got the name of a man who had such a reputation: Jack Manning. I found him in a little restaurant eating ham and eggs one morning. I said, "Mr. Manning, I've heard that you're a promoter, and not exactly a good one, but you're a money-getter. Mr. [So-and-so] suggested that I find a promoter and travel with him."

He said, "Well, I'll tell you. Don't travel with me if you've got any money because I'll get it." And I later learned that was true. He said, "How bad do you want to learn the oil business?"

I told him I didn't have much to do and that it was a fascinating subject.

He said, "You can drive me around. Spend a week with me—I'll pay your expenses to drive. The only thing you've got to do is keep your damn mouth shut. I don't care how ridiculous the argument is, don't you ask me to get into the oil deal."

He was a good-looking guy, about 55 years old. He always wore beautiful gray suits and a beautiful gray cowboy hat. His trick was to go to oil well, turn a valve, and get his fingers wet with crude oil. He'd flip his hat with oil, and then he'd flick a little on his coat as if he'd just walked away from a gusher.

He was supposed to show some wrestlers from Chicago an oil lease in Cumberland County. I was supposed to be the driver, and I was to act like I didn't know anything, that I was stupid. With a Cadillac full of wrestlers, we went to where there were old oil wells. When we went in the gate, a switch was pushed and the wells started pumping. Only one well was a producer, but when the prospects would climb up a ladder and look in the tank, oil would pour out of a 2-inch pipe. Six pumps would be going, and when the prospects looked around the landscape, only one of the pumps would be pumping. That one would only pump if it had been allowed to rest a few days so the oil seeped in. We would drive through the gate, switch on the switch, go down to the woods, and all of a sudden there was the oil lease. You point out that oil well. All the wells are pumping. You drive up to the tank, go up the ladder and look in—geez, the oil's gushing in there. All coming from one lousy well. And Jack picked up $5,000 checks from each one of these wrestlers.

When we got back to the room, I said, "Jack, why don't you let me in on that deal?"

He said, "You goddamn dumb son of a bitch. I told you to keep your big mouth shut and never ask to get in on an oil deal!" And he told me what was going on. And I said, "Jesus, what if the police get after you? What if these wrestlers ever find out about this?"

He said, "Hell, nobody's going to get after me. Those wrestlers are looking for tax deductions. They'll just write it off. They can't do anything with me. I'm not responsible if five of the wells quit overnight."

Soon, I found out that Jack was going to sell a block of leases to a woman in Washington, D.C., named Mrs. Henderson. She was a very rich lady, a widow. Jack was going to trade her a whole big block of leases in the rough part of Kentucky in exchange for an apartment house, cash, and an orange grove in Florida. I heard Jack talking to somebody else about it, and I thought, "Could this be for real?" I said to Jack, "Jack, this sounds like a good deal. How about me? When are you going to get me into a good deal so I can make some money?"

He said, "Your deal is to travel with me and learn this business and keep your goddamn mouth shut. This is a closed deal. You can't get into it."

I got suspicious and I checked with some oilmen and found out that the leases weren't in oil country, they were in coal and lumber country, and if I wanted to I could go see [So-and-so], one of the officers of the company. So I did. I said, "Does Jack Manning have your property lease?"

"No, we don't lease it to anybody."

So I knew this was a real swindle. When I went home to Washington, I went to Mrs. Henderson's house on Massachusetts Avenue on Embassy Row—a great big place. She came out and I said, "Mrs. Henderson, my name's Poppelman. I'm a real estate developer out in Fairfax, and I've run into an oilman that I think you're dealing with—a Mr. Jack Manning."

"Oh, yes," she said. "He's such a nice man."

I said, "Well, you won't think so when I tell you something. Jack Manning does not have the lease he says he does. And not only that, he's the biggest oil crook in Kentucky."

She said, "Oh, you oilmen are all alike! You just want to get him out of the way so you can get my money!" And she chased me out of the house.

As I went down the steps, I yelled back at her, "Who's your attorney? I'll go talk to your attorney."

She said, "What do you want to talk to him about?"

"I'm going to tell him about the big crook you're all mixed up with."

She told me his name, and I went to see him—told him the whole damn story. The next afternoon on the front page of the *Washington Post* was "Oil Hoax: A prominent real estate developer of Falls Church, Virginia [it didn't mention my name] has revealed an oil swindle in the state of Kentucky." The attorney said he'd get in touch with Mrs. Henderson. When they got in touch with Jack Manning, you know what Jack Manning said? "Let me keep the cash and I'll give you back your apartment house and orange grove." And that's the settlement they made. He didn't even go to jail. He condemned me for telling the lawyer about his crooked scheme, but as long as he had some use for a person, he'd figure, "Well, OK. He double-crossed me. I'll get that son of a bitch later."

In the meantime I had committed myself to Jack to watch an oil well in Scott County in western Kentucky. It was hard to get to. I'd sit on the well, which means be at the well and keep a log. The pro-moter has to turn in sacks of samples every ten feet to the state. So when the drillers washed out the sand after baling out the hole, I would sack up these samples, note the depth and the lease, and see that they were sent to the oil office in Lexington. That was the law. Then I was to notify Jack each night from a pay phone—not a regu-lar phone, but a pay phone. Promoters all used pay phones; they would never use a phone where there could be a record of their calls.

The drillers on the well were a Scotsman—a great big giant of a guy—and a smaller fellow. I was sitting alongside a creek fishing, and all of a sudden I heard a lot of rattling. They hit a gusher at around 450 feet. The oil was going up over the rig. Jesus Christ, we all got excited. These drillers capped the well so it could be shut down. (When they drill, the cable goes down through a sort of a gap.) They got the well under control, and the Scotsman told me, "You get ahold of Mr. Manning and tell him what happened."

Jack was in Rockford, Illinois, living with his eighth wife. (Imag-ine that.) I said, "Jack, we hit a goddamn gusher. The driller thinks it'll do at least 500 barrels a day. What do I do?"

He said, "Here's what you do." He had oversold the lease. He sold probably 50 eighth-interests in that well never dreaming he'd strike oil. He had gone into a wildcat area where there were no wells around and discovered the well. So he said, "Poppelman, you tell

[So-and-so, the driller]: 'Plug that hole three feet below the ground. Cover up the slush pit, plow up the field. Get the rig the hell out of there.' And do it tomorrow—do it as fast as you can."

I said, "Hell, Jack, you've got oil. You're going to be rich with all the land you've got leased around here." He'd probably collected at least $100,000 or $200,000 in investments on that land.

He said, "Rich, hell! You do what I tell you. You get the pumping jack that's sitting there and all the pipe and send that stuff back to the supply house."

I said, "Well, how about me? What about me?"

"I'll take care of you. You do what I tell you and there'll be a cool $5,000 for you."

Of course, I never got the money. But we cleared out and covered over the well so that no one could see it. And it's still covered. I'm the only guy who knows where it is, and I don't know what the hell to do about it. I sometimes think, "I would be an accomplice to fraud if I would go back and lease that same land and open that same hole up." I could still find the spot with the help of an attorney who would go through the county records. The counties all have oil books. If I were to find Jack Manning's name, where he owned the lease, I would know that I was in the right place. But someone would figure, "How the hell did Ray know that hole was there?" And then the person would remember that I used to work for Jack Manning. I could go to jail along with Jack, except Jack has already died in a federal penitentiary. He got caught in California on a swindle. (Anyway, Magnolia Oil Company from Texas leased all the land around there. It was so remote—down in a valley with a creek—that no rumor ever got started about the gusher. You practically had to have a jeep to get down there.)

Jack oversold his leases all the time. He'd sell an eighth interest to a guy in Illinois, another eighth to one in Montana, and another to one in New York, so they'd never get together and find out. It's too much of a load for one guy to fight the battle for all the others, so nobody does anything. In the meantime, Jack would send them a statement that they hit a dry hole, and they would take a tax deduction. Jack told me one time he'd sold as many as 60 eighths on a well. It was so damn remotely located, nobody could even find it. And most of the holes he hit were dry because he didn't want to hit oil. His favorite stunt was to find a dry hole—an old one that had been drilled maybe 50 years earlier—and drill beside it.

But I'll tell you what burned me up. At Christmastime, he called me and said, "Poppelman, I have just traded an interest in an oil deal for a carload of television sets."

I said, "Why the hell don't you take them to a dealer and sell them?"

"Oh, those sons of bitches. I don't deal with them. I'll tell you what I want you to do. Do you have any friends who need a television set?"

I said, "Why do you ask?"

He said, "Well, I'm going to give these away. I don't want any more income. I'm OK. If you've got any friends you want to do a favor for, just send me the names and I'll ship these damn television sets to them."

I was so naive and stupid, I didn't realize what he was after. He didn't have any television sets. He wanted the names of prospects. I gave him the name of a dentist who lived up the street from me in Ravenwood. Later I went to the dentist and asked, "Did you get your television set for Christmas?" He said no. I said, "You were supposed to get a television set with my compliments. I have a friend that was going to send you a television set."

He said, "No, I didn't get one, but do you happen to know an oilman by the name of Jack Manning?"

I said, "Yeah, I know him very well. He's the son of a bitch that was going to send the television sets out. Why?"

"He was here last Sunday, and what a deal he gave me."

I said, "How much did you give him to get into the oil deal?"

He said, "Five thousand dollars. Just $5,000, and I got a piece of a big oil deal."

So I told him the whole story—that Jack was a big crook and so on. And you know what the dentist did? He didn't believe me. He thought that I wanted to keep him out of the deal; that I wanted it myself. I really lit into Jack on that one and told him I wanted the list of people. He gave it to me, and I called them all and told them it was nothing but a damn swindle and I hoped to hell they weren't disappointed they didn't get their TV sets.

The FBI came to see me one time. They had a file on Jack two inches thick. He had started promoting during World War I when he was a young man. He would stand in hotel lobbies in Chicago, dressed in an officer's uniform, and sell oil deals to anybody who would buy. Oil was going to jump up in price; he would tell people about a well and they thought they would get rich. He was selling deals right out of the lobby. He would ask anybody who walked by: "Hey, you interested in an oil deal?" Oil is a magic word.

The FBI told me that at one time Jack owned a big estate in Texas with a private airfield; he had made so much money. They asked me about my relations with him and I told them. And they said, "This guy has been to the White House. You can't believe what he has done. He's been chased out of Texas, out of Oklahoma, and Illinois." They had an incredible record on him.

Jack and I were talking once about what makes a good oil promoter. He said, "Poppelman, you know what makes a good promoter, and you haven't got it."

I said, "What is it?"

He said, "You've got to take the last dime from a little old lady and let her be sitting on the curb, crying, and walk down the street and not give a damn. When you can do that, you're a good oilman." That's what he told me. I couldn't believe it.

Here's another story about Jack. He went into Wayne County, Kentucky, and wanted to get a big block of leases in a certain place. Cordell Hull of the State Department owned the land. Jack came to me and said, "Ray, do you remember when you told me you wanted to get into a good deal? Well, I've finally got one for you. You ever heard of Cordell Hull?" I said yes.

"He owns a lot of land in Kentucky in Wayne County. There are six oil wells on the property. I've got the lease, and that's what you should have."

I said, "What would I do with it?"

He said, "The oil's in the ground, but it lacks gas pressure. What you should do is see if you can pick up a big compressor somewhere and put a compressor on one of those wells and pump air down in there. That'll force oil out of the others."

It sounded fairly reasonable, so I bought the lease from him. I think I gave him $12,000 for it. Charlie Holland, a salesman who worked for me then, had been a captain on a commercial ship at one time. I told him what I needed and he told me, "The navy's got all kinds of old compressors." So Charlie and I went to the navy base at Solomon's Island, Maryland, and bought one. We hauled it down on a great big truck of mine and put it on the lease. After a while I got fed up with all the extra cost involved and I told Jack, "I'll sell my lease if you can sell it for me, including the cost of the compressor."

I had heard that Cordell Hull was staying at one of the big old hotels in Washington; he was sick and in bed. I went to see him, and his wife told me, "You can go in and talk to Mr. Hull, but don't stay too long."

So I told him, "I've come about your land in [Kentucky]."

Mr. Hull said, "Mr. Poppelman, there's no oil there. That dried up years ago."

I told him that I was involved in the lease with Jack Manning. He said, "I'll tell you one thing more. I don't even know who Jack Manning is. Nobody has any lease on my land."

So I went to see Jack. I said, "How'd you like to go to jail?"

He said, "What do you mean?"

I said, "I want my money out or I'm going to go to the county attorney. You don't even have a lease on this property, and I paid you money for the lease." So he sold the deal to somebody else, got the money, and gave it to me. He was a real smoothie.

I had been associated with Jack for about three years before the FBI came to see me. After I talked to the FBI, Jack called me up and said, "Poppelman, you like to sail, don't you?"

I said, "Yeah."

He said, "I've got a chance to trade an oil lease in Kentucky for a real beautiful sailboat down in Florida."

I said, "What do I have to do to get it?"

He said, "Not a damn thing. It'll be mine and I'll give it to you for old times' sake."

I went to Florida to see the boat—a beautiful 70-footer. I couldn't have afforded it. I decided there's got to be something wrong in the story somewhere. So I said, "Jack, this is goodbye. You taught me a lesson. There'll be no oil promoter in this world could ever take me on a deal after my education from you, and I thank you for it." So that was it.

To return to the topic of doodlebugging: George Morris had a pendulum that he'd been working with for 30 years. I was so curious about his scores when I tested him out that I borrowed his doodlebug and tried it out on my dad's property. My father's land and the Babcock brothers' land looked really hot. I made a map of the area around my father's property where Standard Oil had about 20 oil wells and went around checking each well with a ruler. The wider the swing of the circular motion of the pendulum, the better the oil. So I made a notation for each well, such as "Standard Oil's well No. 269—2 inches" or 3 inches and so forth. Then I took the map to the vice president of the Standolin Oil Company and told him, "I've got a doodlebug that tells me about oil."

It seems that his father had been a water dowser—he could find water with a dowsing stick. He called in a geologist and said, "What do you think of Poppelman's map here?"

The man said to me, "Which one of our pumpers did you talk to?"

I said, "I didn't talk to a damn soul; the doodlebug told me."

When we were visiting Sue's mother in Florida I went to a compass company and said, "I want you to take this instrument apart." I wanted to see what was in it. They took it apart and showed me what was inside. The major things in it were two little magnets that were backed up so they would repel each other. I said, "Now, I want you to reverse the magnets and put it together like it was never taken apart." They did that.

I went back to George and said, "Let's check out some of your early findings on wells." We went to two to three counties in which George had previously made predictions, especially on dry holes. I had the information we'd taken before, and we tried it again with the magnets reversed. I said, "George, what do you find now?" He got the same readings as he had before. So I took the doodlebug back to Florida and had the compass company reverse the magnets again back to the original configuration. Then we checked again— same results. It didn't matter how the magnets were arranged.

One day while we were in Florida, Sue and I and some friends were on the beach and we played a game. They would hide a can of oil in the sand. Then I'd use the doodlebug to find the oil. One of the girls said to me, "How come your doodlebug goes to that one can of oil but not to that bunch of automobiles parked along the road? They've each got more than a quart of oil in the crankcase." I thought, "Jesus Christ, what a question." But I didn't know the answer.

Another day I was in a restaurant in Florida with a guy named Fred Taylor, and he told the owner, "Poppelman's got a gadget here that finds oil." So the owner hid a can of oil in his storeroom and had me find it. He was so impressed he wanted to put $40,000 into an oil well with me.

I said, "I'm not sure yet why this thing works. I don't think the doodlebug has a damn thing to do with it." I went to the Library of Congress and started reading a lot of books and found out there was a Frenchman who wrote a book claiming that the subconscious mind has a way of agreeing with anything you want to do. Something about the human body responds, and there is no affinity between the device you use and what you're looking for.

I joined the American Society of Dowsers, which had been just formed, and started talking to all the members to see what they were

Demonstrating the correct way to hold a
dowsing rod, December 1963.

doing. They had all kinds of weird ideas. One guy's divining rod
wouldn't work unless he had a squirrel's foot tied on the end of it—
the squirrel's foot would intercept rays, he thought. It's all psycho-
logical. Many people have gadgets that'll do things, find things, or
send messages—like Ouija boards. But there is something about the
human body that responds to oil or water or whatever, and I still
don't know what it is. Albert Einstein once said, "It'll take a greater
mind than mine to explain the phenomenon of the dowsing rod." (I
read that quote in a book.)

I was a trustee for the American Society of Dowsers for eight years, and I checked hundreds of water diviners. Some of them were masters at finding water; they would locate big flowing wells every time. And I met a man who could use his divining rod to find a penny in the woods. No matter where you would hide it, he could find that penny. We checked him out to make sure he wasn't a fraud. One of the trustees in the American Society of Dowsers who was with the Atomic Energy Commission did many experiments to try to figure out how it worked. He was going after it in a physical way; and I thought of it as a mind power.

I finally told George how I had fiddled with his doodlebug. We were in a motel, and I said, "George, I've got to make a confession. You deserve to know." He lay on the bed and cried like a baby. From then on, he was never worth a damn as a dowser. As long as he had believed in it, it worked for him.

I came to the same conclusion as the Frenchman who wrote the book: Dowsing rods have no affinity to water in the ground; they merely accommodate your thinking. If you want to play with a certain doodlebug, it'll work for you. I found that to be generally true. I was really startled when I was in a muddy field once divining for oil. I got to a place where the divining rod not only turned down, it was pulling me down into the mud.

Chapter 20

Befriending Alvin York, and Dowsing Wells with Willie Pyle in Kentucky

During my travels in Kentucky and Tennessee exploring for oil, I made friends with Sergeant Alvin York, one of the greatest war heroes of World War I. He was living in Pall Mall, Tennessee. I met him through his cousin, Willie Pyle, a so-called "hillbilly"—a native of the Appalachians—whose primary occupation was growing tobacco. On Sundays he would preach to his congregation about the evils of tobacco, but the majority of his income came from tobacco.

On the side, Willie was a talented dowser. He had made his brother Earl rich by dowsing for oil. Willie would always get a dry hole if he drilled for himself, but he could find oil for other people, including me. One day Willie drove me to Tennessee to meet Alvin, who was living in a beautiful home with large dormer windows. It was the dream home that he had always wanted—on the Wolf River alongside very rich soil; that soil could grow anything. For all his bravery in World War I and all his generosity to a lot of people, the state of Tennessee had given him the land and built the home on it. Alvin was a national hero, and there were always five or six cars parked near his house. People wanted to meet him and shake his hand. And he was very cordial; he'd never turn anybody away.

I had seen the motion picture about his life in which he was portrayed by Gary Cooper, and the story was quite fantastic. I was sort of shocked when I met Alvin York because he was bedridden. He'd gained considerable weight being in bed so much, and his face was sort of red; he looked like anything but a hero. He was a quiet fellow, very jovial, very cordial, and I questioned him a little about his life—the early manhood I'd seen portrayed in the movie. He was reputed to be a great hunter. He had the ability to shoot the eyes out of a squirrel in the forest. He was noted for his marksmanship. He would always win the contests they called turkey shoots, where they'd shoot rifles at targets to see who would win a turkey. I enjoyed our talks about his boyhood.

He refrained from dwelling on his exploits as a soldier because he didn't believe in killing people. It was against his personal morals to kill people for any reason, but his petition to be a conscientious objector in World War I had been denied. We talked very little about the war. When I was introduced to him as an oilman, he paid particular attention to me because he had hoped someday that some oilman might want to drill on his land. He even suggested maybe I'd like to. I would have, just to have an excuse to talk to him more; I was fascinated by him. There were a lot of questions I wanted to ask him since I had also served in a war, but all he told me was that he had dreaded going into battle and that he had captured 150 German soldiers after capturing a German general and convincing the general that his men should surrender. He told him they would not be killed if they surrendered. He was just arguing for what he believed in: that you should not kill people unnecessarily. The German general was sold on the idea, and Alvin York captured 150 German soldiers. I would say that Alvin York saved the lives of all those German prisoners because they would have been shot if he hadn't brought them in.

We became friends, and I agreed to a temporary arrangement with him to drill an exploration well on his property in Scott County, Tennessee. But before we consummated the deal for drilling a well—which I didn't want to do, but I would do for him—he died. When I think back through my life of all the people I have met, including five presidents, I would say that my visits to Alvin York in his home, even when he was laid up and sick, were the most impressive. He was the one man that I really appreciated seeing. He had a certain magnetism about him; he had a divine aura. He fought in one of the fiercest battles of World War I, in the Argonne, in the thick of it, and wasn't even wounded. I think I developed a lot of courage from meeting Alvin York. When I was building houses and I'd run into problems, I'd think, "Jesus Christ, Alvin York was a human being like me. I can do what I have to do; I'll just do it like he did."

There were a lot of shallow wells in the northern part of Tennessee along the Kentucky line, but Scott County itself didn't have a lot of oil. Tennessee was not a good place for shallow oil wells; Kentucky was. I only drove one deep well in Tennessee and it was too expensive and too much trouble. The formations were too hard. The new rotary rigs that were being used in Texas and Oklahoma liked softer formations. The old-fashioned cable tool used in the early days could break up the hard formations, but rotary rigs would pulverize the rock as you drilled down. Tennessee had some wonderful wells in the early days, about 1860, when Standard Oil was there, but it never became a good oil state. It would have been expensive for me, and difficult, to drill a well on Alvin York's land, and the odds were very high against my hitting oil there. I might have had to drill 50 oil wells to find a good producer. It was really a project for a major oil company, not for me as an individual.

The American Society of Dowsers had decided (as an experiment) to drill an oil well in a very remote section that had never been tested before. We picked a place near the Tennessee line and got opinions from three different dowsers. The dowsing rods were very affirmative, but they just indicate oil is down there; they don't tell you how deep you have to go. All the dowsers chipped in money to drill the well down to 1,200 feet. When we got to 1,200 feet, the formations looked good—a geologist would be happy with it—but we did not have anything but a show of oil. The geologists we talked to thought we should bring in a rotary rig and go deeper if we wanted to really find the oil. But when we compared the formations in Texas with those in Tennessee, we realized we would not get oil in the formations we found in Tennessee. For instance, a formation 10,000 feet deep in Tennessee would be on about the same level as a 1,000-foot well in Texas. Instead of passing the hat among members of the American Society of Dowsers for more financing, we'd have to go to a major oil company, and they weren't interested in such a proposition. So the well was plugged at about 1,200 feet. Although geologically it was a success, it was a failure as far as hitting oil was concerned.

I had abandoned geologists in favor of dowsers. I never got a good well when I used a geologist. I got good oil formations—geologically, it would be a big success; usually it would look like you were right on top of oil—but economically you didn't have a quarter. The only time I ever hit oil, where I would call it a good producer, was when I dowsed to find it.

Here's how you dowse a well: First you hold the dowsing rod in your hand (this comes after a lot of practice). You want to get the location from where you are standing, so you start turning on a 360-degree turn. When the dowsing rod bends or moves down, you know you've got the direction. Then you walk in that direction, or sometimes you can even talk to the rod: "Am I within a half a mile?" No. "Am I within a mile of it?" Yes. The rod goes down for "yes" and stays still for "no." That's the way I used to do it.

I would dowse first and then, with my own money, lease up a lot of land and drill my own well. Then if I got a dry hole I'd just drop the leases and go somewhere else. I was a wildcatter. I thought big and I missed a few times when I could have really made it big. I wasn't too interested in a 10-barrel well. I would usually sell it out to somebody else or sell it to the farmer on whose land it was—let him have all the income from it, because then he could take care of it.

If a farmer had about a 100-acre farm, and I drilled a well and got 10 barrels, I would retain interest in the rest of his acreage, but I'd let him have that well for the price of my drilling costs. All farmers can use an extra water well, and usually wherever you drilled, you would find water somewhere before you got to 100 feet. So you would case off that part of the well with pipe and then go on down with another string of pipe inside of that looking for the oil. If you got a dry hole you'd pull out the inner 6-inch casing, and the farmer would have a 10-inch pipe down to the water. Usually I would give it to him because I had investors' money in there and if the farmer was a good guy, I would just say, "OK, Joe, you've got a free water well here."

The first thing I'd do when I worked in Kentucky was go to the county attorney and let him represent me. I would give the sheriff a donation for his next election because it's always good to have the sheriff in your corner. Second, I would go to the church minister— usually there'd be just one church in a little area—and make a donation to the church. Each time I approached a farmer about his land, he would run to the minister or to the county sheriff to check on me.

By then I had a reputation already as a good guy, so it was quite easy for me to get a block of leases.

I remember drilling an oil well in Cumberland County, Kentucky. We got down to around 1,200 feet without hitting oil. The driller thought it was time to give up and plug the hole. I took my dowsing rod and went in the woods by myself and said, "Now, all along you told me there's oil. If there is oil where our rig is standing, I want to know how much deeper we have to go," and I counted down. I was so surprised—it said 12 feet. I said to the rod, "You mean to tell me that if we drill 12 more feet we're going to get an oil well?" BAM! The thing went down like that. I went back and told the driller, "I want to put up money for you to drill another 12 feet."

He said, "Twelve feet?"

"Yeah, 12 feet. My dowsing rod said that if we go 12 feet, we'll get oil." It was wintertime and there was about a foot of snow on the ground. The driller started telling his men to rack up the tools and get ready to knock out another 12 feet and then go home. I was apprehensive, of course, and I figured that the dowsing had gone to hell. I took a little walk down the creek just to get away from the rig, and all of a sudden I heard somebody yelling. Darned if they didn't hit oil at 12 feet. I pumped that well for several years and finally sold it.

Once I was staying in a motel in Cumberland County, Kentucky, and a Japanese geologist was in the room next to me. He worked for a syndicate out of Indianapolis, Indiana, that was drilling for what they called a knox dolomite formation in Clinton County, which is south of where I was operating in Wayne County. Clinton County had some big wells in the early days, and this group from Indianapolis was looking for one of those big wells; they weren't interested in the shallow stuff. The Japanese fellow wore contact lenses, which he was always losing. We developed a system: If he lost a contact lens in his room, he would bang on my wall with his shoe and I'd come running in there and help him look through the carpet for his lens. We became good friends. One Saturday he came to me and said, "I'm drilling a well in Clinton County. So far we haven't hit the oil. I've got some investors coming down from Indianapolis. They'll be here tomorrow. I need advice on whether we should go deep or just plug the well. I don't know much about dowsing, but you have a reputation of being a dowser. Do you think you could give me an opinion?"

I agreed to help him, so we went to the site. I brought a pendulum on a string, and I just talked to it. When I would say, "Should we go deeper?" the pendulum would whirl around. I told the geologist, "Listen, somewhere down there there's got to be a hell of a lot of oil. This pendulum of mine is going crazy." I recommended that he drill down 200 more feet, and that's what he told his investors they should do.

On the second day of drilling, the investors from Indianapolis were at the well, and damn if they didn't hit a gusher. The oil went clear up over the top of the rig—it was one of the biggest wells ever found in Clinton County. There was so much oil they had to get bulldozers in there to make ponds, and then they brought in trucks to suck the oil out of the ponds. The geologist got such a reputation out of finding that well that a major oil company gave him a big job down in South America.

Of course, I had told him, "If we do hit oil, I don't want you to tell anyone how you found it. Keep your mouth shut. I don't want to be swamped with a million guys wanting me to find oil for them. This is a favor between you and me. I want you to get the credit for finding oil if we do find it." So that's the way we worked it.

Willie Pyle had an interesting way of dowsing. He didn't use the type of instrument other dowsers did—a pendulum or a forked branch; he had a special device that he designed himself. It was a piece of a branch with an arm like a pointer, about a foot long and sharpened on both ends. On the end of the pointer he would tie a little piece of rag that was saturated in oil. He would hold that with his two hands so that the stem would turn, and the arm would always point to the direction he should go to find the oil. As he'd walk, the arm would point. It would go around clockwise for "yes." For "no," it would go around counterclockwise. Willie found over 150 shallow wells up in northern Kentucky using that device.

As I said, he made his brother rich but never himself. He believed there was a reason he should not have so much money. But we were driving down the road together one day when he said, "Raymond, do you know anything about investing money?"

I said, "Well, I don't play the stock market. My gambling is in the oilfields. Why do you ask?"

He said, "Well, I have a little tobacco money, and I'm wondering how to invest it. It's in the bank."

I figured he probably had $25 or $30. I said, "How much money do you have, Willie?"

He said, "Oh, a little over $50,000."

I thought, "Jesus Christ. I've been picking up the tab, buying his gasoline—he's got more money than I have." So I told him that he should take the advice of his local banker and stay out of the stock market. He had enough money to retire on.

One day I asked him, "Willie, in addition to dowsing, what else can you do?"

He said, "Well, I can talk to animals."

I said, "How do you talk to them?"

He said, "I talk to them through my mind."

I said, "Can you give me a demonstration?"

He said, "Yes. I own a mule. He's down in the pasture some-place. If you'll wait a minute, and just leave me alone, I'll see if I can get the mule to come."

Pretty soon, I looked down the valley, and damned if there wasn't a white mule plodding up there; it came right up to Willie.

Here is a fantastic story about Willie. I was in Albany, Kentucky, near where Willie lived, and I had trouble with my Ford car. The engine was making a racket. There was a storm warning for snow that night. I wanted to fix the noise in the Ford before I took off to get back to Nashville to an airport to fly back to Washington. The mechanics worked overtime, but they couldn't find the cause of the noise. They took everything apart and put it together, and they couldn't find it. On my way out of town, I was passing Willie's house, and I thought, "I'll stop and chat with Willie a few minutes before I leave." I pulled up in front of Willie's house and was invited inside. We sat in the living room. Next thing I heard was a bunch of bees outside of the window. I said, "Willie, what are those bees doing out there?"

He said, "Well, I have a lot of bees, and during the day some snow has melted and iced over the little inlet they use to go into the beehive. I've got to go out and break the ice and let them inside."

I said, "When they want to get your attention, do they always come to the window?"

He said, "Yes. They have a line from the beehives all the way up to my window, and they buzz so loudly they attract my attention. Excuse me and I'll go out there and break the ice for them so they can get back in their hives."

Well, that was interesting. When he came back, I said, "Willie, I'm having trouble with my car. It's making a noise. I just hope it can get me down to Nashville to catch the airplane."

Willie got up off his chair, went across the room, and picked up a big ponderous Bible; I'd never seen such a big Bible. He lay it on his lap, opened it up, and put his hands on it. And that's all he did while we were talking. We talked about oil; we talked about a lot of things. Finally I had to leave. I said, "Willie, I've got to go."

He said, "Just a minute. I'll walk out to the car with you."

He closed the Bible and put it back on the shelf. We walked out to the car, I turned the engine on—smooth as silk. It never made another peep.

Willie wore ragged clothes, and once I wanted to buy him a pair of overalls. He looked so damn poor, if you didn't know he had $50,000 in the bank. He had a different insight on the world than I did. If I would make a suggestion about something, he countered with something that was usually better. He was very popular with his friends. If you'd go to town with him, he could walk down Main Street and know everybody. He had wonderful stories to tell. He told me about an old man who used to live in that area. If you put a letter on his head, he would put his hat over the letter. He'd sit there, and after a while he could tell you what was in the letter. Once, the letter was written in Spanish and he still deciphered it through his mind.

Willie was religious in his own way. I believe he used religion in his dowsing. A person could have written a good book if he'd gone down to Tennessee and just lived with Willie and recorded everything he did. Everything seemed to be a little different—peculiar. I would say to myself, "Gee, maybe I should ask Willie," especially after he took the noise out of my car. That had to be a connection with some divine force because I had three mechanics in Albany work all afternoon and they couldn't fix it.

Another interesting story: I was in line to check out of a hotel. The woman in front of me (I don't remember her name) was arguing with the clerk, who wanted to kick her out of the hotel because she hadn't paid her last week's rent (she was renting by the week). (Hell, it was only $25 in this cheap hotel.) They gave her until 2:00 in the afternoon to get the money or get out.

I'd heard that she was from Monticello, a town that I stayed in a lot. So I said to the clerk, "This woman from Monticello—what's her name?" He told me. I said, "You're going to kick her out for $25?"

He said, "Yeah."

I said, "Hell, put it on my account; I'll take care of it."

So I did her a favor, but I didn't tell her. A little later, she got a job in Monticello leasing land for H. L. Hunt, the big Texas oilman. She came to me one day and said, "Ray, you've got 2,000 acres down in Wayne County. What are you going to do with it?"

I said, "I want to get rid of it."

She said, "I represent H. L. Hunt. I can lease it for you."

I said, "OK. But if I let it go, you can go down and lease it."

She said, "No, you did me a favor back up in Green County. I want to help you. I can lease your 2,000 acres to Mr. Hunt."

So I said, "I'll take $1 an acre for it." I was going to let it go anyway, so she brought me $2,000 I hadn't counted on.

A man by the name of Phillips of the Phillips Oil Company came to Burkesville, Kentucky, and checked into the motel room next to mine. He was dying of cancer, and he'd put out an order to all hospitals, clinics, and doctors: He'd give them $30 million if they could cure his cancer. No takers. Imagine that. He came to me and said,

"Do you happen to know somebody who can drive me around during the day? I can't drive anymore."

I thought of this woman, and she agreed to help him; she became his caretaker and grew very close to him. He died and left her $2 million and a beautiful oil painting. And all that happened within a year. All because of that $25.

I wound up making enough money on oil to pay off the mortgages on Ravenwood so I could build the Lord & Taylor department store, and I made money to live on. Instead of going fishing, I went fishing for oil. I had a lot of fun, met a lot of wonderful people, and wound up drilling two oil wells in Texas that kept me going for 20 years.

The Texas oil wells that my father traded me came in when I needed money most, as I increased my income through real estate. The wells eventually went to saltwater and were plugged. But for 20 years I received royalty checks for my share, and the royalties that I gave to my brothers and sisters helped them, too. Coming after the Great Depression, it was a blessing in disguise. Our family still owns the Texas land; it's leased. But with oil producers buying oil from the Arabian governments cheaper than they can pump it down in Texas, our government thinks that we should keep our own oil in reserve and buy Arabian oil. So there's not too much activity in Texas at the present time. There are many wells pumping, but it's not an aggressive business like it used to be. Some operators have drilled deeper and found a big gas deposit, so it's possible that one day when the country is hard up for new energy and needs more gas, there'll be another big boom in Texas with gas wells, but not so many oil wells.

PART 6

Travels in Europe
(May–September 1964)

CHAPTER 21

A Dowsing Convention in England, a Visit with the Poeppelmanns in Germany, and Sightseeing in Holland, Belgium, and Paris

In May 1964 Sue and I embarked on a four-month tour of England and the European contient. We went to England because I had agreed to give a talk there, and we wanted to see Germany and to check out the Poeppelmann family. We figured we might as well drive around the rest of Europe while we were there—we drove more than 6,000 miles throughout the Continent—and spend some of the $5,000 Sue had inherited from her aunt and $10,000 I had picked up unexpectedly from a real estate deal.

When I was doing some research at the Library of Congress, one of the curators had said to me, "Could you be related to the Poeppelmanns of Germany?" and I said, "Yes." He said, "Did you know you had a famous great-grandfather there?" I said, "No, I didn't know it." So he gave me a rundown on my great-grandfather, who had been the architect under August the Strong [1670–1704] for the German Empire and lived at the palace from the time he was 18 years old till he died. He did all the designing for the palace work in Dresden and became known throughout Germany. I wanted to go to Dresden to see the Poeppelmann palace buildings. And then in April 1964 I received and accepted an invitation to be a guest speaker at the British Society of Dowsers.

That May we flew from Dulles Airport in Washington, D.C., to England on American Airlines. In London we checked in at the Rembrandt Hotel, which was located across the street from the Victoria and Albert Museum. At the hotel we were treated rather coolly at first. I asked the concierge, "How much money does it take you to smile?" He said, "In your money, about a dollar and a half." So I gave him the equivalent of a dollar and a half, and from then on he was all smiles and very gracious—he gave us a wonderful room and was our friend.

The president of the British Society of Dowsers was Kenneth Merrilees, who had been a colonel in the British army. He was a personal friend of the Prince of Wales; they hunted together. He called me and gave me the details of their convention, which would be about two weeks later at Tunbridge Wells.

Sue and I had about two weeks to enjoy London. It took us only a few days to learn how to use the subways. We took the typical tours to Buckingham Palace and the museums, but we also had a list of recommendations from a former British Broadcasting Company chief who had been transferred to Washington, D.C. He told us which places to see and what restaurants to eat at. It would take a book to write about everything that happened in London, but generally we had good luck. Buckingham Palace was, of course, very interesting. We saw the changing of the guards. The Coldstream Guards, with the tall bearskin caps and red jackets, who guard Buckingham Palace are the same unit I served with in China in 1927.

I liked London. The Londoners' backyards were so prim and

neat. I went down one street that made me believe there was such a thing as reincarnation. The whole place looked so familiar to me, I didn't want to leave it. I liked the landscaping but not the people in London. For instance, the London tour buses would separate people by nationalities. The guide would call out, "British people, please board the bus." They got their choice of seats. Then people from the other nations were allowed to board, one nation at a time. The British had to have first choice of the seats always. Along the tour we passed a monument, and the guide said, "This is dedicated to the wonderful British soldiers who fought the Germans and won the war." Then she turned toward me and Sue and said, "Of course, Americans helped, too."

I had two suits made at a tailoring shop that the American Airlines pilots had told me about. The tailoring shops there are quite formal. Fitters decide what type of clothes you should have and how the fitting should go. They require special tips for their services. One particular fitter may work for several tailoring shops, but he's a private individual and you pay him separately. He came to the tailor shop in formal clothes; he was very meticulous. It cost about $25 to have him measure me, but when I received the suits a few days before we left London on the plane, I found them to be perfect in every way. No alterations were needed; the fit was perfect. The tailoring was wonderful and the price was very reasonable—you could get a suit made of the finest material for about $150 at that time.

After touring London—and we saw it all, including Windsor Castle (which was the highlight of the tour) and all the other sights that tourists normally see—we rented a car to drive to Tunbridge Wells on the eastern coast of England for the British Society of Dowsers' convention. There were about 500 in attendance and the meeting lasted three days. My speech was well accepted. I talked about how oil dowsers were used in the oil fields and about the 25,000 dowsers in America who were considered water dowsers. The attendees were surprised to learn that there were dowsers in the United States. In the large dining room I noticed that the British dowsers were dowsing the menu to see which food they should have! Colonel Merrilees was very friendly to me. He drove an old Rolls Royce and had a beautiful mansion somewhere in England. He invited Sue and me to come stay with him, but time did not permit us to do so.

From Tunbridge Wells we toured the West Country of England, which is beautiful. By that time we had learned to drive on the left side of the road, and even though the roads were narrow we got along fine. We stayed at Glastonbury, a town with an old, famous cathedral that was just barely standing. Our hotel had been part of the old Glastonbury Castle, and our room was 600 years old. The hotel had interior staircases made of stone—no elevators. Stonehenge was probably the most interesting sight in the West Country.

We next flew to Stuttgart, Germany. We had ordered our new Mercedes-Benz car in the United States and had set a date to pick it up at the factory in Stuttgart. We stayed in a very fine hotel in Stuttgart before we picked up our car. We had two days to rest and sightsee. One day we climbed to the top of the Needle Tower, which is one of the tallest in Europe. We went to a camera factory and I bought a camera at a very cheap price. And we had dinner at the famous Allzepost Restaurant, where for the first time in my life, I tasted bear meat (it came from the Black Forest). We went through several beautiful art galleries—Germany is full of beautiful art galleries. And we visited the Daimler Benz Mercedes Museum—a very large museum with wonderful old cars dating back to before 1900.

The following day we picked up our car at the Mercedes factory outside of Stuttgart. We took a tour of the factory and were shown in detail how the car was assembled. The German system was different from the American one, in which all the cars are on an assembly line and are hauled around continuously from one mechanic to the next; no one ever stops the assembly line. If a car on the assembly line has a problem, it is tagged for someone else to fix later. In Germany, the cars were assembled on dollies that would not be moved until every detail was correct. Each dolly would be moved from station to station, which is a little slower than our way of doing it, but the Germans were perfectionists.

When we got the car, our mechanic took us on a ride and showed us how to drive it. He drove fast and skidded around corners, revving the engine through the gears. I thought he was going to tear it to pieces but he told me, "This is the way you drive a Mercedes. Don't baby it. Don't lug it around. You'll clog up the ports and you may have trouble. Don't try to break it in. We have already broken it in at the factory. We have put 500 miles on it already." I had seen how this was done when we made the tour. Each car rotates on rollers for 500 miles while the engineers and mechanics check everything out.

It was probably about 2:00 in the afternoon when we left the factory and got on the Autobahn headed for Wiesbaden, Germany. On the way, a Masseratti passed us doing about 150 miles an hour in the fast lane. There are no speed limits on the Autobahn. The fast lane is for the real fast cars; the second lane is for cars doing 70 miles an hour. In the slow lane you would be arrested if you did less than 50 miles an hour.

The following day we toured Cologne, which had been completely demolished by our bombers during World War II. Our bombers had torn out one corner of Cologne's famous cathedral, which was probably the oldest large cathedral in Europe, dating back a thousand years. The United States repaired the corner. We drove on through Bonn, which was once the capital of West Germany, to Bad Gotesburg, which was the diplomatic section of Bonn, where my grandfather's relative, Harry Poeppelmann, resided.

His home was just a few doors from the Arabian embassy and the British embassy. (He was one of the affluent Poeppelmanns.) We checked in at the Dreesden Hotel, which was one of the great hotels in Germany. When Adolph Hitler and Richard Chamberlain, the prime minister of England, met for a conference before the start of the war, they held it at the St. Petersburg Hotel across the river from the Dreesden; Chamberlain stayed at the St. Petersburg on one side of the Rhine River, and Hitler stayed in the Dreesden on the other side. During the war, 300 French officers (who were prisoners) were housed at the Dreesden Hotel. They lived like kings.

We made arrangements with a clerk from the hotel to be our interpreter and driver, and he drove us to Harry Poeppelmann's home. We joined Poeppelmann and his wife, Theese, for lunch that day. He was quite a remarkable person. He had a collection of fine oil paintings in his home and had many friends, having been at one time a headmaster of a German university. It was through Harry Poeppelmann that the "Poeppelmann Chronicle in Germany" was put together, which I had a copy of and which was of great help when I wrote my book about the Poeppelmann family. He was an intelligent fellow and could speak many languages, but because of his age (he was 85 years old) he mixed up his languages.

A few days later, Harry and Theese arranged to take us across the river to the St. Petersburg Hotel, which was the most elegant one I'd seen in all of Germany. Poeppelmann was received like a man of great importance, with the waiters and other staff flocking around him. We had a wonderful dinner and the finest of wines, and at least six or seven waiters waited on the four of us. I never saw such attention in my life. We were escorted up to see the suite that Chamberlain had used when he came to the St. Petersburg.

We visited the Poeppelmanns in Bad Godesberg again the next day. They were preparing to go to Denmark to their summer home. (A lot of the Germans had summer homes in Denmark. Many of them had taken their fortunes out of Germany during the war and invested them in Denmark for safety reasons.)

On Sunday, June 7, we set out for the place known as Grandorf, the Poeppelmann residence. Along the way we stayed in a little town called Bad Essen. The town had no hotels, but a policeman directed us to what they call a *pension*—a home in which rooms are rented. The price was very reasonable and included breakfast, and the house was immaculate and clean. From Bad Essen we proceeded to Grandorf. Grandorf was a large timbered house with a thatched roof. All the timbers inside the house were engraved with history about the building, which had been built in 1224 and was a historical landmark in Germany. The Catholic Church at one time controlled most of that country, and the story is that a Catholic bishop had been accosted by bandits or enemies; and the Poeppelmanns, who were peasants working in a field, rescued the bishop; and in return he gave them 5,000 acres and built this big mansion for them.

As Sue and I approached the building, I saw a boy in the barnyard and gave him a letter of introduction that Harry Poeppelmann had given me. Poeppelmanns were still living in the big home in Grandorf, as they had done for centuries. The boy went in the house, and when he came out, the whole family, all dressed up in their Sunday clothes, came to greet us.

The house itself was probably 150 feet long and had many rooms, and one part of it was a barn. In the early days, the animals were kept in the same building. You'd go through the front door and walk through the barn part, paved with cobblestones, until you eventually came to the second part of the building, which would be the house. The heat from the animals helped heat the house and also protected the animals. The barn was kept very clean; you could almost eat off the floor of that barn. Steel wasn't available to those who built Grandorf, so the ceiling of the building was made of huge timbers—they were a sight. The dining room table was probably 20 feet long, all hand-timbered. All the furniture was handmade centuries earlier. With its vast acreage and big barns, the property of Grandorf was almost a small empire.

We sat down to a big lunch with the Poeppelmanns. I had the honor of sitting at the end of the table, and the head of the family sat next to me. We had a question-and-answer session that lasted for a couple of hours. It was in the late afternoon before we proceeded to another Poeppelmann landmark, which is known as Gut Lethe— the place where my grandfather was born. Originally, in 1300, Gut Lethe was a castle, but the castle had been demolished. It was another small empire with vast acreage.

The law of the land in Germany when Gut Lethe was in existence was that the eldest son inherited everything—it was never divided among the children. (I think there were 16 children in the family at one time.) So out of 16 children, the oldest son got all the property. My grandfather, Arnold Poeppelmann, was raised there, but not being eligible to inherit anything, he and his brother Clemens left Germany for the United States.

Of course, many questions were posed to me, including "Whatever happened to Arnold Poeppelmann?" They were surprised to learn that I was Arnold's grandson, and they appreciated hearing my rundown on my grandfather and his brother Clemens.

Eugenie Rolfs, great-granddaughter of my grandfather's youngest sister, was an actress in East Germany in the 1950s. She was very helpful in compiling the historical material of the Poeppelmanns for use in this book.

The Gut Lethe Poeppelmanns were very kind to us. They referred us to a city called Cloppenborg in northern Germany, which is about 40 miles away from Gut Lethe and Grandorf. In the museum, which is known as the German Museum of Antiquities, we met the curator, who was overjoyed to find that finally an American Poppelman had come there. He showed us a big thick book that had all the history of the Poeppelmanns. The museum had many artifacts from the early church that had been built at Gut Lethe around 1400. We were told a lot of facts about the Poeppelmann family we'd never heard before, and the curator took our names and put them on record so that if any Germans ever wanted to know anything about the Poppelmans in America, they'd have it there. Later that came to fruition because a second cousin found me through that record and called me.

On Tuesday, June 10, we left Germany for Holland. (People now refer to Holland as the Netherlands; they don't use the word Holland much anymore.) We saw beautiful scenery between Germany and Holland, and just over the border we visited a town called Apeldoorn, which was the site of the summer palace of the queen of Holland.

On June 11 we drove into the city of Amsterdam. We had trouble finding our designated hotel—we had no map—but once we found it, we had the best food, and on our second day we found a very fine restaurant. We were surprised to find that if you ordered a steak in this restaurant the waiter would come out with the chef and would ask you how you liked the steak so it could be cooked properly and what you didn't like; that information was registered in a book the chef maintained. And you would be given a card with a number so that for all succeeding visits you merely presented the card and the culinary department would know exactly how you wanted your steak; it would always be perfect.

We found Amsterdam to be a little world of its own—lots of canals and bicycles by the thousands. If you sat at a sidewalk café when the factories were letting out, you would see thousands of bicycles on the main street and a few cars. I'd say 90 percent of the traffic was bicycles when we were there. The food was great, and boat rides on the canals were very interesting. We went through a diamond factory, which was known worldwide, called Bonnebakers. To get in, you had to present credentials because they don't let in just anybody—visitors were greeted at the front door and escorted to an interrogator who asked: "Who are you? Where are from? Why are you here?" We took a tour of the factory and saw how they split diamonds. Expert diamond cutters are paid good money because if they make one bad move it could mean thousands of dollars' loss.

I had made arrangements to meet the famous architect Baron von Hoevel. He was a real baron and a famous naval architect for yachts and boats. We were to meet in his hometown of Volendam, a quaint city on the edge of the water. Baron von Hoevel was about 70 years old, with slightly gray hair, and very polite. We talked about the boat—I wanted a 40-foot motor sailor with 50 percent sail, 50 percent power. He suggested that to save the tariff, we should bring the boat into the United States as a used boat. In order to use it, he suggested that he could arrange the crew, and he'd go with them himself and spend one summer in the fjords of Sweden. With his diplomatic power, we would have no trouble getting in and out of Norway. I thought that was great. We generally decided on what I should have and he agreed to make up a preliminary drawing for me for $300.

He also suggested that a fellow by the name of Rikkers might be a good guide for us as we toured the rest of Holland. Rikkers lived in a new home, which was different from American homes. For instance, the laundry room and the bathroom were together. The showerhead was in the center of the room and the water came down in about an 18-inch diameter circle. You would stand in the middle of the room and the water would run down the floor drain—there was no bathtub. After you took your shower, not only did you wipe yourself down but you would wipe down all the items in the room that might have gotten wet such as the laundry tubs. It was quite an experience—the bath area was so roomy you could walk around in it.

Rikkers turned out to be a wonderful driver and could get us discounts in the restaurants. He took us through many quaint towns in Holland and even drove us along the top of a dike. It was an eerie experience—out the right side window we saw the North Sea lapping up against the dike, and on the other side, 20 feet down, there was a whole countryside. If that dam ever broke, the whole nation would be under water.

We heard a lot of war stories about the Germans. In fact, Rikkers told me that when he was a boy, the Germans came through Holland and destroyed everything in sight. They flattened 29 city blocks of downtown Rotterdam. It had to all be rebuilt. Most of the people in Holland had only boiled grass to eat during the war. The Germans took everything from them.

We found that Europeans are really proud of their heritage. They revere their famous art galleries, they like their museums, and they like good restaurants. Instead of gulping down a lunch in 15 or 20 minutes, as we do in this country, they take two or three hours to eat. They enjoy life, and they're not worried about the stock market and who you're going to meet for lunch.

From Rotterdam we went to The Hague. At the Palace of Peace there, arguments between nations are submitted to 15 judges who settle the matters. The palace was donated by Andrew Carnegie, the American steel magnate. The town also has a famous miniature city; all the buildings are only about 18 inches high. We toured the House of Commons and the House of Lords. And in Holland we saw tulips blooming throughout the countryside—it was gorgeous, though it rained most of the time we were there.

We continued on to Belgium and drove to the city of Brussels. The first place we went to see, on someone's suggestion, was Fort Breedonk, about 12 miles outside of town. It had been a German concentration camp. After I went through that camp and realized what really happened—the ovens and gas chambers and all—I was, for a long time, ashamed that I had German blood in me. I couldn't believe that human beings could treat other human beings in such a manner.

Next we drove to Paris. We went to the Folies Bergère, which I liked, and to the Left Bank, where the beatniks and artists hung out. We went to the Moulin Rouge area. There may have been 500 artists on the Seine's north bank every day, selling their paintings to tourists for peanuts. The place I most enjoyed was Napoleon's Tomb. The display is absolutely fabulous. We also took a bus tour to Versailles and went through the Hall of Mirrors, where the peace treaty was signed after the war.

At the famous Louvre museum, I went to see the Mona Lisa. I was all alone. I remembered that when the famous painting was brought to Washington and hung in our National Gallery (it used to be the Mellon Gallery, but he gave it to our country, so it's now known as Washington's National Gallery), the only way you could see the Mona Lisa was to get in a line four abreast and walk slowly past it; you couldn't even stop to look at it. It was guarded by marines. Twenty thousand people a day were coming to see Mona Lisa. In Paris I was able to stand in front of Mona Lisa all by myself—I couldn't believe it.

After many weeks of touring, we got to the point where we didn't want to do a damn thing but stay in our room and rest. Sue got tired quicker than I did, so I had to be careful about wearing her out. When we left Paris, I decided that some day I would rent an apartment there and stay a few months, I liked it so much. Although certain parts of Paris are very dirty, there's just something about Paris you have to like. It was difficult to leave because I knew that I was leaving a lot behind I hadn't seen.

CHAPTER 22

Adventures in Switzerland,
a Toothache in Italy,
Return to Holland, and Home

We next crossed over into Switzerland, heading for Lausanne. In Switzerland the scenery and the architecture changed, and we found that the cars also changed as we went along; once again, we saw German Volkswagens and Mercedes Benzes and BMWs. Lausanne, in a mountainous area, was home to watch factories. We stayed at a gorgeous hotel called the Beau Rivage Palace, in a room overlooking a lake.

The Beau Rivage Hotel had a unique way of parking cars. The employees were not allowed to drive guests' cars, so four men would come up with a dolly and jacks. They would jack up your car, run the dolly under it, and then hand-pull your car to a parking space. I asked the manager, "Why do you park like that? We don't do that in America."

He said, "People who had trouble with their cars used to come to our hotel, let us park them, and then complain when they got the car back that there was something wrong with the car—they would blame us for it. With all these expensive cars coming in here, we decided we were not going to mechanically touch them. This is why we pull them into the parking place with the jack and dolly."

Every 25 years the town holds a big exposition called the Swiss National Exposition, and we happened to be lucky enough to arrive in town in time to experience it. From the hotel we could ride free cable cars over to the exposition.

Our travels took us from Lausanne to Berne, the capital of Switzerland, and on to a famous ski resort in the Alps called Interlaken. There we rode a tram that took us up above 11,000 feet. Even in summer the peaks were covered with snow. Driving through the high Alps of Switzerland was absolutely a treat to last a lifetime. On July 1 we arrived at a beautiful little town called Andermatt, which was a short ride from Interlaken.

We continued down the Andermatt mountain range into Como, Italy. The ride over the St. Gotthard Pass was very difficult, but the scenery was absolutely gorgeous. We spent the following day touring Lake Como, which was lined around the shoreline and in the hills with beautiful villas, all with red roof tiles.

From there we drove south to Florence, Italy. The highlight of our visit there was a little town outside of Florence where Leonardo da Vinci had lived. His home had been made into a small museum. We celebrated July 4 with other Americans at Harry's Bar, a popular place in Florence, which was covered with American flags. We took a bus tour of the city and went to the galleries. After a heavy rain, Florence was very beautiful. Because of traffic and trash, some cities get pretty crummy looking. But after a rain a city changes complexion. On July 6 we went to Leonardo da Vinci's house a second time, and we noticed that all his writings were what they call "mirror writings"—backwards. Some people think that was all automatic writing, that his genius made writing that way effortless.

From Florence we drove to the west coast of Italy to the town of Pisa, home of the famous Leaning Tower. When I stood at the base of the tower looking up, I was very frightened. It appeared that the tower was falling on me. From Pisa we decided to take a boat to the island of Elba, where Napoleon was exiled in 1810. Our car was put on the ferry by driving it onto a netting that had been laid out on the dock; the net was hoisted onto the ship. Sue couldn't watch because she was so afraid the ropes were going to break and our car would end up in the sea.

Elba was a hidden paradise. When our boat came in at night, the whole little port city came out to greet us. Our car was taken off the boat on the net and put onto the dock. From there we drove up the top of a mountain overlooking the harbor. There we found the Plaza Hotel, the only hotel on the island. We saw no Americans. The room had a fantastic view of the whole harbor.

When we went down to breakfast the next morning, we learned that nobody in the restaurant could understand English. A woman sitting at a table opposite us happened to be one of Europe's leading dress designers. She was German but could speak English and Italian. She came over to us and said she noticed we were having trouble with the language, so she had breakfast with us. She said, "I know Elba very well because I come here every year for my vacation. I like it because there are no tourists. Perhaps we should team up. I'll show you the Island of Elba, and you can drive since you have a car." So that's what we did, and we became great friends. Her name was Edith Selma. She took us to see Napoleon's home, and then we drove in the mountains to some villages. Some of the streets were so narrow we had trouble getting my Mercedes through. The island was fringed with small private beaches. We would seldom see more than two or three people at any of them. It was a great place to hide out.

We left Elba on July 8, heading for Rome. We arrived in the city at 6:30 in the evening, right at the busy traffic time. Little Fiat cars buzzed around us like bees. But the drivers were very careful not to cause an accident. If a driver's insurance card is taken away because of an accident, the driver can't drive anymore. The car is impounded until the driver's green insurance card is returned. So although it appeared that we were going to be hit a thousand times going through Rome traffic, we weren't.

A wonderful thing happened to us in Rome. I wanted to see Brioni's famous haberdashery, which was reputed to be the finest clothing store in the world. When Sue and I came to the store, we met a salesman who had been a prisoner of war in Arkansas during the war. He was treated so well there that he welcomed us; he was happy to see Americans come into the shop. (Few tourists went there because most can't afford the clothes.) Mr. Brioni, the owner, happened to be in the shop. He had received a letter from a manufacturing magnate from Chicago—an order in English. Since I was an American, he asked if I could read the letter. Well, the letter looked like the marks made by a chicken walking over the paper! I never saw such horrible writing. But I figured out what the order was. I deciphered it and wrote it out for him. It took me about an hour to do it.

In return, he wanted to know what he could do for me. I said, "Well, I'd like to buy a couple of your beautiful suits." I told him I'd only be in town a week, and he insisted that I be fitted. Mr. Brioni said, "We'll shut down the plant and do your suits first." They made two suits for me and two for Sue.

In addition, the salesman who had been a war prisoner asked, "What size shoes do you wear?"

I said, "Ten and a half."

He said, "We have some tailor-made shoes here that a movie director from Hollywood had ordered, but he never came after them and he never told us where to ship them. Would you like to buy them?"

I tried on a pair, and they fit me perfectly. Whoever had ordered the shoes was my twin brother. I said, "How much are the shoes going to cost?"

He said, "How much do you want to pay for them?"

We finally agreed on $20 a pair, and I took all four pairs. They were supposed to be a hundred and something a pair for the movie director. In addition to that, the salesman loaded up a sack of free socks—there must have been ten pair in that sack. I said, "You can't do that."

He said, "Americans were good to me; I'll be good to you."

When we went to see the opera *Aida* at the old Coliseum in Rome, I had an unusual experience. In the men's restroom were old ladies with towels. When a man stepped away from the urinal, a woman would run over and wipe his penis for him. At all the restrooms along the highways in Italy, women were there with the men. They worked for tips. I never saw anything like it. One old lady at the Coliseum was a little too enthusiastic. According to Sue, the women's restrooms had fancy dressing tables and an attendant would do anything you wanted—fix your hair, straighten your dress or hose—anything for a tip. The services were unbelievable.

In Italy and France it was difficult to tell if a woman was a prostitute. If she was beautifully dressed, she was probably a prostitute. They were gorgeous creatures. I saw two of them in a Paris hotel lobby. I went up to them and asked if they could speak English. They said no and pointed to a bellhop. I went over to him and asked him, "Those women, who are they? They're so beautifully dressed."

He said, "You want one?"

We took a bus tour out of Rome to the beautiful Tivoli Gardens, which has 300 fountains all lit up at night. We also went to the catacombs, rode on the Appian Way, visited the Vatican, where we saw the Sistine Chapel and Michelangelo's beautiful paintings on the ceiling. We were just leaving the Sistine Chapel when I asked somebody about a restroom and was told to go down some steps. I did, and at the bottom was a sort of half-cellar area. There was a little tiny restroom with one urinal and a cubicle with a private stool. The whole area was about eight feet square. I had the whole room to myself. I start to open my fly and realized I had my shorts on backward. So I thought, "What the hell. This is a good time to change them." I took my pants off and was just starting to change my shorts when the damn door flew open. A whole mob of young priests who had been on a bus tour—about 40 of them—barged in. They all had the same urge at the same time. I backed up against the wall, but I couldn't move. I had to wait until they all got out before I could get my shorts and pants back on. What a time!

We left Rome on July 15, the middle of summer, and headed for Naples. In Naples we went to Pompeii to see the ruins under Mount Vesuvius. We wound up in a little town south of Naples called Sorrento, which is on the cliffs overlooking the ocean. The hotel we stayed in was the Camella—a beautiful little place. It had gardens running from the hotel clear to the cliffs overlooking the sea, which are about 100 feet high. An elevator took people down to the beach to board a boat to go to the island of Capri, which we did. Capri is a mountain sticking up in the air. It's beautiful, but the road going to the top is treacherous. The last few hundred feet, we had to ride on something like a tram. At the top is Villa St. Michele, which is very famous. We also visited the famous Blue Grotto, which we got to in a low boat. We had to duck our heads as the boat entered a great big cave. The water is a beautiful brilliant blue.

While we were in Capri I was suffering from a toothache, so I asked the hotel manager to recommend a dentist somewhere around Capri or Naples.

He said, "Which way are you going?"

I said, "Well, I'm eventually going to Venice. I'll be going up on the Adriatic side of Italy." You have to visualize the boot: We were now on the instep part of the boot. We still had to go across the toe, down the Amalfi coast.

The manager said, "If you're going toward Solerno, you should go up to St. Giovanni, a town on a mountain, and see Padre Pio. He's a famous healer. He can heal your toothache quickly."

I had read a book about the famous stigmata of Padre Pio. At 20 years of age, he developed sores like Jesus had, and no one could cure him. They were always bleeding. But there never was any infection. He wore brown gloves with the fingertips cut off. I told Sue, "Here's a chance for us to get to see Padre Pio; let's go." So we went on across to the heel of the boot and up the backside of the mountain where the little town of San Giovanni was located, where Padre Pio, the famous healer, lived. We got to the top of the hill and the little town about 4:00 in the afternoon. I told the woman at the little hotel where we stopped, "We've come to see Padre Pio."

She looked at her watch and said, "If you can hurry, I'll get somebody to take you up before 5:00 Mass. He'll be in church in a few minutes. Leave your luggage here; we'll take care of it." Then she called a man to take us to the church.

The church was full of people—there were no seats left, but there was some standing room along the right wall next to about 20 young men in Franciscan robes, opposite the altar. Sue and I went in and stood next to them. Mass had just started.

Padre Pio was standing just a few feet from us, so I could see him very well. When he raised the chalice, he would take off his brown gloves, which hid the bleeding marks on his hands. Then he brought the chalice down, put the gloves back on, and went on with the ceremony. After the service the congregation started leaving the church.

The 20 men next to us were priests from the town of Milano who had come to get a special blessing from Father Pio. I noticed a door on the side and thought it went outside, so I told Sue, "Let's follow these men and take a shortcut out of the church." The door went to an anteroom in back of the church where the young priests were going to be given a blessing. I got through the door and they cut Sue off—no women allowed. The young priest in charge of the door thought I was with the priests. Inside, we waited a few minutes for Padre Pio. The room was about 15 feet wide with a small altar. He knelt down at his altar and was there for about 10 or 15 minutes. In the meantime the church attendants lined up the men from Milano and me and in two rows, kneeling on pillows. Padre Pio got up from his altar, walked along the rows, and started blessing each priest. When he got to me, I looked up at him—I wanted to see him. It seemed like he was looking right through me. He touched me on the head. I had put my hand up—I think I was about to move my hair or something—and I touched his hand. As he went out the door, all the young men who were being blessed started jumping up and whooping and hollering and hugging each other. I finally went back out the door I came in. I asked one of the young priests, "What should I do now?"

He said, "Well, you can go back to your hotel. The church is pretty empty now; go back home." Sue was waiting for me in front of the church. A man was with her. In a book I have about Padre Pio, there is a story about a pilot and his crew who had the mechanism shot out of their bomber when they were over Italy. A vision of Padre Pio guided them. They made a landing they thought was impossible, and ever since that episode, one of the pilots had gone to see Padre Pio every year. He was in front of the church talking to Sue when I joined her. Sue introduced me to him.

I said, "Well, hell, I read about you in my book."

Sue had told him I'd had a toothache. He said, "Well, how did you do?"

I had to think. I said, "There's no toothache. It's gone." And, in fact, it never did come back.

(When I got home, I went to my dentist and told him about my toothache and being blessed. My dentist pulled out some old X-rays. He said, "This is what we have on record." It showed my tooth canted a little bit. "Let's take a new X-ray and see what you've got." The X-ray showed the tooth straight up! I think it was instant healing.)

The pilot suggested that we visit a New York socialite who had been healed 40 years before by Padre Pio when he was a young man. She left New York and built a big beautiful pink house in the little mountain town; it was known as the Pink House, and all Americans were welcome to come there. So we went to see her. Her name was Mary Pyle. She was quite a woman—very gracious, and she served us refreshments. She told us many stories about Padre Pio. She said, "At one time over 2,000 pairs of crutches were stacked behind the church from people that had been healed by him." She said that she had been cured of some incurable disease; I guessed it was cancer. And because of that, she decided to spend the rest of her life with Padre Pio. Then she told Sue, "If you'd like to have a blessing from

Padre Pio, tomorrow he's going to bless a group of women, and I'm sure if I write a note to a certain priest he'll arrange for you to join them."

So she did, and we found the priest she mentioned and gave him the note. On the following morning, we went to the church and sat in an anteroom on wooden benches. Padre Pio was blessing a wedding in the main part of the church, so we waited. The anteroom was packed with women—there must've been over a hundred of them in there—and a few men, including a boy in a wheelchair. We waited and waited, and finally a young priest said, "Padre's coming," and he opened the door. The first thing the father did was bless the boy in the chair.

The women broke into pandemonium. The ones in the back were crawling over the ones in front of them, all fighting to get Padre Pio to touch them. They were yelling and screaming. The priests who were escorting Padre Pio grabbed him and took him out a side door, brushing past me on his way out. The young priest grabbed me and said, "You get out of that door, too, before you get squashed," so I went out the side door and Sue came right after me. I never saw such a scene in my life. The women went out of their heads. When they realized they were in the same room with Padre Pio, they couldn't contain themselves.

After we left the church and went up the coast to a place called Rimini, our luck changed for the better. Although they hadn't had a room for us at the famous Rimini Hotel, they had a cancellation just before we came in. We got a beautiful room with a beautiful view of the Adriatic Sea. We went on to Venice and everything clicked for us there. The hotel that we were supposed to stay at was a rattrap, but we found a new hotel called the Byron on a beach about 10 miles north of Venice and got a good room there. After that blessing from

Padre Pio, everything started working our way; we couldn't do anything wrong.

Padre Pio became so famous that many nations—including the United States (in a move headed by Mayor LaGuardia of New York City)—sent money to build a big hospital up on the hill beside the church. Padre Pio made daily visits up to the hospital. The last I heard, he was being considered for sainthood.

Sue was getting homesick, and it had been so hot and muggy that we decided we would head north from Venice, back through the Alps toward Holland. Our tour took us through the northern Italian Alps, and to Salzburg, Austria, and to Vienna. We spent several days touring Vienna, including the Schoënbrun Castle, which was absolutely gorgeous. The weather turned cool and Sue began to feel better.

From Vienna we proceeded on to Munich, Germany. It was quite a long ride, 237 miles on the autobahn at high speed. We arranged to see the dress designer that we met at Elba—she came to our hotel, took us to the opera and to some very fine German restaurants at which we did not see any tourists. She had designed a special dress for Sue and had it made. It was waiting as a gift when we arrived. She knew Munich—it was her hometown. She told us the good places to go and the ones not to waste time with. In return, she was supposed to be our guest when she came to America, but we never did get together again. That was the last we saw of her. She was great.

We continued on to Zurich, a beautiful city, and then to Heidelberg, Germany, where we stayed three days. We went through the famous castle on one day and did some general sightseeing on another day. The food was great in Heidelberg, but after traveling for a couple of months, food didn't taste as good to us anymore. It took something extraordinary to interest us. It was the same with the sightseeing; we were bypassing a lot of stuff, and we were anxious to get back to Baron von Hoevel to see our boat plans. So we cut our visit in Heidelberg a little short, although it is a fabulous city and very interesting historically.

We drove back to Bad Godesberg, hoping we would see Harry Poeppelmann, but he was still in Denmark. We drove on to the Netherlands, returned to Volendam, and met with the baron. I mentioned to him that Sue had been very tired and was getting homesick, and he said, "I know a place you will enjoy." In the town of Apeldoorn—we'd been there before—there was an old castle that had been restored to a hotel, called the Hotel Kasteel de Hooge Doursche. We had a recommendation from the baron and got a beautiful room in the castle. An orchestra played at all the meals except breakfast. The food was wonderful, the décor and gardens were beautiful, and it cost us just $12 a day for the two of us. (Recently I told my second cousin Eugenie to stay there, but the rooms were over $300 a night!) Anyway, thanks to the baron we got a room there and stayed for about a week. We didn't do anything but rest. I always wanted to go back there.

At the end of the week Baron von Hoevel and I had a luncheon appointment to discuss the preliminary drawings for my boat. The plans were beautiful—they showed a steel hull ship, sloop-rigged, with a diesel engine. He had talked with some people who were willing to sail with us to Norway once the boat was built. The following day, he took us to lunch at the Dutch Royal Yacht Club, where the queen's yacht was located. We had a wonderful lunch and toured the yacht club. I told the baron that we would be going home on the Holland-American Line on the *Rotterdam*. He said he would call the steamship line and see that they took care of us. Then we parted and headed for Rotterdam.

Rotterdam had been bombed so badly in World War II that the whole town was still under construction. We could see our ship from our hotel—it was just across the park from us. Every day Sue would go down and get as close to the boat as she could just to look at it. She was very homesick.

While we were resting in Rotterdam, I took a train ride back to Leiden to talk to Dr. Tromp, the author of *Psychical Physics*, which was considered among all the parapsychologists the greatest book ever written about dowsing. He also was a representative to the United Nations from the Netherlands. We had a long talk, and he admitted to me, "You know, it wasn't until after I published my book that I realized I should never have published it. I was on the wrong track. I said dowsing is a physical element, and it is not. There is no affinity between the divining rod and the water." He believed that the thalamus gland can be blocked off by emotional conflicts, shutting off dowsing reactions, and that muscles move by subconscious control. Tromp was skeptical of Padre Pio as a genuine stigmatic, but he pressed me for facts and asked to see some of the books about Pio that I had brought. One of the questions Tromp posed was, Why do dowsers need a rod? It's not necessary since dowsing can be done at a distance. In other words, if you dowse on a map, what does it have to do with being there physically? Tromp also believed that there are biological mysteries surrounding the body—that many things about the body are mystical, especially our minds. He believed all persons are just as spiritual as Padre Pio, but Pio had some way of using it whereas the rest of us don't. He said to me, "Before you came I had my secretary hide a silver coin under one corner of the carpet in this room. Can you tell me which one it is?"

I said, "Yeah, but what I want to know is, can *you* find it?"

He said, "It's under that corner, I think," and it was. He didn't have to use a divining rod. He had studied so much on the subject that I think it rubbed off on him.

Tromp presented me with manuscripts of several experiments he had done, and autographed them for me; I donated them to the American Society of Dowsers. He and I had dinner at a very fine restaurant: Coq d'Or.

On August 18 we boarded the *Rotterdam*. A bon voyage message from Baron von Hoevel was waiting for us. We first crossed the North Sea to Southampton, England—a choppy ride.

Aboard ship I ran into someone I knew from Bakersfield, California: Jimmie Icardo. He had taken his children to Italy to meet their grandfather and grandmother. I had gone to high school with Jimmie's brother Al. The Icardo family was very poor; they were Italian farmers. While I played football, Jimmie peddled potatoes and vegetables from house to house after school. Al had since made millions of dollars in the farming business in Bakersfield and had a string of race horses. Jimmie and I became good friends during that crossing. Every day we would have a massage and a steam bath and mix with the crowd during the boat drills and during the entertainment aboard ship.

Sue, being tired from her long trip in Europe, preferred just to lounge around and take life pretty easy aboard the boat. When we got to New York City, the 1964 World's Fair was going on. Sue wasn't keen on seeing it, but I was, so I checked into a hotel while Sue flew directly to California to meet my brother Clyde, who helped her pick up our car at San Pedro Harbor.

PART 7

Later Years (1964–present)

CHAPTER 23

My Mysterious Illness
and How I Was Healed

The morning after we landed in New York City, I got on a subway that I thought was going to take me to the World's Fair, but it went to Belmont Racetrack instead. I decided, "Since I'm at the race track, I may as well stay here." I sat down next to a guy who had all kinds of racing forms. He'd say, "This is the horse to beat," and I'd get the number of it, run down, and put a $2 bet on it. When I got back to my seat that guy would still be working on his forms. Then he'd bet on a different horse, but my horse would win—the horse he told me to bet on. He gave me four races in a row, but he never bet on one winner himself. He got so damn mad he got up and left. And I had won $80, starting with $2.

I finally found out the right way to get to the fair, and the next three days I went there and had a wonderful time. Then I went back to Virginia. The Lord & Taylor building was coming along fine, but some addendums had to be made to our contract, and I had to be there with the lawyers before I could go to California. But eventually I flew to California to join Sue. She was living with my sister in San Fernando, and that's where I stayed for a few days.

My brother-in-law Neville R. Lewis, an attorney, had a client who was a prominent farmer in Bakersfield—by coincidence, I had gone to high school with him. He and Neville owned a piece of land they wanted to sell, and it would be much more salable if it had a water well. So they asked me to stay in California a few extra days and find them a good water well using my dowsing skills. I overexerted myself—I had felt some pains in my shoulders while dowsing, which I figured was just due to fatigue—but I suggested a location for the well. They got a good water well and sold the property at a good price.

Sue and I drove our Mercedes back to Florida to visit her mother and some friends (including a particularly good friend, Robert Plimpton, who was then president of the American Society of Dowsers). We were staying in a motel in North Palm Beach when I woke up in the middle of the night to use the bathroom and found I couldn't get out of bed. Poor Sue called our family doctor, and he suggested that we try to get back up to Washington, D.C., right away. So Sue drove me back, and I checked into a Washington clinic that was headed by an old university friend who had been at one time a top surgeon at the esteemed Mayo Clinic in Rochester, Minnesota. (The clinic was sort of a satellite of the Mayo Clinic.) My muscles were atrophying—they were losing strength. I could barely hang onto a pencil.

The staff worked on me as an outpatient for about a month. I took a bus or taxi from my apartment in Arlington into Washington each day. One day the doctors brought me into a conference room and said, "We have not been able to diagnose your problem. You picked up something in Europe, but we can't figure out what it is. We think you should go to the Johns Hopkins Hospital in Baltimore and see if the doctors there can help you."

I was given a room at the very eminent Johns Hopkins Hospital, and more than 40 doctors checked me over and tested me during the course of two weeks. They got suspicious when they interviewed me about what I'd done in Europe. When I mentioned that I had eaten bear meat, they suspected I had gotten trichinosis from the meat. At the Washington clinic where I'd been previously, the doctors took five biopsies from each shoulder where I'd had pains when I was dowsing in California. On those places the tissue looked like it had been burned with electricity. That also caused concern among the doctors at Johns Hopkins. After they had done every type of test they could, they still couldn't arrive at a diagnosis. They referred me to the man they considered to be the best muscle doctor at that time, Dr. Pearson at the UCLA Medical Center in California.

I had heard about a clinic in Florida and decided to try it before I went to California. It was situated near Venice, Florida, at a place where water flowed out of an extinct volcano. If you dived into the water, you could only go down a few feet before the force of the water would throw you up, but you could float like a log on the surface. I spent two weeks at that clinic and found some relief when I'd exercise.

We traded in our Mercedes and our old Studebaker for the most comfortable car we could find, a Chrysler LeBaron, and headed for California. (The new car had a problem, however—if we slowed to 20 miles an hour, we'd hear a fluttering noise that was very annoying. None of the dealers along the way to California could find the source of the trouble. They all thought it was the air conditioning.) When we got to California, we stayed with my brother-in-law, Neville, until I got a report from the UCLA Medical Center. By coincidence, Neville hosted a party for some of his clients at his home, and one of them happened to be a retired vice president of Chrysler

Motor Corporation. I told him about the LeBaron's problem and he decided he'd take some action. He had the factory send out two troubleshooting mechanics. They leased space in the Chrysler dealership in Santa Monica and practically dismantled my car. They had the engine all apart and could find no trouble. When they got to the transmission, they found that where one gasket was usually installed there were double gaskets, and it was the vibration of the transmission between those two gaskets that caused the fluttering noise.

Dr. Pearson suggested that we take an apartment on the beach near the hospital because he wanted me to exercise on the beach. We found a place called Edgewater Towers in Pacific Palisades, between Santa Monica and Malibu Beach. It was a very swanky place. Cliff Robertson, the famous actor, had the apartment above me.

One day Dr. Pearson called me and said, "Ray, we're giving you further tests. We have all the records from Johns Hopkins Hospital. We think there's only one way that you can ever be cured." I was told I could do just a few activities each day—mostly walking and swimming. Then I learned about a business problem back East. I was in negotiations for a property I was going to lease for an office building, and Sue had to go back to Virginia and handle it for me. I was alone in this swanky apartment house. I went swimming every morning, and sometimes Cliff Robertson would check me with a stopwatch to see if I was gaining or losing time because I'd try to make two laps faster each day. I hired an aide who would take me down to the ocean, which was just a couple of blocks away. There I had to walk in water up to my knees. At first I could walk about 100 feet at the most. Then I began to improve. I could walk—shuffle, really—maybe half a block in a beautiful park on the cliffs of the Pacific Palisades. I was very discouraged.

The hospital sent a nurse over to help me with my meals while

Sue was away. Neville Lewis and my sister lived out in the San Fernando Valley, an hour's drive away with all the traffic.

Every day I was taken to UCLA Medical Hospital. Dr. Pearson finally said, "Ray, there's nothing we can do for you medically. You have to cure yourself by physical therapy. We want you to swim, we want you to walk in the ocean up to your knees every day, we want you to get up and walk, walk, walk." So that was my program.

Sue came back and drove the car home, closed the apartment, stored the furniture, and flew back and joined me. I would walk and walk and walk. And the soreness finally went away. After three months I got so I could walk five miles. And no medical doctor ever arrived at a solid diagnosis as to what I had.

While I was still being treated for my muscle problem in California, a newspaper reporter who was interested in dowsing came to see me. He said, "Poppelman, there's a story that's upset the medical world: A minister in the San Fernando Valley in Encino has healed a girl who was born blind. I have talked to him, and he's going to have a healing procession in about ten days; I have put your name in. I think it's worth a gamble."

The reporter wanted me to meet the minister before the healing services started. I found him to be a very jolly, friendly little fellow, an Englishman. We didn't talk much; I just told him that I was having trouble—I'd picked up some disease in Europe, and the doctors thought it was probably trichinosis from bear meat—and I was on my own with the physical therapy that could save me. Later that day, we went to the healing service (my sister and brother-in-law and a friend were with me), which was held in a big gymnasium. The place was filled. As we waited, the minister came in. He had transformed himself into a Chinese person. He spoke Chinese, he shuffled like a Chinaman, his facial expressions were those of a Chinaman. He could well pass for Chinese. And he went by the name of Yu Fang. He had two assistants with him. In the center of the basketball court were 19 stools arranged in a large circle. I eventually had to come down and take my position on one of the stools.

The first boy he called down was deaf. Yu Fang healed him so he could hear a watch tick across the room. I was on my stool. There were women on each side of me. The minister, Yu Fang, took a stool opposite me. He was in a deep trance and spoke in Chinese, though one of his assistants translated what he said into English. The assistants took my coat off (I was wearing a business suit) so that Yu Fang could put his hands on my body, and he went over my whole body and found the scars from my biopsies. I thought, "How the hell does he know I even had any operations?" A surgeon at the Washington Clinic had done biopsies on my calves, legs, and shoulders, and a surgeon at Johns Hopkins had taken a biopsy from my back. There's no way the minister could know about the biopsies or see the scars through my clothes. And I thought, "The guy must be really extremely psychic." (Later I asked the newspaper reporter if he knew I had had biopsies, and he didn't, so I know he didn't tell Yu Fang about them.)

He pulled up my shirt from my pants and ran his hand down my back, and when he got near my tailbone, he started talking in Chinese, and his hand was like fire. It was so hot I could hardly stand it. His assistants reminded him to talk to me in English, and he told me that I had fallen on my tailbone while ice skating in South Dakota. Well, I had taken a lot of spills because we used to skate on what we called sloughs. But how could he have known that?

Anyway, I started squirming. I said, "I can't stand it. What do you have on your hands?"

The assistant said, "He'll be finished with you in a few minutes. You're being healed."

Then he came around the front of me and said, "You've got special powers."

I said, "I don't think I do, or I wouldn't have been sick for all these months. The doctors can't find anything wrong with me."

He started speaking Chinese again. Then he said, "I think you're going to be OK." When he was finished with me, he moved over to the next person to be healed, and I thanked him. Then I got up and put my coat back on, and one of his assistants escorted me back to where my sister and brother-in-law and their friend were sitting.

Before we left the arena, he handed me a "prescription" for dealing with problems: his business card with his address and phone number. "Any time you have a problem, you call me and I will see what I can find out for you," he told me.

I said, "How will you be able to help me over the phone? Can't I talk to you directly?"

He said, "I don't do this directly. I go into a trance, and another personality, a Chinese fellow, takes over. He knows the answers. I will refer any questions you give me to Yu Fang. It's best to do it at night. You can probably concentrate better and you'll be closer to your subconscious mind at night, before you fall asleep. Just before you fall asleep you get the best results," he told me.

We got to the car, and much to my surprise, I said, "Let's stop somewhere and get a bite to eat and something to drink and maybe even find a place where we can dance a little bit." They all thought I was crazy, but I insisted that we go dancing, so we stopped at a place in Van Nuys on the way home. Then they took me back to my apartment, and I insisted they hang around and have whatever I had to offer them for drinks. They couldn't believe how differently I was behaving. Before we'd gone to see Yu Fang I was depressed and negative about everything—and now I was the life of the party. My brother-in-law thought maybe I'd been hypnotized. As a consequence, I went back to Dr. Pearson and told him what had happened. He checked me over and had me do some exercises I couldn't do before. He had heard about the minister but couldn't offer any explanation.

Things started to change fast. A friend wanted me to go to Reno, Nevada, to a UFO convention. I went and was feeling so well that I went on up to Banff, Canada, to Lake Louise along the Fraser River to Victoria, and to Vancouver, sightseeing. I came back home and had no pain. I went back to Dr. Pearson and said, "I'm back to normal. I can't believe it. I hope the pain doesn't come back."

He said, "Well, now you can worry about me."

I said, "What's wrong with you?"

He said, "I have cancer."

That was a shock to me; he certainly looked healthy. He died two years later of cancer.

To continue with my story: Dr. Pearson said, "Ray, for the rest of your life, you must be very active. Do as much physical work as you can. Try to do something that's fun for yourself, and do it as much as possible." I told him that I would like to live in Oxford, Maryland, because it was a fishing village that had transformed into a yachting center. During the Revolutionary War the little town of Oxford on the eastern shore of Maryland was headquarters for the British Fleet. In my sailing days I always liked to sail to Oxford. He said, "If you like Oxford, just go and live there."

Sue, in the meantime, had flown back out to California. She was ecstatic about my situation. We drove the big Chrysler back as far as Nashville, Tennessee, when we had trouble with the air conditioner. We had to leave the car with a dealer in Nashville for a couple of days, and while we were waiting we noticed across the street a little tiny building with just one car—a Silver Shadow Rolls Royce. An old man was sitting there—he was the salesman. I went over to see what he would allow on a trade on my Chrysler for the Rolls Royce. We got within $1,000 of making a deal. He said, "I want you to look back some day and remember I told you you'll be sorry that you didn't buy this Rolls Royce for $16,000."

Sometime later I called Vern Cameron, a famous dowser who lived in the Lake Elsinore area, and told him how I'd felt pain while dowsing and then got so sick afterward, and he said, "Never dowse more than 15 minutes without taking a break. You overdid it and it backfired on you. Your problem was not bear meat. It was from dowsing."

Dr. Pearson had advised me to lay off dowsing for a couple of years. Then I found that even without using the divining rods, I was getting impressions. I remember one time at the Will Rogers ranch in Santa Monica, a fellow by the name of Fred Kimball, a psychic, said, "Ray, can you show me where the water is here with a divining rod?"

I said, "I don't need a divining rod. It goes here, there, and there."

He said, "How do you know?"

I said, "I just feel it that way."

I found a dowser in Kentucky who was a farmer. His hands were callused, and he said, "If I use a divining rod too long, it pulls the calluses loose and my hands bleed. I can work with shovels and tools and never have any trouble, but when I use a divining rod, the calluses come loose on my hands. It's a different kind of a physical thing."

I tried contacting Yu Fang a few times, and it seemed to work. Whether my problems would have resolved themselves without going to Yu Fang, I don't know, but it seemed that after I first made contact with Yu Fang, my whole life changed. I wouldn't even have to phone him; I would just concentrate on the Englishman, imagine that I was talking to him. "Reverend [So-and-so], I have a problem. Would you see what Yu Fang has to say about it?" I would present my problem, and then a thought would come to me. The general idea was that the healer was contacting some ancient Chinese psychic who knew all the answers to our problems. It seems fantastic, but it worked. If there is such a thing as mental telepathy, then that's what we were using.

Chapter 24

The American Society of Dowsers

My experience with dowsing began while I was a student at the University of Maryland. I had made friends with Bud Avery, a wealthy fellow whose mother liked to entertain. Bud invited me to one of her parties, and she had arranged to have a vaudeville actor from a theater entertain her guests. He would sit at a table in the kitchen with one hand on the door—it was a swinging door that opened to the dining room. On the opposite side, the guests would line up. He had a pendulum that would swing one way for no, another way for yes, and would tell him whether a man or a woman was at the head of the line.

I was put in the kitchen with him to see that he wasn't cheating. There wasn't any trickery. He told me where he learned to dowse: Two fellows in New York City set up an office and charged $25 to tell a woman whether she was going to give birth to a boy or girl. They had a lot of electrical appliances in their office to fool the subjects. They also had a pendulum, which they used while they held a subject's hand—it was the dowsing phenomenon at work. He learned from them how to do it. Later, I heard of George Morris, the doodlebugger who used a pendulum in the oil fields. Through the years, I researched dowsing and read a lot of books relating to the subject, and I learned of the British Society of Dowsers.

Then I found out that the American Society of Dowsers was being organized. Some reputable people were on the board of trustees. The vice president of the American Sugar Refining Company was one, and a fellow who was with the Atomic Energy Commission was another. So I joined the organization and went to the meetings each summer in Vermont, and I found out that, by God, there was something to it. I agree with Einstein: It was something beyond human control. It was a phenomenon that deserved research. As I studied more, I learned that there were dowsing societies in Australia, India, and a few other places around the world. I also found out from my own experiments that it was not physical; it was something else.

The American Society of Dowsers originally was mostly a group of farmers making a social event out of getting together. As the years went by, there were fewer farmers coming to the meetings and more parapsychologists and professors. I spoke at one dowser convention in Vermont and claimed there was no affinity between the divining rod and what the dowser was looking for—water, ore, lost objects, lost people, or anything else. I almost caused a breakup of the society because most of the water diviners and farmers believed that the divining rod intercepts rays or something like rays. As long as you stayed physical when you were talking, they would go with you. When you got away from the physical part and into something else that they didn't understand, you'd lose them as listeners and you'd get into big arguments. But our society evolved from water divining with a forked branch to the same people using nylon rods. There's no water in a nylon rod. The advantage of a nylon rod is that it'll bend but won't break.

I attended my first meeting of the American Society of Dowsers some time in October of about 1960. Somebody told me that a famous dowser named Chet Turner was going to be there. He dowsed people's deaths for hospitals. (In Vermont, it helped to be able to plan when people were going to die each winter because the ground froze so deeply it was hard to dig graves.) At the time, I was involved in a real estate deal. It would have been better if I could have put some of my income into another year for tax purposes, and I was worried about the health of my stepmother, Anne Mitchell. So I asked Chet Turner when I met him, "Could you come to my cabin tomorrow morning [we were all staying in cabins grouped together] and do some dowsing for me? I'll pay you."

When he came over the next morning, I told him, "I have a stepmother in poor health. It would be better if I get my share of inheritance next year. I have to make a decision about when I'm going to sell property." He brought in a forked branch that was about three feet long. I never saw such a big thing. He sat on the bed and held the rod down and was dowsing my stepmother's death—first the year, then the month, then the exact date—May 1 of the following year. Each time he got an answer, the rod came down, BANG! on the table next to the bed. If there'd been a rat under it, it'd be dead. It went down with tremendous force.

Then he fell back on the bed, and I wondered what happened to him. I said, "What's wrong?"

He said, "I had a vision your stepmother's changed the will in your family."

I said, "Are you sure about that?"

He thought a minute and said, "When I get visions like that, they're true."

I wrote a letter that very day to Neville Lewis, my attorney in San Fernando, California—he's got it in his file somewhere—to tell him what happened. "Anne is supposed to die May 1, and she has changed the will."

I got a call from Neville a few days later, when I got back to Falls Church. He said, "I talked to Anne and she did change the will, even though it's illegal." My father's will had stipulated that when he died, the estate would stay intact as a subsistence for Anne. When she died, it would be distributed among the family. But Anne had changed the will so that a nephew of hers would get everything in my father's estate.

A few days later, Anne called my brother Clyde and said, "I want you to take me to my lawyer in Van Nuys." She changed the will back.

Seven months later, on May 1, she died.

Sometime later I tried my hand at dowsing. A neighbor in Ravenwood named Virginia Samples, who lived across the street from me, had lost a dog one morning and came over to see if I could help her find it. I tried to dowse a map of the area to see where the dog was. It showed the dog was back at her house. I said, "Well, I'll tell you, we don't have to look far to get your dog. He's over at your house now." And he was.

Virginia's mother lived in Tennessee, and Virginia had made several sudden trips down there fearing her mother was going to die. I remembered my experience with Chet Turner. I thought, "Hell, I've had some of this dowsing rub off on me—I'll just see what I can do to help Virginia." She had gotten her fourth notice that her mother was sick, so I dowsed for her to see if she needed to go back to Tennessee. The dowsing rod said, yes, she should go home. She went back to Tennessee and called me. She said, "Well, it looks like the same old thing. I get down here and then she seems to feel better."

I said, "What's your phone number?" So by myself, in my office,

I dowsed to see if Virginia Samples' mother would die. I got a certain date, a certain time in the afternoon. I called her back and said, "Virginia, keep this under your hat, but your mother, according to my dowsing, will be dead on [a certain day] at 2:30 in the afternoon." On that day I got the call—her mother had died. I almost fell off my chair when she told me I'd hit it within an hour. I got so scared that I've never tried dowsing someone's death again.

One of my assignments for the American Society of Dowsers was to try to secure tax-deductible status for contributions to the society. I went to a lawyer I knew in Washington, D.C., who was a friend of the secretary of the Treasury. Through that connection, I got an appointment with the chief of the tax-exempt division of the Internal Revenue Service. On the day of my appointment, I was allotted 15 minutes to present my case. After I finished, the chief got up from his chair, came over to me, and said, "My father was a water diviner in Tennessee. He located wells for everybody in our neighborhood. I have never understood what made the divining rod move. Your presentation deserves a follow-up." He called his secretary and said, "Call [So-and-so] and tell him I'll be a little late." Then he called in four attorneys and told them, "I want you to talk to Mr. Poppelman and review all the material he's brought here. I'm convinced that the divining rod needs research." Then he said to me, "I don't think you're going to have any problem getting your exemption."

I called one of our trustees, a lawyer who had tried to get the same exemption, and he couldn't believe what had happened. He said, "My God, this is the biggest breakthrough our society's ever had." One woman wanted to give us $1 million, providing I would be responsible for the money and see that it would go to research, not into somebody's pocket. From then on, the society grew to include several chapters in the United States, including a large one in Los Angeles. Litton Industry donated a lot of money to the foundation.

Prior to my trip to Europe I had, as a trustee, agreed to help the American Society of Dowsers with an exhibit for the 1964 World's Fair in New York. The State of Vermont wanted to have a painting of a typical water dowser using a divining rod in its exhibit because the headquarters of the American Society of Dowsers were in Danville, Vermont, and the state's senior senator, Senator Landers, was interested in the society. I was appointed as a committee of one to find an artist.

The first artist I thought might be good for the task was Grandma Moses, so I traveled to Eagle Bridge, New York, to see her, and learned that she had died a few years before. But the Moses family had several other artists—particularly the son, Forrest K. Moses, whose work I really liked. I decided to buy one of his paintings but couldn't decide which one I liked best, so Forrest told me, "Just take four or five of them with you and send back the ones you don't want. Live with them a while." That's what I did. I paid him for one and took three others with me. (I later sold the other paintings for him.) Forrest Moses did not want the job of painting a dowser, but he recommended a couple of artists for me to speak with.

I finally found an English artist living in Burke, Virginia, who was married to a retired admiral. Her name was Mary Ferguson; she was recommended to me by the owner of the leading art gallery in Washington, D.C. I went to see her and told her that time was of the essence—the painting had to be ready in a few months. She agreed to do the painting; her fee would be $5,000, and she wanted me to find the subject—a dowser farmer (because most dowsers were farmers dowsing for water). To save time, though, she decided that I would pose in the typical stance of a dowser holding a divining rod and she would add to the painting later to make me look more like a farmer. I posed for some sketches before I left for Europe, and while I was vacationing she was planning to do the painting so that it would be ready for the fair. However, she had a death in her family in England and had to return there before she finished the painting.

I also wanted her to paint my mother's portrait from a photograph, so we made a deal. She would do my mother's portrait for $1,200 and throw in my painting for free. When it came to discuss the frame for my mother's portrait, I said I'd have it done in a French Provincial style by a certain gallery in Washington. But Mary Ferguson's husband, the admiral, who had a workshop, liked to make picture frames. He offered to make the frame for me at a nominal fee if I could find him some good walnut boards.

In my travels in Kentucky, I had met a hog farmer who had a lot of good walnut boards in his barn. I wrote to him and told him what sizes I needed for my frame, and that I needed well-seasoned lumber, not knowing what I would get. A few weeks later the postmaster called me and said, "We've got some awful stuff that belongs to you—some boards from Kentucky that are covered with hog manure. If you want them, you come and get them."

I got the boards, and sure enough, they were well seasoned: He had taken them off an old pig pen! I scraped the manure off after I got them home and then took them to the admiral. He thought they were great. After he ran them through a planer and sanded them down, the boards were beautiful. They had wonderful grain. And he made a beautiful frame for me. So the farmer had the right idea. If you want something really seasoned, get it from a pig pen. The painting, which is very beautiful, is still in that beautiful walnut frame (it now hangs in my nephew's legal office, and it receives a lot of comment).

The painting of me
done by Mary
Ferguson for the
American Society of
Dowsers.

As for the painting of the dowser for the fair, I lucked out and got it for myself. And I've never come across another painting of a dowser. The exhibit substituted photographs of conventions we'd had in the past, particularly of a famous water dowser named Henry Gross. He had gone to Bermuda and located three water wells on an island that was not supposed to have any water. So it all worked out fine. The exhibit was well received, and Senator Landers was happy. You start out in one direction and usually wind up in another. Personally it was a break for me because I got a nice portrait of myself for the family.

The Washington chapter of the American Society of Dowsers was the first one organized after the original one in Danville. We had quite a few members in Washington, including Art Souder, who had a pretty high position in the Department of Agriculture. He wasn't quite as advanced in his thinking as I was—he still believed that there was something in the wood of the divining rod that helped dowsers divine water. He was having a big party at his farm in Sandy Spring, Maryland. The dowsers were going to teach others how to dowse in Souder's woods; he knew there was underground water because of springs that he'd dowsed.

He invited people from the Smithsonian, the Library of Congress, the Department of Interior, the Department of Agriculture, and another group involved with water research to attend. Art had quite a delegation of guests coming out for the afternoon. There must've been 200 people there.

Art asked if I would give a little talk because there were going to be a lot of professional people from different government agencies there and I seemed to be well read on the subject. I spoke about the idea that dowsing not only applied to water but to many other things. For instance, in France dowsing is used in the medical profession— dowsing the ailment plus the remedy. Several hundred books have been written on the subject. I pointed out that dowsers could make decisions and do other things with a rod. And I quoted authors who had made arguments in support of this idea. One guy popped up— he seemed to be the skeptic in the crowd—and challenged me. He said, "I've got so much money in my pocket. Can you tell me how much is in it?"

I said, "Well, this is sort of unusual. First of all, I've never dowsed for people's money. But just for kicks, let's try it." I used my pendulum, which swings negative until I get to the proper thing, then it'll change course and swing to indicate yes. I thought since the guy traveled to get to the farm, he must have a bundle of money in his pocket, so I started with $1,000: "Does he have less than $1,000?" Yes. I worked the amount down to $200 plus. "Does he have more than $200?" Yes. Then I thought I could hit it right on the nose. I said, "According to my pendulum you have [X] number of dollars."

"Wrong!" He wasn't going to give me credit for the fact that I was very close. I asked my pendulum, "Is that right? Is the money that he has on his body [so-and-so] number of dollars?" The pendulum said no, so I said, "My pendulum still says that my figure's right—you have to have an extra $2 in your pocket somewhere." And he about fell over. He said, "I cannot believe that." He fished out the $2 bill he carried for good luck. And the crowd went crazy.

Here's another interesting story about dowsing. When the United States had trouble in Guantánamo Bay, Cuba, in 1964, our military base there was getting its water through a 6-inch waterline, and Fidel Castro was threatening to cut off the supply. The question came up, Why don't we drill our own wells down there? Then the newspapers and television stations got in on it: Let's send some dowsers to Cuba and dowse our own wells! Channel 5 in Washington decided to host a demonstration on water dowsing. When my name was suggested, the TV producers figured, "Since Ray Poppelman is a dowser and he lives near the Iwo Jima Monument, and he was on Iwo Jima, we'll have a demonstration at the monument." The monument is in a big park with woods around it. First the producers had me dowse at a spot where there would be a water well, where there was a good stream of water. A reporter with Channel 5 was a skeptic. He said, "If dowsing will find anything, if I throw a quarter in the woods, could you find the quarter?"

I said, "Yeah, that would be easy," and I found it. Everybody clapped. The reporter was still skeptical. I had found a stream of water where the divining rod would go down. The cameraman wanted to set up the camera just across from me so that he could get a close-up of the rod going down. But rods will break—they'll go down with such force that the branch will break. This time of all times, when the rod went down and I raised back on it, one of the branches broke right in front of the camera lens. The cameraman got the damndest picture of it. We broke for lunch, and the reporter came over to me and said, "That was a hell of a trick. How did you break that branch? How can you hold the end and make that branch break way out there?"

I said, "Oh, sometime I'll teach you how to do it."

The story was aired while I was in Europe, so I never saw it, but everybody told me about it. They kept asking me, "How did you break that branch like that? No wires on it or anything?"

I've run into more odd experiences with dowsers. I met a farmer who said that his dowsing rod wouldn't find water but could find copper. To test him, a friend of mine kept him occupied in his barn while I went outside and hid a copper penny. He came out of the barn, took his rod, and went around and around to determine which direction to go. When he got the direction of the penny, the rod went down. He kept walking and walking, watching his rod, until he found the penny. But the only thing he could find was copper. Well, that was in his mind. What would be the difference if it was copper, silver, or gold? Nothing else would work for him because he believed he could find copper.

Once—this would have been in November 1962—I was on my way to Kentucky to check on an oil well and decided to get a hotel room in the town of Monticello. My friend George Morris, the doodlebugger, lived there, so on my way to the hotel I stopped at his house. His wife, Ruby, told me, "George is upset; he had a bad dream last night."

I said, "I'll talk to George about it." When I asked him about his dream, he told me, "I dreamed that President Kennedy was shot." This was in the morning. I left George's place, checked into a hotel, and went out to the oil well. I came back to the hotel for lunch and a girl in the lobby said, "Did you hear the news?"

I said, "No, what news?"

She said, "Kennedy was shot."

Now, how many people in the United States had that same dream? If you had sent out a bulletin on TV that said, "All you people who dreamed that Kennedy was going to be shot or somehow knew he was going to be shot, please let us know," you'd probably get hundreds of them. You might also get a lot of quacks. But George was psychic. Once George was in Monticello and I was on the other side of Cumberland County, and I was sick as a dog during the night. I didn't know where to get a doctor. It was about 2:00 in the morning, and lo and behold, the phone rings. I thought, "Who the hell's calling me at 2:00 in the morning?"

It turned out to be George. He said, "Are you feeling bad?"

I said, "Yeah, why?"

He said, "Well, I just suddenly woke up and got the notion that you're not feeling well, and I thought I'd call you."

The American Society of Dowsers was invited to send a representative to the parapsychology convention, and I had the honor of being selected. The famous parapsychologist Dr. Rhine of Duke University was attending the convention, and by coincidence I was seated at the breakfast table with him and his wife. Dr. Rhine's assistant had been a guest speaker at one of our dowsers' conventions. I told Dr. Rhine about having worked with his assistant on some experiments and hearing him speak at our convention. We got to talking about sleeping, and I told him, "I didn't sleep very well last night."

He said, "That's a natural response of your body. Tonight you'll sleep very well. Your body now knows what to expect when you go to bed tonight."

I thought, "Well, I'll have to remember that."

I talked to Mrs. Rhine about her interests. She had been conducting experiments with girls at a school for students with arrested intellectual development. A series of cards with symbols: a star, a circle, a cross, a wave, and so forth—25 in all—would be put face-down in front of the girls. The researchers gave the girls rewards—candy bars, mostly—for correct answers. One girl could correctly call every one of the cards if she was given a whole candy bar. If she was told, "Now give a bit of your candy to your little friend there," her score would drop commensurately with the amount of candy she gave away. Mrs. Rhine argued that motive could be a factor in psychic studies for that reason. It was a good argument.

CHAPTER 25

Moving to Oxford, Maryland, and Adventures as an Art Agent

In 1965, on the suggestion of Dr. Pearson in California, Sue and I moved to Oxford, Maryland, on the eastern shore of Chesapeake Bay. We picked Oxford for several reasons, one being its great location between New York, Baltimore (which had good hospitals and restaurants), and Washington, D.C., where my business was located. (I was afraid that if I stayed in Washington I'd be tempted to go back into the building business. I really didn't want to do that.) So, at the age of about 55, with my income from Texas oil wells, the rent from the department store, and rent from my office building, I had enough security to retire. Having no children, we were not obligated to anyone, and we didn't owe anybody any money.

(Sue and I didn't have any children because Sue had a medical problem. She thought that we should adopt children, but I had found among my friends so many problems they had with children that it discouraged me from getting too serious about it. I figured some day we would adopt, but we procrastinated through the years and got to the point where we said, "We've gone this long, we might as well just leave it alone." Now I am probably a little sorry about it all, but it was part of my destiny and I didn't worry too much about it.

Not having children gave me facilities to help other people. It's one of the negative parts of my life, but I can't grieve about it. I loved my wife too much and couldn't imagine divorcing her just so I could have kids, and I wasn't ready to interrupt my life with strangers through adoption.)

There was just one apartment building—with only eight units—in Oxford, and most of the residents were wealthy people who had given up their big homes and wanted to live in a small, quiet place. I became good friends with a resident named Bill Valliant, who was an heir to one of the first six families that moved into Oxford when Chesapeake Bay was first settled. He was a banker and owned a fleet of fishing boats along with some property. He even said he would support me if I wanted to run for Congress. I said, "What chance would I have?"

He said, "With my connections with the Duponts and my money and my friends and our organizations, it's just a case of whether you want to do it or not."

I said, "What would I have to do for you?"

He said, "Just protect the fishing rights of the commercial fishermen in Chesapeake Bay, and you can be a congressman. Of course, you'll have to give up some of your fun."

I said, "No, I don't want to do that; I'm retired. I don't want the glory of being a congressman with all the damn headaches."

Our apartment was small, but the building was next to the Oxford boatyards. The wild geese were plentiful, the fishing was good, the sailing was good, and we were happy there. I liked the people. They were laid back. Once you made a friend there, he would always be your friend. And I liked the lifestyle, the fishing and the crabbing. I loved crabs, and we were in a part of the Chesapeake Bay that was home to the finest of crabs. I employed a boy who was a professional crabber to work on my sailboat. He would take me out crabbing on weekends. In fact, he called me recently. He's now an old man and wanted to know how I was getting along.

I liked the nature of the eastern shore. I liked the wild geese, which would come in the fall from Canada, going south to get out of the cold weather up north. Great flocks of geese would land in our area because in the early days farmers didn't have the machinery that they have today and when they harvested the corn, about 10 percent of it would end up on the ground. The wild geese learned to come for it. Not all the geese would go south into North Carolina; some would stop in the Chesapeake Bay area. Across from our apartment was the big estate owned by Bill Meyers, who was a University of Maryland graduate. He had duck blinds that Bob Hope, Bing Crosby, and others in the movie crowd used to rent from him to hunt wild geese.

I trained some of the wild geese by feeding them. I would throw corn out on my dock and could go out to the geese; but if anybody else approached them, they'd fly away. Geese were never afraid of the watermen once they knew them. I would wear the same clothes every time I fed the geese. If I drove from my apartment house through Main Street to the end of town, the geese would fly just above my car all the way. They'd follow me because I had fed them. Once a goose made a nest right by the front door of our apartment house because she knew she'd be protected there. While a goose is nesting, two male geese take turns watching and protecting her. So beside our stoop was a nest with a mother sitting on her eggs and a male goose sitting ten feet away in the lawn, watching to keep muskrats or other animals from attacking the nest. When one male would go away, the second one would take over. It was very interesting to watch.

A flock of bluebirds came in to the Oxford boatyard area that adjoined our apartment house. I was walking along a dock one day, and I looked down and saw a piece of 2-by-4 floating in the water with a little bird on it. The bird had hit the wire of one of the shrouds of the sailboat that came down from the mast to the deck. It was injured but got onto the wood. I picked up the bird, took it to our apartment, and gave it to Sue. She put it in a shoebox and fed it. She put the box out on our balcony so the bird would get some sun and fresh air. And you know what happened? A whole flock of blue-birds—the rest of the flock—appeared. They all stayed until the bird was healed; then they flew away. They took wing and we never saw them again.

I felt that I might want to live forever in Oxford, I liked it so much. So I had bought a lot in downtown Oxford—a low frontage on water with my own dock. A retired schoolteacher owned the house on the property, which was about an acre and a half, but the back part of the property was what I wanted, on the water. I paid $17,000 for the lot, which was submerged part of the time at high tide.

I enlisted the services of a wonderful man by the name of John Bailey, 75 years old, to put in the pilings and bulkheads. I had to put a bulkhead around my property, on what they call the fast water line. That's the farthest point where the grass would grow; the far-ther out your grass would grow in the water, the bigger your lot was. I went out to the last blade of grass. I had John Bailey put a bulkhead around my lot, which would be like a peninsula. Then after that I had him dredge out with a dredging machine all the mud from the channel onto my lot to fill in where the bulkhead came out. So I raised the general level of my lot from, say, two feet above sea level to about six feet by putting in the bulkhead and then filling it in. I made a beautiful lot, which I sold later, after I left Oxford, to a Mr. Stanley, who owned the Stanley Tool Company of America and who had bought the lot next to mine. He was a multimillionaire. He paid me $150,000 for a lot that I had about $40,000 invested in. To keep neighbors away, he built a beautiful Colonial-style, architect-designed *tool house* right in the middle of that beautiful lot!

Bailey pointed out that the people I'd meet on the eastern shore would be different from people anywhere else I'd lived. He said, "I'll give you an example. When I was a young man there was a famous boat-builder on the Virginia side of the eastern shore. He would build a rowboat for $6. I ordered a rowboat from him and I kept waiting, but he didn't show up. One Sunday he appeared in a horse and buggy with his wife; he had ridden 40 miles up, and he still had to go back, to remind me that costs were going up and he'd have to charge $7." He said, "These are the kind of people you're going to be running into."

We confirmed that when Al Icardo and Neville Lewis came to visit me in Oxford. They wanted to see some of the backcountry, so we went through a wild refuge area on a long road with big ditches on each side. The ditches were full of water. A man was sitting beside the road, fishing out of the ditch. After we passed him, Al said to Neville, "What the hell is that crazy bastard doing there fishing in that ditch?"

And Neville said, "I don't know. Maybe there are some special kind of fish there. Let's go back and see." So we turned around and went back, and Neville walked up to the old man and said, "Well, how are you doing?"

The old man said, "OK."

Neville said, "What kinds of fish do you catch here?"

The old man said, "Oh, there's no fish in here. I just like to fish."

And Al said to the old man, "You mean to tell me that there's no fish here and you know it and you're still fishing?"

"Yeah, I like to fish."

I suppose if you like to fish, what's the difference whether you sit beside the ditch or beside the ocean if fish are not biting that day?

When I moved to Oxford, a lot of University of Maryland alumni were living in the Talbot County area. Word got around: "Did you hear the latest? Ray Poppelman's living in Oxford now. He's one of us." The first thing that happened to me was that I was inducted into the Tred Avon Yacht Club. Practically everywhere I'd go at the club, when I was introduced to someone I'd be asked, "Are you the Poppelman who played for Maryland?"

"Yeah."

"Gee whiz! Maybe we can have lunch one day."

So I made friends in Oxford. As I mentioned, Bill Valliant, who was the political power boss in town, wanted me to run for Congress. I used to sail with him. I would go out on his houseboat on weekends. The only thing I had to do was keep my nose clean and be friendly to everybody. I always remembered my coach Curly Bird's advice when I first went to Maryland. He said, "Ray, to get along in this world, no matter who you meet, whether you like them or not, make them think that they're the greatest person in the world. Fuss over them; make them think they're important to you, and you'll be a success."

And that's what I did in Maryland. When somebody would ask, "Are you Ray Poppelman the football player," I'd say, "Yeah. Were you at Maryland?"

"Yeah, I was there. My father used to go there." Then the conversation would turn to the father.

I remember when Curly Bird, who later became president of the university, and then governor, came to Oxford in his big governor's yacht. It docked at Oxford, and all the politicians went down to the dock to meet him. The first thing Curly Bird said was, "Isn't this the town where Ray Poppelman lives?" So they summoned me and I went aboard the yacht.

But the people in Oxford generally were clannish. If you had a grandfather who was "somebody" in Maryland, you were in. As an outsider coming in, you were pretty well scrutinized. So you had to have friends who talked you up with their friends. And you had to be friendly yourself. You never knew if the stranger you were introduced to was a very important person. I used all the tricks I was told to use because generally I wasn't a very social guy. I was not an extrovert; I was too much of a loner. I had to get rid of that loner aspect to get along with people.

Here are some of my tricks: If you're drinking or eating with a group, you pick up the check. You're not just buying drinks, you're buying goodwill. It works. When you meet somebody, you don't talk about yourself; try to get the discussion focused on them. "Do you live in this area?" Yes. "Gee whiz, that's wonderful. Where do you live?" and they tell you. You just keep talking about them. If you are talking to somebody and you see a stranger in the crowd, you ask the person you're talking to, "Who is that fellow over there?" Then you say, "Geez, he's a nice-looking guy, isn't he? What does he do?" And, "Gee, I'd like to meet him sometime." Eventually the person you were talking to will go over to the stranger and say, "The guy that I was talking to over there is Ray Poppelman. He was a famous football player in Maryland. He wants to meet you." That way, you sort of stay in the background, and a friend brings a friend to you.

I'll give you an example of how to make friends. Our apartment house had a vacancy, and a guy named Jim Ivans moved into the apartment. He was general counsel for one of the big Texas corporations that controlled all the gas pipeline companies that operated out of Texas into the northern cities. Ivans was using the apartment as a temporary residence until he got a big estate downriver fixed up. He'd been on fast transatlantic ocean races years before and was a famous sailor. He didn't tell me that when we first met. He didn't have a sailboat, but from his balcony he could look down and see mine. One day I was working on the boat when he came down and started talking about my boat. I said, "Yeah, I don't know too much about sailing. I've only had this boat a few years." I knew he wanted to go sailing. I said, "Would you like to go sailing sometime with me?"

"Oh, yeah. Gee," he said. We no sooner pushed off then he had all the sails up. He was a real pro. He finally told me he was a blue-water sailor who'd done a lot of ocean racing.

I said, "Any time you want to use my boat, you don't have to wait for me. Just come down and use it." So he had that privilege. After he moved out of the apartment I found out who he was from the manager of our apartment house. Later he came out with a big, beautiful 60-foot yacht. He'd always invite me to his yachting parties. I had made a good friend.

Once my nephew John came out to visit me and Sue, and I told Jim, "I've got a nephew who's coming from California. He's an attorney." To make a long story short, Jim Ivans suggested that since John was a young attorney starting out, maybe he had better come down to Texas and join their corporation. Eventually Jim could have him assigned to California and he would be a big corporation lawyer. John's father objected to the idea. His father wanted him to be in his office in California. Had John gone with Jim Ivans, he'd have been a big-shot lawyer.

Having lots of friends was a problem sometimes. In Washington, I had been active in a homebuilders' association and I had been a real estate broker as well. There are only seven days in the week, and when you have several hundred friends, from golfing partners to professional colleagues, you give up an awful lot of your time to social activity. When they say, "Let's have lunch," you can't turn them all down. So to have any retirement time for myself, I had to get out of Washington. Oxford was a great, great move. There I had friends in activities that would help me physically, and I had more of a social life than I ever needed. All I had to do was go down to the yacht club if I got lonesome. There was always something going on there. But I had to be careful in Oxford—I was on racing committees and others. Many of my free days would fall on weekends when they were hosting big regattas, and I'd have to help out at the club.

Soon, fishing wasn't enough for me, and sailing wasn't enough. I wasn't quite satisfied, and needed something else to do. As had happened before, coincidence had an effect on my life. As I mentioned, I had met the artist Forrest Moses when the State of Vermont needed a painting for the World's Fair. I had wanted to buy one of his paintings, so I took four away, kept one, and sold the other three for him. He was charging $150 and I sold them for $300, and I got to thinking about selling art. I was in Florida with my friend Robert Plimpton, who wanted us to rent a plane and watch an Apollo rocket being launched at Cape Canaveral from the air. The government would allow planes to fly up to five miles high during a launch, but the planes had to be seven miles away from the launch site. Robert suggested that since we had rented a four-person plane, we bring his uncle along for the flight. His uncle was a curator of a big cultural center in the heart of Palm Beach, Florida, with art galleries and had everything.

We watched the launch from the plane, which gave an entirely different perspective than you see on television. (When the rocket leaves the ground and zooms up, you see it for only about three or four seconds; it goes so fast. The television cameras can follow it up quite high, but in real life, it just goes VOOM! It's out of there fast. That was a great experience.) While we were in the plane, I was talking to Mr. Plimpton, the curator. I said, "I have a Forrest Moses painting I want you to look at and tell me what you think of it." After the launch, he looked at it and said, "It's got a touch of Grandma Moses in it. It's not bad." I told him how Forrest was selling his paintings for $150, and he said, "If you want something to do, and you like art, why don't you get to be his agent?"

I said, "Is there such a thing?"

He said, "Yeah; you take Forrest to his attorney and have him make up an agreement."

So that's what I did. I went to see Forrest and told him that I'd sold three of his paintings for $300 apiece and that I wanted to be his agent. He agreed to meet with me and his attorney, and I told his attorney that Forrest would get 70 percent and I would get 30 percent. His attorney said, "You've got it backwards. Forrest has all the fun. All he's got to do is paint the paintings and you've got to sell them. You're the one that should get the 70 percent." We made up an agreement on that basis. So for the next eight years, until Forrest died, I was his agent. I had connections with Lord & Taylor in New York through the vice president, and the company agreed to sponsor a show of Forrest's paintings in its Fifth Avenue store. The show was a big success. Eventually some of his paintings sold for as much as $4,000.

I was using all the tricks I could and listening to people who knew about art. I read a book about a man who faked paintings. He said one of the tricks to selling art is to be sure to "psych" the buyer by using the color red in the painting—that would make the painting sell faster than other paintings. Forrest was painting his barns gray—just raw wood. It was authentic, but the gray didn't have the feel that the red did. So I went to him and said, "Forrest, we've got to get you to paint some red barns and red houses. Somehow we've got to get red in the paintings. As an experiment, here's a painting that we have had at Lord & Taylor for a couple of months. You've got three gray barns in there. I want you to take out two of the barns and make them red."

Forrest didn't want to do it, but he said he would consult with an artist friend of his in upper Vermont, a portrait artist who had painted Eisenhower's picture and Grandma Moses' picture. His flat fee was $25,000 a painting. We discussed the red aspect and he said, "Poppelman's right. The red won't be authentic because they didn't use paint in very early Colonial days. They just used raw wood. But the red will excite a buyer more than gray." So Forrest agreed to change two buildings in the painting to red. I thought it looked beautiful, and I took it back to Lord & Taylor, and they sold it within a week. So we changed all of Forrest's paintings. I had him put red in them somewhere. I didn't care what it was—just as long as he added red to the paintings. Our sales really picked up.

Another trick we used was one we learned from Grandma Moses: Paint subjects that had a connection to the buyer. For instance, a buyer would look at a Forrest Moses painting in Lord & Taylor and say, "Geez, that looks just like my grandfather's farm." Also, most people like water, so we always tried to include a stream of water, which ties a painting to fishermen and the natural world. I told

Forrest, "Just don't paint pictures of woods and one barn or some-thing. Put workmen in, put the cows in, and chickens—make it as natural looking as a farmyard looks, because practically everybody in America in the early days was related to farms. They weren't city people.

And then we would get a frame that would bring out the paint-ing. I could take a painting to the experts at Heydenryck that I didn't like too much, but by the time they got through putting a frame on it, you wouldn't recognize the painting. The framing was so beauti-ful that it was like a new painting.

My art business did well. I had shows at Lord & Taylor's new stores in Atlanta, in Houston, and in Boston. People liked the Ameri-cana aspect of Grandma Moses' paintings, and Forrest's work had some of her characteristics. By the time I ended my art-selling career with Forrest (he died of prostate cancer), I had his paintings selling for up to $4,000, and many galleries wanted them. I didn't have to go out and peddle them; propositions were coming to me over the telephone.

I also represented my nephew, Richard Luney, who was selling animal pictures in the Laguna Beach area. He was what you might call a street artist. I liked Richard's paintings, and I showed one of them to an art director in New York. We were quite good friends—she would do anything I would ask her to do. She said, "Well, Ray, if you want, I'll ask Mr. [So-and-so—a vice-president of Lord & Taylor] about it." I had Richard send me some photographs of the paintings, and the art director liked them, and so did the vice presi-dent of Lord & Taylor. So they agreed to fund a show for him. They spent $2,000 for an ad in the *New York Times* announcing: "Free to the public, not by invitation, Richard Luney, a famous artist from California."

Richard rounded up about 25 paintings, all of different animals. On the day of the show, he had on a dark red velvet Armani suit, artist-style. He was the artist everybody wanted to meet: and he was a good-looking man. In fact, one old lady came up to me and said she would buy one of Richard's paintings if Richard would let her hold his hand for a few minutes! The art director for the *New York Daily News,* a beautiful redheaded girl, invited Richard to spend the night with her in her apartment in New York City. He was so afraid of it he backed off. He had committed himself to go to dinner with Johnsie Bailey, Sue's niece, and somebody else. He missed the boat there. But much to our surprise, the show was a big success. I thought Richard had it made, but you know what he told me? He said, "I don't like the city of New York." He didn't want to show his paintings there, even though we sold his first painting for over $3,000. Money was pouring in. *National Geographic* wanted some of his paintings. But he wanted to be a big frog in a little pond in California instead of a little frog in a big city like New York.

Forrest Moses was close to 60 when he began painting. He told me that when his mother became famous, somebody asked him, "Forrest, why don't you paint?"

And Forrest said, "Why should I?"

"Well, maybe you've got a touch of your mother's talent."

A man said to him, "Look out the window and paint what you see." So Forrest did, and the man liked the painting. So Forrest started painting. Forrest would sit all the children (as they got older) down at the table. He would give them his paints and say, "Now, paint me a picture of what you see out the window." Of all the children of the Moses family, there were three or four that had Grandma's touch. None of them went to school for art, and they'd never been in a gallery in their life.

At that time his mother was selling her paintings at the local drugstore for $5 and $10. She recorded her sales in a book. Years later, at the Hammer Gallery in New York City, they sold one of her paintings for 60-some thousand dollars. I got the title and the number of it and checked it in that little black book. She had originally sold that painting for $10, and she put two stars next to the entry. I asked Forrest, "What do the two stars mean?"

He said, "Oh, it means a big sale." So the painting that she had sold in Eagle Bridge, New York, for $10 eventually got to New York and sold for around $60,000.

Another story of how the value of her paintings grew came to me from Betty Moses, a granddaughter of Grandma Moses. A little old man who had a small piece of acreage used to take care of Grandma Moses' garden for her in his spare time. One Christmas, as a present, she made a painting for him because she couldn't afford to buy presents. Years later, the man had bought a farm that had a mortgage on it, and he couldn't make the payments, so the land was being sold off at a sheriff's sale. (First, the farm is sold, then the animals, then the stuff that's inside the house.) Wilford Robertson, a nephew of Grandma Moses who was also a good artist, painted a scene of the auction sale. Two New Yorkers who were there had heard about Grandma Moses—her name had made it around New York through her agent, Otto Kallir. They saw the painting Grandma Moses had done for the man and bid against each other until the top bid for the painting paid off the mortgage. The mortgage was canceled and the man's farm was saved. I paid $300 to Wilford Robertson for his painting of the auction scene. I took it to the Lord & Taylor gallery in New York City. Some time later, a collector from Europe was going through the gallery. Of all the paintings Lord & Taylor had, his attention settled on that painting of the auction scene. On the back of it Wilford had written a story about the scene. The fellow bought the painting for $650.

Grandma Moses had started painting quite late in life. She was a maid and a housekeeper until she got ill. She was sick in bed and to pass the time, she started painting scenes out of her bedroom window. She had such a bad case of arthritis that she had to hold a small potato in her hand; she would push the handle of the brush through the potato to give her a little relief so she wouldn't crimp her fingers so much. And that's how she painted.

She painted only scenes that she could either remember or see. All her paintings represented scenes of Americana of New England. Her style was very different from anyone else's in the art world at that time. Otto Kallir had a lot of trouble selling her paintings in the beginning. They sold for $200 and $300 in New York. One day she talked a gallery into letting her show the paintings, and some art experts came in and liked her work. Another man contacted Grandma Moses and made a deal for Christmas cards and drapery and dishes and stuff. After that, her painting started gaining popularity. She had a certain touch that people liked, a softness. She painted what she knew about American life—that's what touched the Soviets. The Russian farmers could relate to everything she painted in her paintings.

One time I helped out Tom Moses, a great-grandson of Grandma Moses. A boy had found a painting that Grandma Moses did on old-fashioned oilcloth; it was an Indian scene. It was in an old railroad caboose car in Troy, New York. Between the windows there was advertising space, but somebody had put her painting in between the windows, and eventually some kids going through the old car took it out and threw it along the railroad track. A boy found it and gave it to his father, and his father recognized the signature,

Moses, and gave it to Forrest Moses, who gave it to Tom. Tom had it under his bed. Tom had been arguing with his wife about buying a new car, so he came to me and said, "Raymond, I've got two Grandma Moses paintings: One, Grandma gave me, and another one was found on the railroad tracks in Troy, New York."

I said, "How much do you want for the good painting that your grandma gave you?" He sold that to me for $1,200. Then Tom said, "See what you can do with this oil painting that we found." I took it to the Heydenryk Gallery in New York City and had it cleaned up and put in a beautiful frame, and I sold it to an art museum in Bennington, New York. I sold it to the museum for $4,000 and gave Tom the entire $4,000. He bought a new car and saved his wife from leaving him.

Grandma Moses' paintings had been very successful in the Soviet Union, and our State Department liked the idea that we had "softened up" the Cold War through art. Otto Kallir was originally from Russia, and he had connections there. The State Department wanted her to have another showing there, but Kallir was ill and had taken Grandma Moses' paintings off the market. He was not capable of going to Russia. The State Department wanted me, as a substitute, to take Forrest Moses' paintings over. I spent two years preparing for a show in the Soviet Union. I had Forrest paint 36 paintings, and I stopped my shows. I had the house of Heydenryck in New York City do the frames; they were the world's best framers and did the framing for the National Gallery in Washington, D.C. We had the collection all ready and were going to be accompanied by a man named Beers who had a singing family—they had been to Russia on a very successful tour—and knew some people at the State Department. The Beers family singers would accompany an exhibit of Forrest Moses paintings, and Beers would be in charge of the delegation. The State Department also agreed to take Sue along as a secretary.

In the fall of the year, I got a telephone call that Mr. Beers had been killed in an accident. With Beers, the man in charge of our delegation, killed, the whole project folded. I didn't think I was capable of handling the whole thing. It broke my spirit when that deal fell through. I was devastated and even thought about shooting myself. That Russian show would have made me in the art business. I had contacts with leading art galleries in Scottsdale, Arizona, and Palm Beach (I was getting ready for a big show there, especially after the Russian exhibit), and the Public Broadcasting Company was going to send cameras with us. The *Christian Science Monitor* wrote up a big article for me. There were telephone calls from all parts of the United States from people who wanted Forrest Moses paintings. I figured after the Russian show I would push his paintings up into the $35,000 range. Then, about six months after Mr. Beers was killed, Forrest died of cancer. I gave up my contract with the Moses family and was determined to leave art.

However, the following year, W. Carman Davis, the head of the Art Academy of Eastern Maryland, was giving art lessons to Sue, and I started getting interested in his paintings. He was quite an artist and was famous on the eastern shore. His paintings had been shown in the United States capitol rotunda and in the state capitol at Annapolis. However, about the time he was getting enough acclaim to charge decent money for his paintings, he died. After he died, which caused distress in the county, his wife got sick and was in the hospital. I went to see her. She wanted to know if I would like to buy her collection of her husband's paintings, which I did. Her attorney was also a member of our yacht club, and he decided that I should have Carman's collection for $17,000. Before I left Oxford, I

WHO'S WHO

IN AMERICAN ART

1976

Edited by JAQUES CATTELL PRESS

POPPELMAN, RAYMOND JAMES
 ART DEALER, COLLECTOR
b Marvin, SDak, Mar 6, 07. Study: Univ Md, BA(bus admin, econ); self-taugh vis Libr Cong, Washington, DC & art mus throughout the world. Pos: Artists' rep for descendant artists of Grandma Moses family, including Forrest K Moses (son), Betty Moses (grand-daughter) & Thomas E Moses (great-grandson). 68-73;, agt for Richard Luney & Betty Moses, currently. Specialty: Primitives and wildlife. Collection: Primitives of the Grandma Moses family; Indian art by Fritz Scholder; African animals by Richard Luney; various others. Mailing Add: 142 Neptune Ave Encinitas CA 92024

R. R. BOWKER COMPANY
A Xerox Education Company
New York & London

My citation in the 1976 edition of
Who's Who in American Art.

sold a lot of them to get my money back, and I made a deal with the attorney to discard any paintings that were below the standard that Carman had reached in his paintings.

He had a studio in back of his property, and it was full of paintings in different stages of completion. In my agreement, I think I had title to 130 paintings. I agreed with the attorney that I would destroy 30 of them. Those I took to the Oxford boatyard, where they had a band saw, and I cut them up jigsaw style and threw all the pieces in a big barrel. That night, two workers in the boatyard went in and fished all the pieces out of the barrel, put them together, and glued them onto pieces of plywood. So I found that there were two types of paintings circulating around Oxford: the band-saw type and the originals. I sold enough Carman Davis paintings to get my money back. (I still have about 75 of his paintings. At the art shows I always sell three or four.)

CHAPTER 26

Leaving Oxford for California and Nevada

A t this point in my life, I realized that I was an outsider on the eastern shore. I was just a friend of the people who were the real natives of the land. And I knew my sailing days were over. Sailing on a very calm day when the breeze is light is one thing, but when you get out into open water and a storm comes up, if you don't have some extra hands aboard, it's hell to handle a big sailboat. It was time to leave Maryland. I longed for California. I had not forgotten California.

So I sold my boat, and for my last year in Oxford I joined a crew of a large class-A boat, a 60-foot boat. I was a member of the crew on one of the big yachts that sail, for instance, from Annapolis to Newport Beach. One year I sailed with Dr. Dolan, a friend of mine, on a class-C boat, which was about 40 feet long. I was in on a big race from Annapolis to Norfolk, an overnight cruise. I went as a navigator—I would set the courses and so forth. Every four hours we would change the deck crew. There'd always be the navigator and four other crewmen on the deck.

We got down to the lower bay area and the wind sort of died. I had remembered going to Florida one time with Captain Dick, the

419

man who built my boat. He said, "Any time you get a light breeze in the center of the bay, work your way over to shore and you'll pick up a fresh shore breeze. That's a phenomenon of the winds in the Chesapeake Bay." I had remembered that, and when hundreds of boats were out in the middle of the bay, I suggested to Dr. Dolan, "Let's get over towards the western shore, just outside of the fish stakes, and we'll pick up a breeze." In the early morning, just before it got daylight, we moved on over by wind (you never used power). We went toward the western shore, and the closer we got, the more breeze we got. We went flying into Norfolk and were the first boat in. We won the fleet honors.

That was very exciting. But it was hard work. And I figured, "Well, some day I'm going to die, and I'd better get back to where my relatives are so I'll have somebody at my funeral." I told Sue, "I think we should move back to California. We've got a pretty good income coming in now, and we'll find a place down near San Diego and do a little traveling and be with my brothers and sisters."

We agreed that we would give up the eastern shore and the cold winters and go to the ideal climate of San Diego. So we moved from Oxford to Encinitas, California, in about 1973. I had mixed emotions about moving. I'd been living in so many places and had so many friends. I didn't want to leave my friends in the yachting crowd in the eastern part of the United States, and I didn't know exactly what to expect in the western part. California had changed so much. There was such an influx of people that I'd go back to my hometown of San Fernando, and, hell, I wouldn't know anybody. The people there were all new, and the old people had gone away. That was one of the disappointments I had. I'd ask about friends of mine that I knew in high school, and I couldn't find anybody around; they'd all scattered. That wasn't quite the way it was in the East. In the East, you might have grandchildren living in the same house that their great-great-grandfathers lived in. If you knew a family back East, you figured you could go back there and find somebody.

After I left Oxford, I got a call from Mr. Stanley, who had bought the lot next to me. He said, "Have you ever thought about selling your lot?"

I figured if I could get $70,000 for it I'd be lucky. I said, "Well, I don't know. I don't think I want to sell it. I don't know what kind of a price I'd want for it."

He said, "I'll open the bidding and offer you $150,000 cash for it, or you can have the money any way you want it. All I'm going to do is get the lot to keep somebody from building on it."

I said, "Well, I'll think it over, Mr. Stanley."

That was a bargaining strategy. If I'd said yes too soon, he would've figured he'd offered me too much. Then later he'd say, "I've thought it over—I'll only give you $125,000."

I called my attorney and said, "Neville, Jesus Christ, I've been offered $150,000 for my lot."

He said, "Did you take it?"

I said, "No."

He said, "You goddamn fool, call him back."

So I wrote Mr. Stanley a nice letter and told him how I had carefully built the lot. I had three septic tanks I had taken care of and had filled, and I had all the debris taken off the lot, and all the fill that I put on the last three feet in the lot came from a cornfield where they were putting a road in. It was all pure topsoil. I built up a hell of an argument.

He wrote back and said, "Not only do I own Stanley Tool Company, I also own a brokerage house in New York City. We have a guest apartment in [a certain location]. Any time you go to New York, you're welcome to use our apartment. And whenever you come to Oxford, you come and see me." He also said, "By the way, I am going to Portugal next year with my wife. Maybe you and your wife would like to go with us." He was a real nice guy.

So that was the end of my life in Oxford, which was pretty well built up when I lived there. Most of the property in town was owned by rich people, but most of them don't live there. I do get homesick for it. It was a part of my life that was very sweet. I had everything I wanted; the only thing that I never could figure out is how my planned art show in the Soviet Union blew up so badly. Of course, a lot of people told me that possibly it was the best thing that could have happened to me: Russia's a long way off, and it was during the Cold War—I could have been shot over there or never come back.

Now I think possibly it was a great thing for me. Let's assume that it had been a great show; suddenly I'm thrust into the art world and my life is all art. Would I have ever had the fun of sailing? Would I ever have gotten back to California? Would I ever have gotten to Las Vegas? Would I ever have gotten to Boulder City? I think now that there was a reason for me not to go to Russia. And things had been going so well for me for about ten years that I might have needed a disappointment to bring me back to normal.

We had furniture we wanted to keep, and I had over 100 oil paintings crated in cardboard boxes that had to be moved to California. I decided to take a Ryder truck and have a friend of mine, Sandy Loscomb, who looked after my boat in Oxford, drive the van to California. Unfortunately, the day we were to load the truck, we had a very heavy snowstorm, and I had to summon high school students in an emergency to help us take the furniture from the upper floor of our apartment house down to the truck. I put my sailboat,

Seaflower, up for sale on the opposite shore of the Chesapeake Bay from Oxford, in a little town called Galesville, a yachting center. I felt the market to sell the boat would be better near Washington and Baltimore. And I was very lucky. Within a week, I sold it. So I was free to go to California.

On a previous trip to California, I had made a deal to buy a condominium in Del Mar, north of San Diego. When we arrived in California and went to the condominium, we learned it had been sold to another party. I had no choice but to store the furniture in a warehouse and check into a motel. From there, I searched the beach area. (I wanted to be close to the ocean.) I searched from La Jolla on up to Oceanside, almost near the marine base.

About the time I became very discouraged, I got a call from a real estate company claiming they thought they had a place for me. There was a wealthy family by the name of Petz that had a very peculiar deed drawn by their parents—a will in the form of a deed. They owned a chain of bakeries in Chicago, the largest chain there. The children were allowed to share in this estate providing they were not married. When they got married, they had to give up their interest. That was to keep fortune-hunters from marrying members of the family. Anyway, the family had built a million-dollar home on the beach in Encinitas. Two daughters had retired and were living in the upstairs section, which had four bedrooms and three baths. The third daughter worked with one of the brothers. On the first floor were two bedrooms and a large living room, which came out onto a patio that went to the edge of the cliff with a 180-degree view up and down the beach. The two gentlemen in the family, who were attorneys, would occupy the lower floor when they retired. Until the attorneys were ready to retire, they wanted a pair of "Puritans" to rent the first floor—people who didn't have too many parties and were not drinkers and so on. And so Sue and I were nominated to talk to the owners and see what they'd think about our renting the downstairs. They liked us—particularly Sue. When they asked us how much we could pay for rent, I said $350 was in our budget. The apartment house was probably worth $2,000 a month, but they let us have it for the $350 because all they wanted was somebody to occupy it. When I gave up the apartment five years later, the daughter of Baron Hilton of the Hilton Hotel chain leased the property for $1,500 a month.

So we were quite lucky in getting the place. They had a Mexican gardener who took care of everything during the day; we didn't do much of anything around the house. Sue became quite friendly with the two retired women upstairs. One had been a principal of a high school and the other had been a clerk at the Atomic Energy Commission. Around 5:00 p.m. Sue and I would go upstairs to their apartment, where we'd have cocktails of the finest liquors. Whenever they'd go out to dinner, we would join them at the best restaurants and they'd insist on paying for everything. We lived there for about five years.

The Petzes had no heirs, so they proposed that they would adopt us and we would look after them until they passed away; then we would get the property from the estate. When I told Neville Lewis, my attorney, about the proposition, he said, "Don't do it; you might be looking after them the rest of your life—you'd be sort of slaves to them. And what if you die before they do?" So we backed off. It was quite a sad occasion when we left the Petz family and went on our own, because we were so integrated with each other. We were really a family.

So we split, and Sue and I moved to an apartment house in Las Vegas, Nevada. Many of my friends wanted to know why I was

Sue and me on my 70th birthday, March 6, 1977, in Encinitas, California.

moving to Nevada. The reason was that I was scheduled for a prostate operation when I was living in California. My attorney thought that since there was danger of death (he'd had some clients who had died from those operations), Sue and I should establish residence in Nevada because it had no state income tax, whereas California at that time did. If I should die at least Sue would have a good jingle and the state of California wouldn't be dipping into our estate. So we lived in Nevada for one year, in 1977, in downtown

Las Vegas. I didn't like it—it was noisy at night: airplanes overhead, police car sirens going off, and people coming and going in the casinos.

During that year in the desert, the arthritis that I'd developed while living on the beach in California disappeared. It felt so good to be without arthritis that I decided to try living in Nevada for good. Boulder City was suggested by a lot of people who had lived in Nevada. One reason I chose to live in Boulder City is that I had read a convincing article in *Reader's Digest* magazine about why small towns are best for old people. The reasons given were that old people generally have similar desires and modes of living, there is less crime, neighbors are friendlier, it's easier for shopping, there's less traffic, the taxes are lower, and the facilities at the senior center are better. Las Vegas was nearby if we needed it—Boulder City is only 18 miles from downtown Las Vegas. And because Boulder City is 500 feet higher in elevation, it is cooler than Las Vegas in the summertime. Lake Mead is nearby, and the airflow from it and the Colorado River coming up the valley cools us off some. And Boulder City remains the only city in the state of Nevada that prohibits gambling, which makes it very popular with families.

The main reason, I think, that I chose to settle in Boulder City was that my brother-in-law Neville Lewis, who is also my attorney, liked to fish and he had a mobile home at Lake Mojave, which is 75 miles from Boulder City. I liked to fish too, so I spent many week-ends at Lake Mojave; thirty years ago the fishing was very good there. In addition to that, if I had any legal problems I could discuss them on his boat.

Finding a lot to buy in town took some work. Since the town had started out as a camp for federal workers employed on the con-struction of Hoover Dam, the federal government deeded all the land to the city of Boulder City—the city owned all the land around Lake Mead. If you wanted to buy land here, you went down to the city hall and talked to a clerk.

At that time the city golf course only had nine holes, and there were still three vacant lots around it. One belonged to a miner in Alaska—he was not interested in selling because when he retired he was going to live in Boulder City. A woman in New England had one lot. She wouldn't sell; she was planning to retire here also. So there was one lot remaining, and it belonged to an ex-marine. It was a small lot, 70 feet wide and 150 feet deep, backing up to the golf course.

That's where I got my break. The ex-marine had a radical idea about the house he wanted to build. He planned a swimming pool half in the house and half out; water would be pumped to the roof of the house into a reservoir of about six inches, which would give him good insulation. It was a very technical design. The major water line coming down the street was only half an inch wide, and of course that would not give him enough water for his special house. But the city would not give him a permit because it didn't have an engineer who knew enough about such a radical house. As a result, he put the lot up for sale on bids—the highest bidder would get the house.

When I talked to the ex-marine, I found out that he was sentimental about, and still liked, the Marine Corps, and he was impressed that I'd been on Iwo Jima. So he said that he would give me a tip on how high to bid. He said, "I think if I were you I'd bid $17,000." Of course, that was a very low price. I rushed a check to him and a contract, and in response he came to Boulder City with his house plans, which he was going to include in the sale—he'd give them to me. At first I was sort of impressed with it; I thought it would be nice to be able to walk out of my bedroom and dive into a swimming pool. We sealed the deal, and I had my lot. But it came with some restrictions. You had three years to build or the lot would go back to the city. There were about 30 days left on the original contract for me to rush a house onto the lot.

Because I had experience as a builder of subdivisions and had done some designing of houses, I made a preliminary drawing and took it to an architect by the name of Smith, who was the architect for Wayne Newton's house that was then under construction. When he saw my drawings he said, "You know something about building," so I told him about my experiences. He said, "You're just the man I need. I don't know too much about building, but I made the mistake of agreeing to supervise the building of six big million-dollar houses. I'm in a spot with Wayne Newton's house. I need somebody to look it over and be sure that it is being built according to the plans." Then he said, "I'll make a deal with you. I'll design your house and make it ready to build, if you'll stop at Wayne Newton's house a couple of times a week and be sure they're building the house the way I designed it." I agreed to the deal and in return got a very carefully designed house.

I seldom ever saw Wayne Newton because he was working at night and sleeping in the daytime. Most of our communications were through the foreman or scribbled messages. The job was estimated to cost $750,000. By the time I left, the cost had gone up to about $1,300,000. I couldn't believe the boondoggling that was going on there. It turned out that I became more of a policeman than I did an observer. For example, some gold bathroom fixtures were missing. The supply house claimed they had delivered them. The plumber that was doing the work claimed, "No, they'd never come." By accident one day, I was in the living room and the builder, E. R. Johnson, had his son there as sort of a supervisor. He was just a young fellow; he didn't know too much about construction. I said to the son, "Tell you what. You've got to clean up this goddamn house. It's just absolutely full of junk. They're pushing all the debris over in the corner of the living room and it's a mess. You get better production out of employees if you keep a clean job. Just get a couple of fellows and take all this trash out to the dumpster."

In the process of doing that, they stumbled on some boxes containing the gold bathroom fixtures. When they checked into it, they found out that the driver for the supply house came in after working hours (they had a gate with guards on it). He didn't want to take the gold fittings back so he hid them in the trash pile, but he never told anybody. It was only because I told the boy to clean up the trash pile that we ever found the stuff.

At first, I was resented as being a stool pigeon and a spy for the architect, milling around. But as we went on, I was making suggestions that made sense to everybody. For instance, the entrance hall into Wayne Newton's house is about 40 feet in diameter; it's a big circular hall with a pair of beautiful staircases going up to the right and to the left. The staircases were made in Czechoslovakia out of pure crystal, and they were assembled in a boatyard in Baltimore and shipped out by American Airlines. When it came time to put up the staircases, the front doors were already on and there wasn't enough room for the two sections to come in. They took off the doors and brought in the staircases, but the curvature of the staircase was a little different from the way the walls were framed out to fit. The dumb carpenters were going to tear the staircase apart to fit the walls, and I stepped in and said, "Hold it. It's easier to just tear out the walls to put the staircase in and then rebuild the walls." So that's what they did. It was just stupid stuff a high school kid could have solved.

It was a cost-plus job, so nobody was pushing. They were in the painting process. One morning when I came in to look around to check on the place and keep my promise to the architect, there were nine painters on the job—eight of them standing around the fireplace smoking cigarettes and one guy painting. I went up to them and said, "Listen. Wayne Newton is a hell of a nice guy. He's trusting everybody here; he's paying the bills. I just can't see you guys all standing around here loafing; that's just like stealing money out of his pocket."

One of the fellows said, "What the hell do you care? He's a guy making $90,000 a week."

I said, "Listen, by the time he pays taxes, pays his agent and so forth, it's gone . . . and I happen to know that he had to go to the bank to borrow money to keep this damn job going. I think you fellows ought to give the guy a break." So they all shuffled off and started painting.

It was not my job to supervise the workers; my job was to check that the house was being built according to the plans. Then if there was any deviation, I would go to the architect and tell him. But eventually I would go to the builder directly and tell him if I came upon some miscalculation. For instance, there were Colonial columns going up in front of the house. The portico above was overhanging, but the porch where the columns would sit was short, so that if you put the columns up to the portico above, they'd be dangling in the breeze. There was no foundation for them. A high school kid would think of that. But you know, when you're spending somebody else's money you're not quite as careful as when you're doing it yourself.

A feud began between the builder, the architect, and Wayne Newton. I kept in the background. The upshot was that they moved the architectural drafting department into the builder's office. The house was far enough along so they really didn't need me or the architect any more except for details, and the architect would take care of that.

The design of my house was being completed in the contractor's office. The draftsman had moved in and was doing the work. Wayne Newton came in one day and was looking at the plans for my house. The draftsman said, "This is the house Poppelman's going to build in Boulder City." Wayne Newton liked it and thought it would be a great design for a guesthouse on his property. When he approached me about it, I said, "You can use my plans." Then he wanted me to get some old beams for it, but I refused—I told him he'd have to get some good dry stuff out of Canada because the Japanese were taking all the good stuff out of the West Coast.

Wayne Newton got mad at me, and we didn't talk for a long time. But a few years later a salesman who tried to sell me some screens for my back porch called me. He said, "Hey, Poppelman. Guess what?"

I said, "What?"

He said, "I was talking to Wayne Newton this afternoon. I didn't know you knew Wayne Newton."

I said, "Well, I tell you, Wayne Newton and I are not close. We haven't talked to each other for years."

He said, "Well, he told me that he thinks you're great."

I said, "Hell, he never told me that."

He said, "He said you came on the job and got things straightened out for him."

I said, "I didn't even know he remembered me."

To my knowledge, he never did build the guest house.

The plans for his house were so detailed and so voluminous that when you opened them up they would frighten you. And Wayne Newton was not good at reading plans. He would walk into the house and say, "What's this?"

I'd say, "This is the dining room."

"Well, gee, I don't like it." Pretty soon his workmen would be kicking partitions out and rebuilding.

In the closet upstairs in his personal bedroom, all you would see was a bunch of buttons. If you pushed a button, a wall would turn, and there were evening shoes all the way up to the ceiling. I was there once because the carpenters were trying to figure out a note on the plans: "Closet for 60 pairs of slacks." They were wondering how they were going to get 60 pairs of slacks in there. One panel that opened up was a secret door into a private recording room.

I suggested to the electricians that they put a special outlet plug beside the toilet in the master bathroom so that Wayne could shave while he was sitting on the toilet. Everybody thought that was a great idea. When things are not normal, you can be open to surprises.

The ceilings were made of very intricately paneled squares. Every room had a fireplace; we wondered why in that climate he would need a fireplace in every room. The upstairs was separated into three apartments: one for the baby; another for Wayne Newton and his wife; and one for his business manager, who lived in the house. The basement contained an elaborate wine cellar. Everything in the kitchen was double—double stove, double refrigerator, and double cabinets. The laundry room was as big as my dining room (12 by 15 feet) and all tile. The walls were so jammed with electric wires and electronic equipment, it was unbelievable. Fortunately, the company that did all the wiring in the house knew what they were doing. And Johnson, the builder, was qualified to build it because he was a top man. However, I think he was overloaded and depending too much on his son. That's why the son and I became pretty friendly; he would ask me questions, especially on the plans. He would say, "What is this? Is this a closet?"

I'd say, "No, hell, that's an elevator." I think I did a good job, and I learned a lot. Building methods in the West are entirely different than they are in the East.

I was given a special pass so I could walk in and out through the gate. When my brother and his wife came up to Las Vegas to look around, I took them on a tour of the house after I asked the builder's son, "Is it OK if I bring my brother in?"

"Oh, yeah. Hell, you can do anything you want."

The thing that I couldn't understand was why there was a pond of water at the back of the house. Between the pond and the house was a swimming pool. Then between the pond and the swimming pool was a great big stack of beautiful gray rocks that had been brought up from Southern California. Wayne wanted that particular shade of gray. And on top of the rocks they built a gazebo. Water from the top of the rock pile tumbled down the rocks into the pool on one side and into the pond on the other side. On the back side, in the pond, damned if they didn't have an outboard motor.

The invisible costs that went into the house would be phenomenal today. Wayne was a game guy. If he wanted something, he put it in, and he didn't care what it cost. That's what ran the cost up. It was a big house; I'd say, with both floors, probably 20,000 square feet. All in all, the builders told me the house was running about $1.3 million. It would probably cost $5 million to duplicate it today. The tragic part was that Wayne and his wife built their dream house and then got divorced.

Getting back to my own house: I had come upon a mutual friend who knew Robert McCracken, an old buddy of mine in the Marine Corps who lived in Nevada. (We had played football together on the undefeated 1928 Marine Corps all-marine team.) The friend gave me Bob's address and telephone, and when we got together I told him that I was planning to build a home in Boulder City. I had seen a house that was built with timber ceilings and I liked it so much I decided to have my house designed with timbers if I could find some. Bob said it might be possible to get some beautiful timbers out of an old mining mill that was being dismantled. He had a friend who had a mine in a wilderness area. By law, when you abandon a mine in a designated wilderness area you have to remove all the buildings and material and restore the area to its natural state as nearly as possible.

Through my old buddy, we contacted the owner of the mine, Bob Wilson. He had a big pile of timbers at his mill site, and he drove down one Sunday with a great big truck and a great big trailer full of them. He was alone, and there was no one to help us unload them. I went up and down the street, begging people to help us. We needed at least four men to a timber, with two on each end. A few came up and worked a while and then left. When we had unloaded them on the golf course—and we had to carry them a distance—I called together all the men who helped me and said, "Your reward will be a $50 bill apiece plus a bottle of bourbon apiece." The word spread up and down the street, and all these guys that wouldn't work for me ran up to get in on the deal.

I was lucky enough to get six large loads of 8-by-8-inch timbers around 20 feet long. When we stacked them up along the side of the lot, the pile of heavy timbers was six feet high. They were all around the property and on the adjacent golf course. A woman across the street who was apprehensive about all the timbers wondered what in the hell was going on. She came over to ask some of the workmen I had enlisted to dig footings for my house. In jest they told her that the owner was building a duplicate of the big fort at Fort Laramie, Wyoming. This caused her to panic, and for the next few days there was a "For Sale" sign in front of her house. I went over and explained that the boys were just kidding her about Fort Laramie, and she took down her sign.

The draftsman was a Japanese architect who came out to the lot, measured all the beams, and labeled them according to their length and condition. And I was lucky enough to have the help of my friend Robert McCracken, who was an expert at handling beams from his experience in the mines. Bob stayed with me in a house I leased on the next street. He would come to the lot every day and dress up about four timbers—cut them to length, trim them down nicely, and have them ready to install.

Our problem was that the house had progressed to the point where we had rafters on the roof before the timbers were delivered, and we could not use a crane to lift them over the house and set them in place. We had to set them from the inside by manual labor. The builder made a deal with the workmen of the subcontractors he was associated with, and he got about ten people to come down to our house for free beer after they got off their jobs. The timbers were so damn heavy it took all ten to lift them overhead. The house was really a beer joint while we were putting up the timbers. Everyone would come and have a cold beer, and then the builder would say, "OK, boys, we're going to put up timber No. 17 today to start with." So ten guys would carry in that particular timber and slide it into place as shown on the plans, and the carpenters would lock them in and finish it up. Then the men would have another beer and then

Robert McCracken was an expert with an
axe. Here he is shaping up some old
timbers to put in my Boulder City house
during construction in 1978.

haul in another numbered timber, and so on. All the rooms, even the
atrium, have timbers in the ceilings.

The foundation of the house had been constructed three feet
above ground level, so that from a sitting position inside the house
I could look out and see all of the golf course. We used rock and
gravel fill to bring it up high enough. That meant we also had to
raise the porch. First, we poured a concrete slab about two feet above
the ground level, and then we built a timbered porch using the last
of our timbers, with some air space between the concrete slab and
the timbers to keep the timbers from rotting.

We brought in a very large sanding machine from Las Vegas (the
kind used in bowling alleys), and sanded all the porch timbers level
and smooth. After they were varnished, they were beautiful. Every-

body loves our floor. So we got a beautiful floor and timbers all through the house, and Bob Wilson only charged me for hauling the timbers and for some bulldozer work on the site.

My total bill for all the timbers in the house was $1,700. Bob McCracken would not charge me anything for his work; he said he was just doing it on a friendship basis. But I found out that he had a note at a bank in Tonopah, Nevada, where he lived, and I secretly paid off about $1,800 on the note; so for his labor, he worked off the debt to the bank, and he was very happy about that. And Bob was very good moral support on the job. He kept the men laughing, telling them stories while they were having lunch. He was very popular among the work crew and was a great help to me.

Bob worked mostly in the backyard next to the golf course. Golf balls would sometimes fall near him while he was dressing the timbers. One day a ball came from tee no. 5, a distance of 150 yards, and hit Bob in the back of the neck—you can imagine how much that hurt. Some fellow in a golf cart came racing over and wanted to know where his ball was, and we told him that we wanted to know if he had insurance because he had hurt one of our employees. He said, "I can't worry about your employees; I just want my ball."

I said, "Well, I've got an employee here who got hit in the back of the neck by your ball; you're responsible."

He said, "I'm not responsible for a goddamn thing. I just want my ball."

Bob was listening to this conversation, and of course he was suffering from the pain—and he was working with a double-edged axe. Bob started after this golfer and said, "I'll give you your ball. It'll be inside your goddamn skull when I get through with you." He was chasing him with the double axe and the golfer was running like hell to get in his golf cart and get away.

This device at the rear of my patio was designed principally to ward off golf balls and to protect the full-length windows I have facing the golf course. It was designed by an American architect who had spent several years designing structures for the navy in Japan. He thought we should use a Japanese-style gazebo rather than an ugly high fence.

I ran after Bob and I said, "Bob, don't kill him! Don't kill him! We've got to finish these beams." The guy got in that golf cart and we never saw him again.

In order to protect Bob and the others, I got a notion to use a big bull wheel that was lying out front. We put it in back on the porch to protect against golf balls. The only problem was how were we going to get it back there? It had 13 layers of wood and must have weighed a ton. Bob got five men to help us set it up straight, and we rolled it to the back. Then we set it up on the porch, locked it in place, and there it remains. Everybody asks me, "How the hell did you get that heavy thing onto your porch?"

Of course, I really had to scramble to get that house designed and up in 30 days—and I got a break. While I was still in Las Vegas, a young man knocked on my door and said, "Mr. Poppelman, I have been referred to you by the American Society of Dowsers headquarters in Vermont. I wrote to them to see if they could tell me if there was a dowser in Nevada who could teach me how to dowse."

I said, "I do belong to the dowsers' society, but I just don't have time to teach you how to dowse. I've got problems to attend to right now." At that time the city would not allow builders from Las Vegas to build in Boulder City because there were about 12 small builders in town that they wanted everyone to use. So the city wouldn't give me a permit to build my house. I had gone ahead and put the footings in without a permit to start with. I told this boy, "Sorry, but I can't help you," and he asked, "What's your problem?"

I said, "I'm having a hell of a time getting a building permit from Boulder City. They want me to use one of their builders, but I had a builder lined up." (I was trying to get Wayne Newton's contractor to build my house, but he didn't have an office in Boulder City.)

The young man said, "My uncle is the head of the Mormon Church for the state of Nevada. I can help you." (Boulder City was then basically a Mormon town.)

That changed things! I said, "If you talk to your uncle and can get him to get me set up OK with Boulder City, I'll try to teach you to dowse."

Next thing I knew, they couldn't do enough for me in this town. The city gave me half my building fee back and said I could go ahead and use whichever builder I wanted. I liked Bud Dayton, one of the builders in Boulder City, very much. He had just finished up a couple of houses so he had the nucleus of a good crew assembled, and he needed work for them. He agreed to build my house at cost and to let me be supervisor of the timber work. So I wound up getting to know the community of Mormons in town, and they were really good to me. Bud was good to work with and very cooperative. In fact, he acquired five building jobs just from people coming to see the construction of our house. With that in mind, he never charged me for any extra work—he did a lot of work for me for free.

I can't remember the name of the young man who wanted to learn dowsing, but I went to his house one night. We sat at the dining room table, and I tried to teach him how to use the pendulum. All of a sudden his wife came running out of the kitchen with a broom to chase me out of the house. She didn't want evil spirits in the house, and she figured that dowsing involved evil spirits. So we had to do it out of her sight. As hard as I tried to teach him, he never did learn to dowse. He was absolutely dead with the dowsing rod. The only time it would move was when I grabbed his arm.

The young man wanted to learn dowsing so he could find the source of diamonds that had been described in a book about a pioneer in the days when Las Vegas was just a farm. The pioneer came stumbling back to his farm with a bucket full of diamond ore, claiming that southeast of Las Vegas was a mountain with a black streak running through it, and that black streak was full of diamonds. The ore was taken to Los Angeles and analyzed by a jeweler who said the diamonds were top grade, and that started a hell of a flurry in the area. The young man who wanted me to teach him to dowse also wanted me to help him look for the source, but I didn't have time to do it. I think he did get a water dowser from up north to go with him to look for the diamonds. They didn't have any luck, though.

In 1977 I took out a construction loan of $80,000 and signed it over to the builder. He never asked me for another quarter. He said, "This house was good to me; I've got my crew back together again and I'm making money. It all came from your house. The construc-

A recent picture of the front of my home in Boulder City, Nevada. These are flowering trees.

tion work was so good in your house, people would walk through it, they'd like it, and I got credit for it." Adding the cost of the lot and house together, I paid close to $100,000 in 1977 dollars. Of course, it would cost much more now. The lot alone would go for a couple hundred thousand dollars; the house is worth at least $500,000. I added the flagpole, the gazebo, a lot of concrete work and a lot of landscaping myself.

It's a good house, made with the best materials. Instead of using 2-by-4s in the walls, we used 2-by-6s. Instead of putting in one air conditioning system, I had a double system put in, so there are two separate units. If one fails, I still have the other. Both units are large enough to take care of the whole house. And there's no house in town insulated like it. I used rock wool, two feet deep in the ceiling. I had lived in big houses, and they were a damn nuisance—you had to have two maids and a gardener and a whole damn crew just to live there. I did not want to retire to a mansion or a big house. I wanted a small house, but I wanted it to be different and special.

This was the last photograph taken of my dear wife, Sue Megan Goodwin Poppelman, before her death in 1988.

Just about the time we got the house completed, in August 1988, Sue died. I thought that was an odd coincidence and a real tragedy. Sue had hired Bertha's, a decorating company in Las Vegas, to furnish the house just the way she wanted it. In all the houses we had lived in back East, I guess at least 25, that we built for ourselves, somebody always offered us so much money that we had to sell. We built our retirement home, and as soon as she got it the way she wanted it, she died. Sue had lymphoma, a kind of cancer that spreads

"Welcome Ray Poppelman"—I traveled to Maryland as a guest at the June 29, 1995, game between the University of Maryland and Duke University. I went back as the captain of the Maryland team. This sign was up before the game, when I posed with it. That's the weekend I was inducted into the University of Maryland Athletic Hall of Fame.

from one place to another in the lymph nodes. She battled it for three years. It went into recession several times, but it would always pop up in another place. Finally the doctor told me she had about four months to live, but she died within a couple of weeks of that time.

My life changed drastically after Sue's death. It appeared shadowed with miracles—nothing but miracles happened to me. One event was that I got notice from the University of Maryland that I had been inducted into the Athletic Hall of Fame, which was something I had wanted for a long time. I was a bit saddened and frustrated by the fact that the news did not come while Sue was alive. But, later, I found that she had known about it but didn't want to tell me until the day that I would be inducted. Her niece had visited her and told her that she had learned that I *had* been inducted into the Hall of Fame, and they were going to tell me later. So actually, Sue did know. But I didn't know that she knew, and I was upset.

Another birthday portrait, March 6, 1992.

Epilogue

While I was writing this book, I thought back to a particular day in my foxhole on Iwo Jima. I prayed to God that He would let me live three more days so I could reach my 39th birthday. Not only did He give me the three days, but He added a bonus of 56 years. And it was within those 56 years that my life took on a different style. It reminded me of somebody who had aimed to travel from A to Z but wound up going from C to Q instead. Life got better. What I would plan would usually change for the better, and it just continued that way the rest of my life.

I have come to the conclusion, looking back through my years, that possibly the universe that we see and think is *beyond* us might be *within* ourselves. Whenever I would meditate over a problem or ponder a problem, it seemed that if I'd wait patiently, eventually things would work out in my favor.

After Sue died, I felt generally lost. We had been married for 40 years, and she had worked hard for me. She had faith in me, and it seemed that I was sort of surrendering to events rather than projecting them. I would be patient and wait, and things would happen. I had properties that I had not even thought about selling because I didn't think I'd get a good price for them, and then, out of the blue, I'd get a notice of an offer. And the offers would be higher than I would have suggested if somebody asked me what the price of a property was.

I was beginning to get breaks, and I wondered, sometimes, if Sue, from her new dimension in life, had some influence. I began to wonder if a lot of the things that were happening were created through Sue, in whatever dimension of life she had moved into. I became confused for a while. I didn't know exactly what to do. I just lived on and took things as they came to me rather than forcing issues.

I traveled a little bit and found that conditions were different as the years rolled by. Places that I normally would like to go on a vacation did not appeal to me much anymore, and I became attached to Nevada. I was afraid to make moves on my own. I was always wondering, "What would Sue think about my doing this?" And consequently, I think that a lot of what I call "luck" was from another source.

And I began to be attached more to religion than I had ever been before. I wondered why, on Iwo Jima, I had prayed for three days, and since then the years were rolling by with better luck than I ever had before. And my philosophies about life changed. I began to wonder: The experiences I had here on Earth—were they really real? Maybe I was in some other dimension of life and didn't know it. So I was cautious about everything I'd do. And I began to depend more on my attorney, John A. Lewis, my nephew in San Fernando.

Although I didn't realize it at the time, I had been lucky before Iwo Jima and lucky before Sue's death. When I was living through my life, I didn't feel that I was lucky. I had to work like hell. And I didn't realize when I was getting the breaks that they were coming to me without effort. Just suddenly, things were happening for the best. All my life I had to scratch very hard to make a living. When I was in the building business in Washington, D.C., I faced bankruptcy many times, and at the last minute, some event would happen to change everything. Money would come to me from sources I didn't expect. Sales would pop up at the most opportune time. And I began to wonder about that. Why was all that happening?

Life had never been very easy for me, even during my youth in South Dakota. Everything seemed to be a hardship—the weather, the working conditions, getting to school, everything. And during my years in Washington, D.C., after I quit the government and went out on my own, I did not have a silent partner. I had to scratch along on a pay-as-you-go basis, and the earnings from one house would build the second house, and so forth. I never had a great surplus of money until after Sue died.

It was just amazing how my thinking changed. I would wonder before I made decisions, if Sue would approve of them. And I would ponder propositions carefully. Looking back through the years, from the time I left San Fernando and went on my own, there was some divine force with me—a sort of partner—that was guiding me. There were too many things happening for the good that I didn't expect. During my service with the Marine Corps, there were many times I could have been killed, both in China and on Iwo Jima. But there was always something that came to my rescue. The same was true in financial deals and in the completion of projects—getting the breaks on the weather at the right time and so on. I would have to admit that I was a very lucky person.

I believe there is something beyond normal luck, a divine force that's aware of everything you do and what you need. If I was giving advice to young people today, I would suggest they be just a little more patient: Think about what they'd like to do and be patient about it. Don't jump into things. My financial situation changed for the good—I'm comfortably situated now, beyond what I ever dreamed, whereas at one time in my life I considered myself to be very unlucky. As I was writing this book, I would think about events in my past, and then I began to realize how damn lucky I have been. And I realized, too, there had to be more than luck at work. Using myself as an example, I think a person should try to learn as early in life as is possible that he or she is not alone. No matter what you think, there is some dimension of activity that you're associated with that knows more about life and what's going to happen to you than you do yourself.

When I had to complete almost 40 houses before entering the service in World War II, my creditors began to panic for fear that I might have to abandon my project without paying my bills.

Instead of going to an attorney, I sought the services of Mr. Biederman, a Christian Science practitioner in Washington, D.C., for help. The practitioner listened to my predicament carefully and then fell into a light trance as if he were sleeping. After a few minutes he "awakened" and said, "It is not necessary for you to see an attorney. You will be all right."

On my way home I stopped in at the Arlington Trust Company in Rosslyn, Virginia, a bank I had not done business with before. The banker, Mr. Alan Prosise, listened to my problem and said, "Follow me." We went into a large vault and he put a bundle of cash into a wire basket. He said, "You say you need $40,000 to pay off all your creditors. You will not need that much. I'm putting $18,000 cash in the bottom drawer of my desk. Each morning you help yourself to what you need to settle discounted accounts."

Fearing that I might not come back from combat, the creditors settled all accounts for a total of $18,000. Later, I learned that the banker had recently lost a son in the air force over Germany. He became generous to all servicemen after the war. When I went to see him later, he said, "You know, when I gave you $18,000 in cash, I forgot to have you sign a note and you were a total stranger." My experience was more than luck.

A lot of people are lucky and don't know it—or don't appreciate it. For instance, when my family moved from South Dakota to Minneapolis, we didn't realize how lucky we were. But now I give my father great credit. He had the courage to make the move to improve ourselves. And we improved ourselves again when we moved to California. At the time, we thought it was a catastrophe.

Here is another example: Why should an old lady in northern Maryland suddenly decide that I could have her property, no money down, and give her lawyer instructions to deed the property to me just because I'd done a little favor for her by helping her get a cabin set up? That had to be more than just luck. Something helped me. Getting 20 acres of land at the right time really set up my career in the building business. One moment I had no money to buy land and the next I had the very 20 acres that I wanted. That event had to come from some force, something *more*. You can call it religion or you can refer to God—call it what you want—but something caused me to get 20 acres when I had no money.

Some people would say a lot of my luck had to do with the fact that I was a nice guy and that I helped other people—David Tishman, for instance. Maybe the old lady gave me the land for nothing down because I helped her with that cabin. If I'd been a typical person, I would have just gone down the road and it never would have happened, but here I was.

I like to look at this question the other way: What made me do things that I did? What made me get in an old beat-up car and drive way the hell up in Maryland to talk to an old lady? That's what I'm saying—there's got to be something more than just pure luck. There's got to be some sort of a destiny, whether it's preplanned or planned as a person goes along in life.

Maybe some day I'll have all the answers; I'll find out what the truth is. I have gone to a lot of funerals in my life, and I have grieved about a lot of things. I think of the time I had my first decent amount of money—I think I had $2,000. I was going to see that old lady and give it to her in payment for the 20 acres she'd given me. I drove all the way up there and found out she had passed away, and I never had a chance to thank her. Those are the things that I feel sorry about.

While writing this book, I thought about a lot of people who helped me—thousands of people in my lifetime who helped me in some way. I had a chance to thank only a very few. People in Washington, D.C., helped me, and they didn't have to. I never had a chance to go back and thank them when I was in a position to—never had a chance to do something for them. That is one of my sorrows now. I had a lot of help in college and through my economic difficulties as a builder. It seems like I had help all the time and didn't realize it.

I would like this book to help other people realize that they, too, can look in the mirror and say to themselves, "You lucky son of a bitch." Because everybody's lucky in so many ways they just don't realize. You've got to figure that you're lucky every second of the day—every time your heart beats. Periodically in life a person should sit down and appraise his or her situation. You could stop any person on the street and tell him, "You're lucky as hell." A doctor once told me that there are over 2,000 known diseases that the medical world has to fight. We're exposed to most of them. So if you're sitting here today, healthy as you are, looking back through the years, with everything that's happened, you're lucky as hell, too. You don't have to have a lot of money in the bank to be lucky. If you've got your health, you've got the best of all.

I once picked up a hitchhiker; we probably rode together 45 minutes in the car. By the time he told me what he had been doing and what he was going to do, and where he was going to go, I was fascinated. "Geez," I thought, "what a lucky guy." I think about a guy named Raskob whom I knew at the University of Maryland. His father, who was a Democratic National Party chairman, had built the Empire State Building. Raskob had tons of money. I said something to him once about how lucky he was. You know what he told me? He said, "If you wanted to go out and buy an automobile and you had the money to do it, you could do it, couldn't you?"

I said, "Yes."

He said, "I can't. My father won't let me have a car. I have to call up for a chauffeur."

And I got to thinking about how lucky I was. If I had wanted to, I could buy a car. So each person is lucky in different ways.

I tried to get Raskob into my fraternity at school, and he was blackballed. And he reminded me—"Poppelman, you're the lucky one. You belong to the fraternity. I can't get into a fraternity like that." His father was grooming him to take charge of a textile factory in New England, and he had to attend a sewing class. The guys in the fraternity pictured him sitting in the sewing class and blackballed him. I thought he was lucky to be so rich, and he thought I was lucky. Thinking it over, I *was* the lucky one. He had no freedom.

So there you have it. My life has been a long one, filled with interesting twists and turns and a whole lot of luck. Make that more than luck.

Index

Note: Italic numbers following page numbers indicate photographs.

Lee, W. E., 130
Lejeune, John A., 105, 118, 126, 131–132, 139, 143
Lewis, John A., 448
Lewis, Neville R., 58, 378, 379, 381, 389–390, 404. 421, 424, 426
Lindbergh, Charles, 128
Liversedge, Harry, 99, 130, 235, 260, 262–263, *99*
Lombard, Carole, 160–162
Londos, Jim, 61
Lord & Taylor
   as art buyer for, 409–411, 413–414
   building in Maryland, 302–303, 308, 344, 377, *303*
Los Angeles Rams, 151
Loscomb, Sandy, 422
Luney, Richard, 411–412

M

Manning, Jack, 320–329
Mao Tse-tung, 129
Marine Corps, *78*
   commission in 1943, 196, 209–210
   commission as second lieutenant, 211
   discharge from, 139
   joining, 69–71, 75
   officers' school, 212
   playing football for, 81–84, 128, 131–137, 139, 143, 287
   promotion to corporal, 82, 118, 132, *133*
   promotion to first lieutenant, 249
   promotion to sergeant, 118, 132
   training, 76–77
Marine War Memorial. *See* Iwo Jima Monument
Markel, Joe, 286–288, 289–290
Marshall, George, 61
Marsham, Lord, 101
Marvin, South Dakota, *31*
   barn raising, 27–28
   as birthplace, 3
   family farm, 27–33, *17*
   healthcare in, 33–34
   house in, 27–31, *27*

school certificate from, *22*
   schooling in, 14, 19–25, *20*
Mathiesen, Andrew, 130
McCracken, Bob (Sr.), 134–135, 434–438, *436*
McGroarty, John, 167–168, 171–172
McIlvane, Jim, 298–299, 300–303, 304
Mena, Gomez, 191–192
Merrilees, Kenneth, 348, 350
Metling, Earl, 44
Meyers, Bill, 402
Milwaukee
   Arnold Poppelman's arrival in, 8
   Poppelman household in, 9–11
Minneapolis
   life in, 39–46
   move to, 35–38, *37*
Mitchell, Anne (stepmother), 168, 389–390
Moll, John, 6
Morris, George, 318–319, 329–330, 332, 387, 397–398
Morris, Lieutenant, 214–215
Moses, Betty, 413
Moses, Grandma, 392, 410, 412–415
Moses, Forrest K., 392, 408–411, 412, 415–416
Moses, Tom, 414–415
Motorcycles, interest in, 66–68
Mount Suribachi, 225, 231, 234–235, 237, 240, 246–247, 249–250, 261, *240, 247*
Moving
   from Marvin to Minneapolis, 35–38, *37*
   from Minneapolis to California, 48–51
   to Washington, D.C., 171–172
Munn, Mr., 52, 53, 58
Munn and Poppelman Realtors, 52, 58
Murray, John W.A., 103–104
Muscle problems, 378–382

N

Navy Yangtze River Patrol, 88
New Orleans, football game in 1928, 136–137